ROUTLEDGE LIBRARY EDITIONS:
HOUSING POLICY AND HOME OWNERSHIP

Volume 20

I0130987

THE RADICAL HOMEOWNER

THE RADICAL HOMEOWNER
Housing Tenure and Social Change

IAN C. WINTER

Routledge
Taylor & Francis Group

LONDON AND NEW YORK

First published in 1994 by Gordon and Breach Publishers

This edition first published in 2021
by Routledge
2 Park Square, Milton Park, Abingdon, Oxon OX14 4RN

and by Routledge
52 Vanderbilt Avenue, New York, NY 10017

Routledge is an imprint of the Taylor & Francis Group, an informa business

© 1994 OPA (Overseas Publishers Association) Amsterdam B.V.

All rights reserved. No part of this book may be reprinted or reproduced or utilised in any form or by any electronic, mechanical, or other means, now known or hereafter invented, including photocopying and recording, or in any information storage or retrieval system, without permission in writing from the publishers.

Trademark notice: Product or corporate names may be trademarks or registered trademarks, and are used only for identification and explanation without intent to infringe.

British Library Cataloguing in Publication Data
A catalogue record for this book is available from the British Library

ISBN: 978-0-367-64519-9 (Set)
ISBN: 978-1-00-313856-3 (Set) (ebk)
ISBN: 978-0-367-68530-0 (Volume 20) (hbk)
ISBN: 978-0-367-68541-6 (pbk)
ISBN: 978-1-00-313800-6 (Volume 20) (ebk)

Publisher's Note
The publisher has gone to great lengths to ensure the quality of this reprint but points out that some imperfections in the original copies may be apparent.

Disclaimer
The publisher has made every effort to trace copyright holders and would welcome correspondence from those they have been unable to trace.

THE RADICAL HOME OWNER

Housing Tenure and Social Change

IAN WINTER

Gordon and Breach Publishers

Australia • Austria • Belgium • France • Germany • India • Japan • Malaysia • Netherlands
Russia • Singapore • Switzerland • Thailand • United Kingdom • United States

Copyright © 1994 by OPA (Overseas Publishers Association) Amsterdam B.V.
Published under license by Gordon and Breach Science Publishers S.A.

All rights reserved.

No part of this book may be reproduced or utilized in any form or by any means, electronic or mechanical, including photocopying and recording, or by any information storage or retrieval system, without permission in writing from the publisher. Printed in Singapore.

Gordon and Breach Science Publishers S.A.
Postfach
4004 Basel
Switzerland

British Library Cataloguing in Publication Data

Winter, Ian C.
    Radical Home Owner: Housing Tenure and Social Change
    I. Title
    333.338

    ISBN 2-88449-028-0

For my mother
Gillian Andrea Winter
1939–1992

CONTENTS

PART TWO
HOUSING TENURE AND SOCIAL ACTION:
THE CASE STUDIES

PREFACE

The origins of this book lay in my frustration with what is known as the housing classes debate. This now 27 year old debate has been spirited in terms of its theoretical clamour, with claim and counter-claim from either side of the constructed Marxist—Weberian divide, but has suffered from a dearth of empirical information and thus become increasingly speculative. Furthermore, what appeared to be a fruitful line of theoretical inquiry for urban sociology has largely been abandoned. The research for this book was thus commenced with two explicit aims—to pursue through empirical inquiry theoretical assertions about the sociological significance of home ownership and to extend the Weberian theorising that had begun with Rex and Moore, Haddon, Saunders and Pratt.

Since commencing this research some of the much needed empirical work has been undertaken by others (Saunders, 1990; Forrest, Murie and Williams, 1990; Davis, 1991 to mention a few) and the debate has consequently taken new interesting turns. I hope that the empirical work presented below is found to be equally rewarding, offering, as it does, an Australian perspective on a U.K. and U.S. dominated debate. In Australia home ownership has housed more than 50 per cent of households since 1911 and is enshrined in popular culture as the Great Australian Dream. These facts mark Australia out as an important country within which to conduct such empirical research. On the basis of this research a new theoretical understanding of the social significance of housing tenure is developed—that the meanings and interests of home ownership can lead home owners into radical courses of social action. So whilst this book is intended as a contribution to the housing classes debate, I also hope that it has other dimensions for those whose prime interests lie elsewhere.

First, what may be regarded by some as a perhaps too particular development of a theoretical position (in this case Weberian inspired) is presented as an illustration of the logical interconnection of an ontology, epistemology and methodology. I hope that this is of some use to others who have vainly searched for examples of how such dimensions interlink and the impact they have upon research design. Second, for those grappling with the realist interpretation of causal processes differentiating between necessary and contingent relations, the Weberian concepts of adequate and accidental causality, I believe, offer a powerful and methodologically practical alternative. Third, the qualitative data presented within demonstrate how qualitative data can be used in theoretically informed causal analysis and how the recently available computer programs for qualitative data analysis aid this process to a significant degree.

Throughout the long process of completing this book a number of people have been particularly important in developing my thoughts, or the research project more generally, and I wish to thank them here.

My interest in housing tenure as a topic of sociological debate stems from being an undergraduate and then Masters student at the University of Sussex from 1981 to 1985, during which time Pete Saunders was publishing his (as ever) original thoughts on the topic. The opportunity to endlessly debate this material with him through essays and tutorial papers was too good an opportunity to miss (sorry about that Pete), but it was through this engagement that my interest was fired.

A move to Australia posed the problems of understanding a different housing history, a different political economy and a different cultural understanding of the significance of housing tenure. Commencing doctoral work at the Urban Research Unit, Australian National University a number of people helped in a range of ways in coming to terms with these differences and with the difficulties of beginning a research project of this nature—with particular thanks to Susan Faulbaum, John Short, Roger Jones, Victor Minichiello, Michael Ball, Pat Troy, Max Neutze and Hal Kendig.

The mainstay of this research was undertaken whilst at the Department of Geography, University of Melbourne, where Iain Campbell, Jamie Peck and Michael Webber each contributed to a lively and challenging intellectual environment. Thanks are also due to Martin Taylor and David Hayward for invaluable assistance with the design of the interview schedules, to Rita Anderson and Alice Lowe for assistance with the transcribing and Neal Enright who helped solve many statistical difficulties. Special thanks are due, however, to Ruth Fincher and Mike Berry who provided rigorous and challenging supervision of this research throughout my time at the University of Melbourne.

The ongoing refinment of this work has benefited from helpful comments and criticisms from students and staff in the Urban Policy and Planning program, RMIT, and most importantly from the enthusiasm and support of David Thorns and Peter Williams. The time and energy that David and Peter have devoted to reading drafts, advising on improvements, paving the way with publishers and generally providing encouragement has been and is highly valued.

This research could not have been completed without those people who allowed me into their homes and gave up significant amounts of their time. Thank you to everyone who participated.

Publication of this research has been assisted by grants from the Committee on Research and Graduate Studies, The University of Melbourne, and the Faculty of Environmental Design and Construction, Royal Melbourne Institute of Technology.

Finally, my thanks to Lynne Darkin who has lived with and endured the writing of this book more than anyone else—she has read the manuscript more times than any one is ever likely to, offering helpful advice, numerous improvements and much needed and appreciated encouragement.

Ian Winter

PART ONE

UNDERSTANDING HOUSING TENURE:
THE THEORY

Chapter 1

HOME OWNERSHIP IN WESTERN SOCIETY

Cementing the Status Quo or a Force for Change?

Home ownership has expanded in the Twentieth Century to become the dominant tenure form in many developed societies. In countries such as Australia, Britain, Canada, New Zealand (N.Z.) and the United States of America (U.S.) between 60 per cent and 70 per cent of all households are home owners. Denmark, France, West Germany and the Netherlands have lower overall rates of home ownership, between 40 per cent and 50 per cent, but each has experienced significant growth of home ownership since the Second World War (Ball *et al.*, 1988:91). The national housing histories that have produced these statistical similarities differ widely: whilst more than 50 per cent of Australian households were home owners in 1911, not until 1971 did a similar number of British households own their homes. In the past twenty years, however, the home ownership rate in Britain has raced to 67.5 per cent in 1991 with most of this growth in the 1980s.

Alongside these large percentages of home owners the tenure distribution of other households varies both spatially and temporally. In contemporary Australia 25 per cent of households are in private rental and only 5 per cent in public rental, whereas in Britain the ratios are practically reversed. Whilst in the early part of the Twentieth Century British households were overwhelmingly private renters their numbers have now dwindled to such an extent that private renting is a minor tenure. This variation in the tenure relativities of different nations is indicative of how the 'make-up' of housing tenures is culturally specific. Bearing this in mind and as the social scientific contributions to the understanding of housing tenure are primarily drawn from North America (for example, Pratt, 1986a, 1986b, 1986c, 1986d, 1987, 1989) and Britain (for example, Saunders, 1977, 1978, 1982, 1984, 1986, 1989, 1990) an analysis of housing tenure in a different cultural context can provide an important counterbalance to existing material. Hence, the primary data for this examination of housing tenure are drawn from three case studies in Australia in which we are concerned with the two main tenure groups, home owners and private renters. Secondary data from a range of countries in which home ownership is a significant tenure (the U.S., Canada, Britain and N.Z.) are also drawn upon to examine the relevance of the arguments to be presented beyond the confines of the three case studies and the Australian scene.

One of the key forces behind the growth of home ownership throughout the Twentieth Century has been the bipartisan political support that it has enjoyed. In Britain, most recently, this support took the form of large discounts for those wanting to purchase public housing and it is Mrs Thatcher's benevolence towards public housing tenants that is largely responsible for the rapid rise in Britain's home ownership rate through the 1980s. Was the council house sales program an act of benevolence, though, or was it an act to promote social and political stability? For it is such stability that politicians believe home ownership can magically bestow. The comments of Australian politicians over a number of decades are typical:

> Home ownership generally means better home life, and better home life must unquestionably be reflected in better citizenship. (Makin,

Labor member for Hindmarsh, South Australia, Commonwealth Parliamentary Debates, 1927, 116:669 cited in Williams, P. 1984:180.)

Home ownership is also the basis of national social security. If we desire to rid the community of communism, and to safeguard the best interests of the nation, we must provide every opportunity to the people to acquire their own homes. (Costa, 1952:2354, cited in Kemeny, 1977:48) (Costa, D. 1952 House of Representatives speech on second reading of Loan (housing) Bill (1952)). *Commonwealth of Australia: Parliamentary Debates* (Hansard). Session 1951–53, Vol. H of R.1 (New Series).

[Home ownership] would not only make a better citizenry generally, but also would promote greater industrial harmony. I feel that if a workman owned his house and therefore had a great interest in it, he would be disinclined to be influenced by extraneous matters raised by a few demagogues. (Jones, 1972:120 citing Mr Duggan, Deputy Premier of Queensland, 1953.)

The political 'sales-talk' has been about giving people a 'stake in the system'—a set of property related interests. Such interests constitute a stake in the system due to an association between domestic property rights and the private property rights essential to capitalist social relations. Buying a home has been 'sold', if you'll allow me, as the equivalent in principle of owning a factory or some other form of the means of production. As such, the interests of the home owner are equated with the interests of the factory owner and each, as a central part of the private property relations essential to capitalism is bound to support the status quo.

Portraying home owners as 'stable pillars' of the community, however, not only denies home owners the right to defend their property interests in ways that may be 'improper', it also denies that the defence of such interests may lead home owners into courses of social action that in fact oppose dominant social relations and challenge the status quo. And it is precisely this, how home ownership can provide a basis for oppositional strategies, for social action that is confronting rather than conforming, that this book reveals. In so doing we will develop a new understanding of the sociological significance of home ownership.

This new understanding begins by recognising the interests that are an essential part of home ownership. These interests stem from the economic, political and cultural inequalities that are constructed through housing tenure. It will be argued that these inequalities shape and pattern the experience of housing consumption to create different sets of meanings about the home and neighbourhood between owners and renters. It is these meanings that inform the social action of home owners in such a way that dominant social relations may be challenged. We will discover that tenure interests can lead home owners into social action in public domains, such as the neighbourhood and place of employment, that oppose the current socio-spatial logic of global economic restructuring. From such findings the question of the radical home owner and the title for this book emerge. Whilst the issue of what is radical is fraught with definitional problems, the paradoxical nature of the book title reflects well the counter-intuitive conclusions we shall reach. 'Radical' is understood here as a process of opposition to the status quo. Whether such engagement is in the end absorbed or transformative, reformist rather than radical, or resulting in an 'urban effect' or not, are issues deliberated upon later.

Understanding home ownership in this way is important for it challenges many existing assumptions about the nature of home ownership and undermines the glib association of home owner-ship with responsible citizenship, social stability and industrial peace. Moreover, this understanding of home ownership extends and develops the current social scientific theorising of the signifi-cance of home ownership. Part One, including Chapters 1–5, is structured to reveal the theoretical development, and Part Two, including Chapters 6–9, the empirical exploration through case studies that leads to this new understanding of home ownership.

Whilst Pratt (1989) and Rose (1980) have challenged the incor-poration theory of home ownership (the political 'sales-talk' position), neither offers a causal interpretation of these processes. Their theorising and what is known as the 'housing classes debate' are reviewed in Chapter 2 as we move toward establishing five key

parameters that usefully demarcate a new approach to the understanding of housing tenure.

Chapter 3 examines secondary data from a range of countries to
establish the extent of the economic, political and cultural
inequalities constructed through housing tenure. It will be made
clear that previous attempts to theorise the construction of
inequality through housing tenure have tended to reduce this
process to one dimension of inequality, primarily the economic
and occasionally either the political or the cultural. Rarely has it
been recognised that each of these aspects of inequality is
constructed concurrently through housing tenure relations.
Second, the nature of the data currently available on home ownership illustrate that the subjective understanding of the construction of inequality through housing tenure, what tenure relations
actually mean to home owners and private renters, has been
ignored. Third, it will be shown that the causal nature of the relationship between housing tenure and social action, the impact of
housing tenure relations on householders' activities, remains
unspecified by the current literature.

The key concepts and research strategies of the neo-Weberian
approach adopted are detailed in Chapter 4. The methodology
was designed specifically to overcome the three perceived short-
comings of the existing literature noted above and detailed in
Chapter 3. Weber's original concepts of class, status and party are
re-visited and a range of Weber's methodological concepts, such
as, *verstehen*, ideal types and adequate and accidental causality
applied. Towards the end of each chapter an account of how these
concepts have guided the empirical research strategies is also
discussed. Chapter 4 is thus of broader scope and provides
examples of the integration of abstract concepts into an empirical
research design and of an alternative framework to the realist
method of investigating causality.

Chapter 5 combines both primary data from Australia and
secondary data from a range of countries to detail the subjective
understanding of the economic, political and cultural inequalities
of home owning and renting. A wide range of meanings attributed
to housing tenure is exposed and the causality of such meanings
grounded in the experience of housing tenure.

Part Two focuses upon the three case studies and examines the causal relationship between the meanings of housing tenure and social action across three different locales; the home, neighbourhood and place of employment. Chapter 6 examines participation in a community-based crime prevention scheme and focuses upon social action within the home. Chapter 7 examines participation in a residents' action group with a focus upon social action at the neighbourhood level. Chapter 8 examines participation in an industrial strike and focuses upon social action at the place of employment. In these chapters the causality of the relationship between the experience of housing tenure and courses of social action is examined and the implications of such social action for oppositional strategies and social change discussed.

The book is structured in this way to assist exploration of the understanding of home ownership being advanced here. How the relations of housing tenure can create radical home owners who challenge dominant social relations will thus be established by: first, showing that objective inequalities of an economic, political and cultural nature are constructed through housing tenure relations (Chapter 3); second, examining the way in which such inequalities are interpreted and meanings attributed to housing tenure (Chapter 5) and; third, exploring the causal nature of the relationship between the subjective understanding of housing tenure and social action (Chapters 6, 7 and 8).

Through these chapters this book develops theoretical, methodological and substantive knowledge. Theoretical insight to the significance of housing tenure for social structure and social change is provided through our conclusion that tenure-based social groups engage in oppositional strategies that result in social change. Methodological understanding is advanced through the explicit development of a consistent ontology, epistemology and methodology, drawing upon both qualitative and quantitative data to investigate the nature of causal processes between housing tenure and social action. Finally, substantive knowledge of the importance of home ownership for Australian households and their engagement in a range of courses of social action is provided through the case studies.

Chapter 2

SOCIAL SCIENTIFIC APPROACHES TO HOME OWNERSHIP

The analysis of housing tenure first arose as urban sociologists in Britain attempted to re-define what it was that lay at the kernel of their discipline. Urban sociology had long suffered from an identity crisis with nothing specifically 'urban' being apparent in the problems and issues that urban sociologists considered.

> ...(D)efinitions in terms of size were purely arbitrary and had little sociological significance, while more specifically sociological formulations in terms of peculiarly 'urban' cultural characteristics exhibited an unfortunate propensity to collapse in the face of empirical evidence demonstrating the presence of 'urban' phenomena in 'rural' areas or of 'rural' phenomena in 'urban' areas. (Saunders, 1981, Preface.)

The pioneering work of Rex and Moore (1967) re-emphasised the urban dimension of sociological concerns in a study of housing and race relations by highlighting the scarcity of key urban resources, such as widely desired housing, and the inevitable competition for such resources that would flow from this. Housing tenure thus emerged as one aspect of a housing hierarchy that urban dwellers were competing for with home ownership at the top end and lodging houses at the bottom. By relating housing to an individual's life chances Rex and Moore linked urban sociology with the mainstream sociological concerns of sources of inequality and class conflict. By identifying the essential spatial elements of this conflict, Rex and Moore were able to specify what was 'urban' about their urban sociology (Saunders, 1981, p. 115). Urban sociology was thus re-born and the analysis of housing tenure born.

Since this time housing tenure has become a focus for debates about social stratification. The primacy of social divisions arising from the sphere of production (primarily the labour market) has been questioned through recognition of the increasing importance of divisions arising from the sphere of consumption, such as the housing market. This book moves the theoretical analysis of housing tenure forward again by examining the significance of housing tenure relations for social change. At an empirical level the study of housing tenure remains important due to the ongoing change in housing tenure relations. As more and more countries exhibit high ratios of home ownership, so it is important to understand what this will mean for these nations sociologically.

The sociological understanding of housing tenure over the past 25 years can somewhat crudely be reduced to two different approaches: those who argue that home ownership has collectivist tendencies and those who argue it has anti-collectivist or fragmentary tendencies. These positions tend to ally themselves with Weberian and Marxist thought respectively, although not exclusively.

This chapter briefly details each of the key positions within what is known as the housing classes debate and then builds upon the understanding that has been developed through debate to establish five key parameters which represent the current 'state of play' in the theorising of housing tenure. These will usefully delimit the theoretical inquiry we will pursue through the ensuing chapters.

THE COLLECTIVIST APPROACH

The essence of the collectivist approach is that home ownership is seen to be the basis for the formation of social groups. Home owners are said to share common experiences through their housing consumption that unite them in a significant way. The concepts used to identify these social groups have ranged from 'housing classes' (Rex and Moore, 1967) to 'housing status groups' (Haddon, 1970) and from 'domestic property classes' (Saunders, 1978, Pratt, 1982) to 'consumption sector cleavages' (Saunders, 1990). The key aspect of home ownership around which such social groups are said to form, was at first access to housing and then, in the face of sustained critique, the exchange value of housing.

By focusing upon individual's abilities to gain access to scarce and desired housing resources, we can identify a hierarchy of housing classes ranging from owner occupier to private tenant, the important point being that these divisions cut across those arising from the world of work (Rex and Moore, 1967). Housing class barriers would then be maintained by size and security of income as a passport to credit facilities and thus house purchase, or one's ability to fulfil local authority housing list requirements and thus gain access to the public rental sector.

Rex and Moore's (1967) approach attracted much criticism (Haddon, 1970; Saunders, 1977, 1979). For, as with any analysis based upon the commodity market an infinite number of differing consumption patterns will be revealed. This is so much so that Rex and Moore '...identify five (Rex and Moore, 1967, p. 36), six (Rex and Moore, 1967, p. 274) and seven (Rex, 1968, p. 215) housing classes in the area of Birmingham they studied' (Saunders, 1979, p. 69).

More significantly, it was argued that Rex and Moore had identified housing 'status groups' and not housing classes (Haddon, 1970). The concept remains Weberian yet is crucially different to that of class. For example, '...'classes' are stratified according to their relations to the production and acquisition of goods; whereas 'status groups' are stratified according to the principles of their consumption of goods as represented by special styles of life' (Gerth and Mills, 1948, p. 193). As housing is an element of consumption it was argued that Rex and Moore misinterpreted Weber, for consumption, it is clearly stated, is the sphere from which only status groups may derive. Therefore, 'Haddon's analysis must be taken as a convincing refutation of Rex and Moore's neo-Weberian housing class thesis' (Saunders, 1979, p. 75).

Despite Saunders' acceptance of Haddon's refutation he later develops his own version of housing classes using the concept 'domestic property class' (Saunders, 1977, 1978, 1979). Saunders argues that a real division exists between owner occupiers and tenants, be they public or private sector. The potential exchange value and the rights of use, control and disposal are emphasised as the privileges of owner occupancy. These privileges then form the basis of Weberian property classes, dependent on the proof of owner occupied housing as a source of real wealth accumulation. Stress upon the exchange value of housing, as opposed to access to housing as a scarce resource, differentiates Saunders' domestic property class from Rex and Moore's housing class. (See Pratt, 1982 for a discussion of this.)

Saunders (1979) later developed an auto-critique of this work, that, he argues, renders the domestic property class analysis redundant. The fundamental aspects of his critique are as follows. First, the domestic property class model is not exhaustive or complete. It cannot account for all empirical situations of housing consumption (e.g. housing co-ops and housing associations). Furthermore, it is possible for an individual to belong to more than one domestic property class, e.g. the owner occupier who occasionally lets out a room. Second, the model is static. Class, it is argued, should be seen as a relational concept, yet the model cannot specify any relations of exploitation. Third, the approach '...in the final analysis ... is empirical and descriptive dependent upon the continuation of specific conditions which are external to the analysis itself' (Saunders, 1979, p. 98). That is, the analysis depends upon home owners continuing to realise capital gains through their home ownership. Saunders saw these points as being sufficient to undermine his domestic property analysis. Accordingly, he recast his conceptualisation of housing tenure in the following manner.

Following Dunleavy (1979), Saunders (1984) (1990) applies the concept 'consumption sector' to housing and other consumption processes. This represents a significant widening of the terms of the housing classes debate. Attention is focused on a wider basis of inequality, state intervention generally, to include housing, education, health, transport, leisure, etc. The main axis to consumption sector cleavages is said to be 'public/private'. Those consuming privately-provided facilities enjoy greater benefits than those consuming publicly-provided facilities. Dunleavy maintains that these divisions are primarily ideological, whereas Saunders argues that they are significant material differences. For example, Saunders would argue that one is disadvantaged as a patient in the public health sector when compared to the service one can receive in the private health sector. These material differences, Saunders believes, cannot be satisfactorily explained as ideological divisions.

Meanwhile, Pratt (1982) revitalises the concept 'domestic property class' in a critique of Saunders' (1979) earlier auto-critique. This critique rests on a rejection of the three main 'weaknesses' that Saunders raises:

1. the historical contingency of the analysis;
2. the absence of conflict between all domestic property classes; and
3. the uncertain articulation of domestic property and acquisition classes.

On the first point Pratt (1982, p. 485) raises the questions:

...1) does it appear that the conditions necessary to constitute domestic property classes are temporary, so as to restrict the general validity of the analysis? And 2) if so, as an epistemological statement, is the criticism acceptable?

Pratt's response to the first question is inextricably linked to the second, for having briefly reviewed the arguments for and against the continuation of conditions likely to create capital gains for owner occupiers, she states that:

> ...as long as advanced capitalist societies pursue independent housing policies, the applicability of the domestic property class analysis will vary across political entities... the extent of variation across nations at any particular time is an empirical question. And the fact that it is an empirical question does not betray a fundamental flaw in Saunders' theorising (1982, p. 486).

The inextricable link between these points is of an epistemological nature. Pratt follows E. P. Thompson (1978) in arguing '...that theoretical frameworks should be transformable in response to historical and social conditions' (Pratt, 1982, p. 487).

On the second of Saunders' points, the absence of conflict between all domestic property classes, Pratt rightly points out that '(T)o state that class *ought* necessarily be treated as a relational concept tends toward a Marxist perspective...' (Pratt, 1982, p. 488). Saunders is thus erring from his Weberian starting point towards a Marxist definition of 'exploitation'.

> For a more closely weberian definition we may follow Giddens who defines exploitation as: ...*any socially conditioned form of asymmetrical production of life chances.* 'Life chances' here may be taken to mean the chances which an individual has of sharing in the socially created economic or cultural 'goods' which typically exist in any given society... In class structures the system of exploitation operates through differentials in market capacity. (Pratt, 1982, p. 489, original emphasis, citing Giddens, 1973, p. 130–131.)

Using this explicitly Weberian definition of exploitation, Pratt (1982) argues that the state, differentially allocating 'subsidies' between tenures, acts as a 'source of conflict between tenants and house owners'. The relational tie between classes, according to Pratt, is thus established.

The final of Saunders' points that Pratt tackles is how do we theorise the interaction between the housing and job markets?

How do we conceptualise the 'house-owning factory worker' (Saunders, 1979, p. 97)? Pratt's response is that,

> No claims need be made that domestic property is the *only* source of property which leads to wealth accumulation ... the relations between domestic property classes and other forms of property classes and between property classes and acquisition classes are open, empirical ones—not ones that *a priori* invalidate the domestic property class analysis (Pratt, 1982, p. 493).

Pratt thus argues for a return to the domestic property class analysis and a return to the debate of 1979.

Pratt's most recent work (1989) joins a growing list of articles that call for a new and theoretically more sophisticated look at the role of home ownership. (See Harloe, 1984, p. 228; Gray, 1982, p. 267; Kemeny, 1977, p. 52; Williams, 1984, p. 191; Barlow and Duncan, 1988.)

> First, it has been recognised that the category, housing tenure, must be conceptually unpacked. Second, the conspiratorial interpretation of the process of incorporation has been rejected. Third, a one dimensional causal account of the ideological effects of home ownership has been abandoned for a more fully contextualised understanding of the interrelationships between ideology, politics and housing tenure (Pratt, 1989, p. 295).

Pratt's article (Pratt, 1989) reviews the housing classes debate and argues that home ownership is part of a dynamic process that can lead to both integration into and resistance to capitalist social relations. The understanding of housing tenure in this article moves far beyond the early and crude functionalist theories and presents an interesting position from which to build our own analysis. The main weakness of Pratt's position, however, is that it fails to develop a causal understanding of how home ownership relates to incorporation in or resistance to capitalist social relations and this problematic is in many ways the central task of this book.

In Saunders' (1990, p. 326–7) latest work the notion of a tenure-based class is still rejected as '...home owners themselves do not appear to feel that their class identity is any different because of their ownership of domestic property'. Saunders, however, is asking the wrong question. Concern should not be with whether home owners redefine themselves as middle class rather than working class simply because they are home owners. Saunders is still preoccupied by the relative significance of housing market position *vis-à-vis* labour market position. Rather, the inter-relationships of occupation, tenure, gender, ethnicity, age, etc. in the formation of social groups should be examined. Indeed, a key aim in this book is to establish whether or not housing tenure causes the formation of social groups and if so how?

The collectivist line of thinking, however, has not developed in a vacuum and in fact has advanced due to a sustained critique from those arguing that home ownership in fact fragments other social groups such as the working class.

THE ANTI-COLLECTIVIST APPROACH

The Marxist-informed critique of the concept 'housing class' rests on whether or not home ownership represents an independent source of economic inequality sufficient to affect the distribution of social power. Two key points have been raised. First, that the conditions in the housing market of Britain and the United States in the 1970s, ripe for producing capital gains (the alleged source of economic inequality), were only a temporary aberration in housing market history and, therefore, of little independent theo-retical significance (Gray, 1982; Edel *et al.*, 1984). Second, even if capital gains were not a passing moment, such gains as did exist were merely a reflection of income differences derived from the job market. Capital gains to home owners, it is argued, are propor-tionately larger at the top end of the housing market in which those on the highest incomes trade. This means that the economic inequalities of capitalist formations, grounded in the labour relation, are merely being perpetuated through the housing market and that no (independent) reshaping of inequality is taking place through housing tenure (Thorns, 1981; Forrest, 1983).

In rejecting housing tenure as a source of economic inequality, anti-collectivists argue that housing tenure should be theorised as an ideological division (Clarke and Ginsburg, 1975; Harvey, 1978; Kemeny, 1980). As such the anti-collectivist argument is as follows. Private ownership of housing, which fosters a concern for the dwelling and its contents, has promoted a home-centred-life-style or privatism. This stands in contrast to the street, neighbour-hood and employment public-centred 'life of old'. Second, home owners are locked into the capitalist system through the mortgage debt they have encumbered in order to buy the house. This ensures a compliant workforce, for wages have to be earnt to pay the mortgage to keep the home. Home ownership, thus, fosters conservatism and incorporates households into the capitalist system. Third, because all households cannot afford to become home owners, the working class is divided along tenure lines. This fragmentation thesis has recently been extended to argue that as more and more households become home owners, then, inevitably fragmentation and differentiation amongst home owners will occur (Forrest, Murie and Williams, 1990).

Rose (1980) counters the functionalist tendencies of some of this work by pointing to the changing meanings of home owner-ship over time and the way in which home ownership was strug-gled for by the working class in Nineteenth Century Britain. This struggle, she argues, created a 'separate sphere' or private domain, in which the exploitation and alienation of the workplace could be forgotten.

More recent Marxist-informed work (Berry, 1986; Preteceille, 1986) has moved on from the earlier functional work as well to recognise divisions of consumption as being of a significant material nature, though not independent of production practices. These authors maintain that the primacy of class relations must be recognised in analysing social inequality. (For other Marxist informed commentaries on this subject see Ball, 1983; Bell, 1977; Edel, 1982; Hayward, 1986; Kemeny, 1981, 1983, 1986.)

Our current understanding of housing tenure is, then, signifi-cantly more sophisticated than the early attempts at specifying a housing class. This is largely due to the productive debate between

Marxist and Weberian scholars and the accumulation of empirical evidence. Detailed critiques of the literature reviewed already exist (see Harloe, 1984; Gray, 1982; Kemeny, 1977; Williams, 1984; Barlow and Duncan, 1988). As an alternative to a further critique, the housing classes debate is extended here to develop a conceptual analysis that examines the subjective understanding of housing tenure. On the basis of the current debate we can note the following points which usefully demarcate the parameters to the analysis developed throughout the rest of this book.

TOWARDS A THEORY OF HOUSING TENURE

First, it cannot be assumed that every time home owners' interests are threatened they will respond in a predetermined way. The economic reductionism of the early work of Saunders (1978), whereby it was simply assumed that home owners would automatically defend their economic interests, must be avoided. Furthermore, accounts interpreting the growth of home ownership in a mono-causal manner, for example, that the home ownership rate grew because it was functional to capitalism (Clarke and Ginsburg, 1975; Harvey, 1978), are too simplistic, as shown by Rose (1980). Structuration, after Giddens (1984), is a two way process and tenure as an element of the social structure is reproduced by the intentional actions and unintended consequences of individual agents. Thus, we require a conceptualisation of the relations of structuration between housing tenure and the individual. This, I suggest, should be theorised as the subjective understanding of the material experience of private property rights.

Second, tenure is not the single most important factor in explaining social life. It is not necessarily *the* determining variable. We need to take account of how tenure interacts with other social factors such as occupation, income, family life cycle and gender, to affect the material experience of private property rights and, thus, sift which tenure-based meanings are more or less important at the household level. As different meanings become more or less important then so will different courses of social action be engaged in. This is part of what I assume Pratt (1989) to mean by a 'contex-tualised understanding'.

Third, tenure is only one part of a system of housing provision. To categorise home ownership as a division of consumption is to totally misrepresent the mechanisms of inequality involved. The inequalities produced through home ownership do not lie solely at the point of consumption. They are, rather, part of a far wider structure of provision which spans production, exchange, consumption and reproduction, constructing inequalities through housing tenure (the focus of the housing class debate) and inflated returns to landowners, builders, developers and exchange profes-sionals (Ball, 1986 p. 5; Paris and Williams, 1983). With regard to economic inequality there are a variety of agencies and institutions that operate within the home ownership structure of provision. More specifically, agencies such as the state, banks, building soci-eties, estate agents and solicitors, interact to help shape a housing market in which their actions ultimately play on the price of housing and affect the wealth accumulation of the home owner.

As Ball (1986, p. 5) argues, the economic inequality constructed through housing tenure in Britain is grounded in state subsidies that filter their way through higher house prices to builders and developers; in finance institutions which play a key role in access to the home ownership market and the long-term cost of that entry through interest rates; in exchange professionals who parasitically bid up prices through their intervention; and in the process of production whereby builders provide accommoda-tion space of particular kinds and types to meet their assumptions with regard to appropriate living standards. In this way housing tenure is inextricably linked with the essential capital-labour relation. However, the consequences of home ownership for the social structure are only contingently related to the value relation. Housing tenure relations cannot simply be read off from job market relations for it is the interaction between these markets that needs to be taken into account. With housing tenure it is the subjective understanding of the material experience of differing private property rights and how that understanding relates to different courses of social action that is central.

Fourth, tenure is part of a system of housing provision that is both culturally specific and temporally and spatially variable. (Ball, 1983; Paris and Williams, 1983). Whilst an analysis of housing tenure in an Australian context of the late 1980s may demonstrate an impact upon courses of social action, this is not a generalisable empirical observation.

Fifth, in arguing for recognition of the distinction between the economic, political and cultural axes to power and the fact that they are constructed through housing tenure in particular, I reject the usefulness of a conflation of the economic with the sphere of production and the political and cultural with the sphere of consumption, for this leads to an unhelpful dichotomy of the spheres of production and consumption. Much of the 'housing classes' debate has been posed as a question of whether or not inequalities derived from the world of work or the world of home are more significant. The debate has been carried out in terms of whether divisions arising from the sphere of production or the sphere of consumption are predominant. It is this false dichotomy between production and consumption that has seriously fettered the progress of debate (see Warde, 1990, who argues a sociology of service provision is the solution to this problem). As long as concern remains with whether or not 'class' or 'sector' is primary debate will remain at loggerheads. If, on the other hand, it is recognised that economic, political and cultural power relations operate across markets, we may clarify how production and consumption forces, be they of an economic, political or cultural nature, combine to structure social inequality and the consequences of this for social action.

Our aim, therefore, is to theorise the subjective understanding of the material experience of private property rights. The need for a contextual understanding of tenure is recognised, however, the primary aim is to establish the significance of tenure *per se* not its relative significance. The interaction between housing market relations and job market relations as they are structured by the economic, political and cultural dimensions of power is examined in order to identify the essential causal aspects of housing tenure relations.

Chapter 3

HOUSING TENURE AND INEQUALITY

The empirical evidence that inequalities of an economic, cultural and political nature are constructed through housing tenure is wide ranging. This evidence has been presented in an inter-twined manner, reflecting daily life and subsuming the individual significance of these different aspects of inequality. To redress this, Chapter 3 establishes the significance of each aspect of inequality by conceptually separating the economic, political and cultural dimensions, as far as is possible, whilst also noting the extent to which they interact empirically.

At the base of all tenure inequalities be they economic, political or cultural is the state as the fundamental guarantor of private property rights. Importantly, however, the state cannot generate economic or cultural inequalities, only those of a political nature. In the pure type, economic inequalities are generated through market relations, political inequalities by the state and cultural inequalities through lifestyle relations. It is this distinction between 'base' and 'generator' that underlies the significance of the ideal types. The fact that private property rights are an essential aspect of capitalist social relations also renders a de facto guarantee of private property rights by the state.

ECONOMIC INEQUALITIES

Considering economic inequality as the outcome of control over resources which are primarily monetarily oriented, this section demonstrates how economic inequalities are constructed through housing tenure. These inequalities are fundamentally determined by the housing market, though state intervention can provide bases from which the housing market can generate new inequalities. We shall examine data on the nature of the economic inequalities constructed through housing tenure, for those countries that have a significant proportion (over 60 per cent) of home owners, including Australia, N.Z., Canada, the U.S. and Britain. The Australian material is drawn upon where appropriate to contextualise the later case studies and to attempt some redress of a debate that has been dominated by North American and British contributions.

The following three sections examine the construction of economic inequality between home owners and private tenants and amongst home owners and amongst renters. We shall reveal that: home owners enjoy economic advantages that renters do not, but that not all home owners have access to such advantages all of the time; the causes of this variation remain unspecified and, thus; we need to consider alternative conceptual strategies. One that focuses upon the subjective understanding of housing tenure is suggested.

Economic Inequality Between Home Owners and Private Tenants

The distinction between home owners and private tenants provides the clearest example of the economic inequality constructed through housing tenure. Renters are economically disadvantaged and owners advantaged by their housing tenure, immediately differentiating their tenure experiences. The mechanisms through which this economic inequality occur, in Australia, are four-fold:

1. whilst incomes and rental payments rise with inflation, mortgage repayments are devalued by inflation,
2. as house prices rise home owners have the opportunity of reaping untaxed capital gains,
3. the imputed rent value of owner occupation remains untaxed; and
4. first home owner schemes continue to be funded at the expense of rental subsidies.

These mechanisms redistribute wealth regressively in favour of home owners and against private tenants and have done so in Australia for a substantial part of the Twentieth Century.

Whilst the outcomes of the above mentioned processes are that home owners have access to economic resources through housing tenure and renters do not, the source of much of this economic inequality is of a political nature. The fact that capital gains and imputed rent remain untaxed are political decisions. The fact that government commitment to subsidising home ownership is carried out at the cost of rental subsidies, is also a political decision. The political basis to this economic inequality exemplifies the empirically inter-twined nature of the dimensions of inequality. Such inter-twining though does not deny the analytical value of separating these dimensions conceptually as ideal types. Whilst there may be a political basis to economic inequality, it is the relations of the market that in fact generate such inequalities.

Examining housing costs in Melbourne (capital of the State of Victoria, Australia) over a 50 year period, we can see that in 1932 the costs involved in owning and renting were approximately equivalent at $630 and $720 (per 5 years) respectively (King, 1987, p. 222–223). However,

> The extraordinary leap in house prices in 1949–50, and the reappearance of uncontrolled rental housing around 1950, ended any approximate correspondence between the costs of purchasers and those of renters. The equivalent estimated total costs over the five years for the end of 1952 to 1957 were £–229.10s.0d (i.e. a net *benefit* of £229.10s.0d or $459, rather than a cost) for purchasers,

but a cost of £2,730.10s.0d. ($5,461) for renters (both in 1957 prices). Although both sets of net costs fluctuated over the era, this order of extreme difference nevertheless persisted through the 1950s and 60s (King, 1987, p. 222–223).

In the 1970s the economic gap between owners and renters widened further.

In the speculative boom of 1973–77, the net costs of renters generally rose slightly ahead of inflation, but slightly behind increases in average earnings; for owner occupiers however, capital gains ensured that net costs became net benefits, and real return (on initial outlay and net expenditure) soared to an average 158 percent above inflation over the five years (or 20.9 percent per annum compounded) (King, 1987, p. 273).

Furthermore, the economic gap between owners and renters widens after housing costs have been paid.

Only 3.7% of full house owners are very poor *after* housing, compared to 12.8% of private tenants and 6.7% of all income units. Private tenants make up 40.8% of all income units very poor after housing, although comprising only 21.4% of the total population. In other words, private tenants are twice as likely to be in serious poverty as are other housing groups (Berry, 1977, p. 54).

By 1977–82 owners and renters net costs in Melbourne were again almost equal, after a period of 50 years (King, 1987, p. 273). However, private tenants continued to be economically disadvantaged when compared with owners when examining after housing costs. Though we should note the difficulties of comparing metropolitan data (such as King's, 1987) with aggregate national level data due to the spatial variability of housing market performance (see King, 1987), if we compare the situation in the early 1970s with data for 1981/2, private tenants continued to be the largest proportionate group whose housing costs shifted them from above to below the poverty line; 8.2% of private tenants with incomes above the poverty line before housing were in poverty after paying rent, compared with 3.9% of owner/purchasers, the next largest group (Bradbury *et al.*, 1987).

Figures of this nature about housing tenure have real consequences for the distribution of wealth in Australia:

> The most widespread and striking inequality is between house owners and tenants. Not only has home ownership been encouraged by tax concessions and home savings grants; it has proved to be the surest road to capital gains. The returns to home ownership, in terms of rent saved and capital gains, have been higher than on any other broad class of asset available to the ordinary citizen (Manning, 1983, p. 10).

A further aspect to tenure-based economic inequality, is that home owners accumulating wealth through their housing tenure have the opportunity to bequeath a valuable asset. Renters, on the other hand, have no asset at the end of their tenancy or life as a direct result of their housing consumption.

The economic advantages of owning compared to renting have endured in Australia for a large part of the Twentieth Century with few periods of exception. The construction of economic inequality through housing tenure exists: generally in the form of ground rent and specifically in the form of the favourable tax treatment of capital gains and imputed rent; in the form of mortgage repayments deflated by inflation versus rental payments that increase with inflation, and; in the form of first home owner schemes versus rent subsidies. The combined result is that home owners are economically advantaged whilst private tenants are economically disadvantaged. However, is it clear that such economic advantages apply to all home owners at all times in all places?

Economic Inequality Amongst Home Owners

Capital gains are the key variant in the economic fortunes of home owners within a nation state, though varying state policies differentiate the economic and other experiences of home ownership internationally. There is and has been considerable variation in the extent of capital gains available to home owners over space and time. The fact that capital gains are available at all and more particularly that wealth distribution may be affected by housing market processes, has fuelled the 'collectivist' argument that housing tenure represents an independent source of economic inequality that cross-cuts divisions arising from the labour market. In contrast the 'anti-collectivists' have suggested that the economic inequalities constructed through housing tenure are not independent but merely reflect inequalities generated in the job market. Any variability in the capital gains available from home ownership, will, they argue, reflect variations in inequality that derive from the labour market.

Thorns' (1981) work in Christchurch, New Zealand is one of the earliest analyses of the precise manner in which economic inequalities occur through housing tenure. Thorns argues that,

> Most data available on rates of capital gain ... mask considerable local variation ... related to local market conditions, to the price and location of the property and to the class base of the occupants (Thorns, 1981, p. 205–6).

Thorns suggests that what is really required are data that examine '...capital gains within the home owner group by sub-market location to assess the relative rates of gain and thus their likely affect upon owner occupiers as a property class' (Thorns, 1981, p. 206).

To this end, Thorns conducted research across five different suburbs that reflected a range of housing sub-markets. Most importantly he concludes that '...substantial gains are made from owner occupation', but '...that gains are made unevenly across the various areas of the city' (Thorns, 1981, p. 210).

> The analysis of occupation, household income and capital gains shows that the largest gains are obtained by those in managerial and professional occupations and in the higher, over $300 per week, income categories. This would seem to indicate that gains from the job and housing markets are in fact quite closely related and to some extent mutually reinforcing. It further shows that owner occupation

has brought greater financial benefits to middle class home owners than it has to working class home owners (Thorns, 1981, p. 213).

Several points need to be made in relation to Thorns' pioneering work. First, owner occupiers do appear to enjoy capital gains, although the extent of this appears to vary according to position within the job market. The mere fact that owner occupiers do enjoy capital gains supports the claims of collectivists, such as Saunders (1979), that home ownership represents a significant material division within society. The qualifying statement, that the extent of capital gains appears to vary according to class, is the sort of evidence called upon by anti-collectivists, such as Preteceille (1986), to suggest that the economic inequalities apparent in the housing market are largely a reflection of those derived from the job market. So it is argued, no independent structuring of economic power is taking place through the housing market.

However, it is difficult to arrive at firm conclusions about capital gains on the basis of Thorns' early work. First, the five study areas were identified by means of their distribution of house values; the top end of the scale having 59.9 per cent of its houses worth more than $50,000, the bottom end having 86 per cent of its houses worth between $20,000 and $30,000. This appears to be a satis-factory manner in which to identify study areas but it is problem-atic to assume, as Thorns does, that the identified distribution of capital values reflects the class character of these suburbs. To equate house value with social class and to assume that there is class homogeneity within a suburb assumes too much, for there need be no necessary correspondence.

Second, Thorns assumes that within each of the five study areas housing market processes are uniform. In fact we have no guar-antee that the sub markets he identifies are the lowest level of sub market—there might be sub-markets within the sub-markets. For instance, capital gains may vary according to house type, as much as 'class'.

More sophisticated accounts of capital gains in Australasia have built upon Thorns' early work, examining the housing markets of Melbourne (King, 1987), Adelaide (capital of South Australia)

(Badcock, 1989, 1992a,b,c) and New Zealand (Thorns, 1989; Dupuis, 1992).

King's (1987) account of the housing markets in Melbourne, 1932–1982, is one of the most sophisticated treatments of capital gains yet attempted. King documents the extent of spatial and temporal variation of capital gains and importantly examines the causes of such variations by linking capital gains made in the domestic property market to circuits of capital in the global economy.

The broad picture according to King is that home owners' and private tenants' net costs were approximately equal in the early 1930s and early 1980s but in between these periods home owners have enjoyed capital gains that have climbed as high as an average 158 percent above inflation between 1973–77 (see discussion above). These gains have been distributed unevenly throughout the housing markets of Melbourne, both spatially and temporally, according to the actions of speculative investors. However, King notes that such variation is not completely without pattern for,

> ...despite the spatial switching of uneven investment and development ... there have indeed been quite long-term redistributions of wealth through the medium of housing. And these redistributions have been typically regressive favouring owner-occupiers over renters and, among owner-occupiers, those in more affluent areas over those in poorer. And secondly, differential prices shifts seem mainly to have reflected the relative expansion of the professional workers, one must surmise that any switching of investment...will reflect the behaviours...of groups that enjoy some hegemonic position in the social class structure (King, 1987, p. 274–5).

Following Harvey, King's conclusions concur with the Marxist or anti-collectivist position in the housing classes debate; that the economic inequalities of housing tenure appear, in Melbourne at least, to simply enhance those created through the job market. There is no apparent cross-cutting of job market divisions by economic inequalities constructed through housing tenure.

However, we cannot draw firm conclusions on the basis of this one data set (despite its depth), for Badcock's (1989) study of

Adelaide housing markets paints a different picture. Badcock (1989) examines trends in Adelaide's separate-housing market, 1968–75, to answer the question, what is the relationship between class position and house price inflation? Whilst, like King (1987), Badcock (1989) is keen to specify the generative mechanisms underlying capital gains or losses, his data set covers a relatively short period of time (seven years) in comparison with King's 50 year study. Bearing this in mind Badcock presents conclusions which contradict those of King (1987), in that

> Home ownership does not unilaterally reinforce class position determined in the labour market. It is clear that Adelaide's housing market is actively redistributing wealth in ways that cut across to some degree the pattern of earnings determined by the labour market (Badcock, 1989, p. 88).

Badcock is suggesting that the economic inequalities constructed through housing tenure are sufficient to reshape economic inequalities originating from the job market, though the precise form of this reshaping is unknown. This is the nature of the empirical evidence that many of the Weberian authors, noted above, have used to suggest that home ownership does indeed represent an independent source of economic inequality and thus that home owners can be specified as a specific class, cleavage, or division within the social structure.

Badcock's later and more extensive work (1992a,b,c) details the 'capture of value' by Adelaide's inner-urban residents at the expense of suburban residents. This appears to tilt the balance of the argument in the opposite direction, if we assume that the inner-urban gentrifiers are in an economically advantageous position due to the prior structuring of the labour market. Firm conclusions are, thus, still difficult so let us consider yet further data.

Thorns' (1989) later work in New Zealand concludes,

> ...that home ownership constitutes a base for real accumulation but the rate and extent of this process is not an even one. The ability to gain wealth varies considerably by time, location, level of individual and family income, employment level, and household type (p. 293).

Thorns argues that '...the wealth generated through home ownership is a factor fragmenting rather than uniting social groups and, therefore, is unlikely in itself to be a basis of political mobilisation' (p. 293). This Marxian interpretation argues that the heterogeneity amongst home owners is so profound, due to variables such as time of purchase, location, position in the job market, etc., that home ownership in fact contributes to individualism and privatism, weakening the collectivism of the working class.

More recent analysis of New Zealand's housing market generally confirms this picture (Dupuis, 1992). Since 1970 all home owners in New Zealand have made capital gains subject to variability in the extent of such gains across time and space. The interrelations of labour and housing markets at a metropolitan level account for some of this variability, though not all. Thus, it is not really possible to state categorically to what extent capital gains in the housing market are dependent upon ones position in the labour market.

We have seen that capital gains are reaped by home owners but that there is considerable variation of capital gains over both time and space. Furthermore, we cannot arrive at firm conclusions regarding a distinct patterning to the variation in capital gains or what causes such variations. Whilst King (1987) suggests there is a distinct pattern for Melbourne, Badcock suggests that there is not for Adelaide. We, therefore, require not only further intra-city comparisons of capital gains, but inter-city as well.

If the Australian data are inconclusive as to the patterning of capital gains, has research overseas produced a clearer picture?

Canada

Examining studies of the housing markets in Vancouver 1949–63 (Hamilton, 1976), Vancouver 1965–77 (Housing and Urban Land Development Association of Canada, 1978) and a range of Canadian cities (Royal Trust, 1983), '...the Canadian evidence suggests that access to potential capital gains through house price inflation has not been restricted to middle-income home owners' (Pratt, 1986c, p. 368). These results support the collectivist position of housing tenure being a significant redistributor of economic wealth, rather than simply a means by which job market based inequalities are reproduced or enhanced. Pratt concludes that,

> The wealth opportunities afforded by home ownership do not simply reinforce class differences created within the production sphere. The housing market structures wealth accumulation somewhat differently from the way wealth is structured in the job market, and it is in this way that housing tenure contributes significantly to economic cleavages in societies such as Canada, the U.S. and Britain (Pratt, 1986c, p. 369).

However, Pratt's presentation of the construction of economic inequality through housing tenure, in Canada (1986a) (1986c), is largely drawn from secondary sources. Whilst this is not in itself problematic, it is never clear which economic aspects of housing tenure have been included in the calculations of costs, gains and losses. It appears that Pratt has not offset home owners' costs against the potential capital gains they have access to, which could be a significant amount during a period of high interest rates.

United States

A study of Boston's (U.S.) housing market, 1870–1970 concludes that capital gains in Boston have fluctuated widely over time and space (Edel et al.,1984). Though '(t)he loss of money on reselling one's home was not an experience suffered by a majority of the population ...' (Edel et al., 1984, p. 107); '... the relative appreciation to investment in housing has varied with location in the Boston region' (Edel et al., 1984, p. 126); and finally '...both among different strata of the labour force and between them and top wealth holders, the distribution of real estate value changes helps to maintain relative wealth disparities' (Edel et al., 1984, p. 133).

These conclusions, as do King's (1987) for Australia, support the anti-collectivist argument that the construction of economic inequality through housing tenure is not a process that cross-cuts economic divisions created through the job market but one that reinforces such inequalities.

United Kingdom

Turning our attention to the Britain, Forrest and Murie (undated) caution against any simple assumptions about the relationship between position in the job market and opportunities for wealth through owner occupation.

> ...the relationship between housing tenure and employment or economic position is not a straightforward one...Family life cycle factors, wealth inheritance, inter-generational transfers (including gifts and loans) can all act to 'distort' the simple relationship between labour market position and position in the owner occupied market (Forrest and Murie, undated, p. 6).

Hamnett (1988), commenting on the significance of home ownership for wealth inheritance in post Second World War Britain, states that 'House price inflation has played a major part in the creation of a new class of wealth owners who have little else in the way of assets apart from their house' (Hamnett, 1988, p. 11). In line with the collectivist argument this suggests, that home ownership may restructure job market based inequalities. This is supported further by the work of Munro and McClennan (1986) in Scotland, for they suggest that, '(t)he potential for relative capital gains in Glasgow over the last decade has been greatest at the cheapest end of the owner-occupied market' (Munro and McClennan, 1986, p. 20).

Saunders (1990), drawing on one of the most comprehensive studies of home ownership and capital gains ever undertaken in Britain, concludes that, '...the median home owner stands to lose precisely £1,987.90 every year from any attempt to 'liberate the masses' from the contemporary capitalist system of private property ownership' (p. 203). As one of the main protagonists in the collectivist argument Saunders research was undertaken to provide data for an increasingly abstract debate. His conclusions are that: home owners do make capital gains and not at the expense of other owners as '...housing increases in value at twice the rate of RPI while staying constant in cost measure against real income levels' (p. 202); these gains are not temporary but have been realised throughout this century and certainly since the 1950s; gains are made by all home owners but vary according to location and; home owners are aware of the potential for capital gains and act accordingly.

On the other hand, Duncan (1990) asking 'Do house prices rise that much?', answers '...that capital gains in owner occupation are not as real as they appear' (p. 205). Duncan '...attempts to measure real house prices (i.e. adjusted for inflation) and pure house prices (i.e. adjusted for quality and quantity changes) for Britain since the mid 1960s' (p. 195). Whilst the notion of 'pure prices' introduces an interesting complexity to the debate, Duncan's reliance on national average data poses problems with regard to the spatial variability of capital gains as discussed above.

In sum, it appears that the only firm conclusion that can be arrived at, on the basis of a review of the capital gains literature in Australasia, Canada, the U.S. and Britain, is that capital gains can be realised, however, there is such temporal and spatial variability of capital gains to home owners, that no distinct pattern exists. Therefore, the level of generalisation anticipated in the literature about capital gains from the housing market cross-cutting job market divisions, is inappropriate. Such a conclusion indicates that it is time for a different strategy with which to consider the impact of capital gains.

As an alternative let us consider the subjective understanding of economic inequalities constructed through housing tenure, rather than continuing to try and establish the when and where of capital gains. This approach explores the attribution of meaning to housing tenure and the impact of this upon social action. The significance of housing tenure for home owners and renters them-selves and the impact of this significance upon social life can thus be established.

Two fundamental points need to be made in relation to the work that has focused upon the construction of economic inequality through housing tenure. First, such work tends to focus exclusively on the economic aspects of housing tenure at the expense of examining other aspects of inequality such as the cultural and political. (Although Pratt's (1986a, 1986c) work is a notable exception to this and Saunders (1989) (1990) most recent work implicitly stresses the cultural significance of home ownership). For as will be shown in the following sections, the political and cultural aspects of inequality constructed through housing tenure are equally far reaching in their impact upon people's lives.

The second point relates to the treatment of the incumbents of housing tenure in such work. It is largely assumed that all home owners will act in similar ways in response to economic interests such as capital gains. This takes no account of how these economic interests are of varying importance for different individuals and households as defined by stage of the life cycle, ethnicity or income. In other words no account is taken of the subjective understanding of the economic interests of housing tenure which may differ substantially from the objective economic interests that are assumed to exist. This is important for it is the subjective understanding of economic interests that will affect different courses of social action.

This section has documented the existence of economic inequalities amongst home owners. Not all home owners enjoy equal access to the economic benefits of home ownership at the same time, but different groups of home owners at different times and places enjoy such benefits. The overall patterning of this process, however, is unclear. Let us move on to consider the tenure-based economic inequalities amongst renters.

Economic Inequality Amongst Renters

Though there is little data on the comparative experiences of the construction of economic inequality amongst public, private and co-operative renters, the starting point to investigate these experiences should be the experience of differing private property rights. On this basis there are perhaps two key distinctions that can be made: first, between those in the public sector and those in the private sector; second, between those trapped in private renting and those for whom it is a short term option.

On the first point, the fact that private and public landlords have different economic motivations is significant. Private landlords are in pursuit of profit whilst public landlords are attempting to cover costs, though the latter varies from state to state within Australia and no doubt internationally. This of course has ramifications in terms of the amount of rent the tenant is required to pay.

The distinction between trapped and mobile renters in the private sector is made clear when considering the notion of after housing poverty. After deducting housing costs from private renters' incomes a number of them fall below the poverty line. These households are then trapped in the private rental sector as they are unable to accumulate savings to buy into home owner-ship. As rents rise with inflation they rely upon wages and pensions to maintain parity with the Consumer Price Index (CPI) to simply remain where they are.

The central message of this section is that economic inequalities are constructed through housing tenure. These exist between home owners and renters, amongst home owners and amongst renters. Whilst it is clear that home owners enjoy economic advan-tages unavailable to renters, it is not clear that all home owners enjoy all of these advantages all of the time. The causality of vari-ation in capital gains remains unspecified and hence, an alterna-tive strategy for establishing the social significance of housing tenure is suggested: examination of the subjective experience of private property rights. This suggestion is pursued in Chapters 4 and 5 whilst the following sections of Chapter 3 establish the extent of political and cultural inequalities constructed through housing tenure.

POLITICAL INEQUALITIES

Political inequality is the result of ideal and/or material advantages given primarily by the state. In relation to housing tenure the state guarantees the private property rights of home ownership, differ-

entiating them from the limited private property rights of renting.
The political inequalities of housing tenure relate to differing
rights of control and security. Home owners, for example, enjoy
rights of control over the dwelling far beyond those of either public
or private renters.

The political inequalities that result from different private
property rights guaranteed by the state have received scant attention. In fact, housing class debaters have used the term 'political'
to refer to the political consequences of housing tenure as in political activism, voting, or political attitudes, rather than the political
base of tenure inequalities and how these relate to social group
formation. This section examines how and why private property
rights differ between tenures and how the 'political' has been
treated in analyses of housing tenure under the headings political
activism, voting and political attitudes.

In terms of the relationship between the political dimension and
the economic and cultural dimensions, the guarantee of private
property rights by the state underlies the economic and cultural
inequalities generated through housing tenure. If the private
property rights of exclusive use, control and ownership are fundamentally undermined, then access to the economic and cultural
privileges that go with home ownership can also be undermined.
The state guarantee of private property rights is, therefore, a
necessary precondition of the economic and cultural dimensions
of home ownership, however, it is not a sufficient condition. That
is, the economic and cultural inequalities of housing tenure are
not generated by the state, but by market relations and the relations of lifestyle, respectively. However, without the state's political guarantee of private property rights there would be no basis
from which the relations of market and lifestyle could carve out
their differing sets of inequalities.

Private Property Rights

The general pattern of private tenants' rights in Australia is that
they have limited rights of use, control and security. Use rights are
curtailed through contract clauses that for example ban pets;

control rights are limited as there is no freedom to decorate or alter the dwelling; security of tenure only exists effectively for as long as the rent is paid, typically one month. As soon as a tenant falls into rent arrears all rights are basically lost, hence, security of tenure is effectively month by month.

In Europe and the U.S. a longer term comparative view of tenants rights sees them increasing with the aftermath of each World War as rent controls and security provisions were imposed, and then a general strengthening with the establishment of the post 1945 welfare states (Harloe, 1985:267). In France the old controlled sector of private rental accommodation provides lifetime security of tenure with rights of inheritance of such leases. More recently three year leases have been the norm. In Denmark the tenant has been recognised as the weaker of the partners in negotiating a contract and thus given a degree of protection through limiting the grounds for eviction. In the Netherlands two to five year contracts are typical with disputes resolved through the courts. In the USA, as in Australia, tenants rights are a State (and local) rather than federal matter. In New York there exists a controlled and a liberalised sector as is the case in most of the European countries reviewed by Harloe (1985). Whilst tenants in controlled apartments have security of tenure and rights to a renewed contract, those in the liberalised sector have security for the contract term but no right to a renewed contract (Harloe, 1985:267–276).

The legal status of renters is limited and yet there are doubts about whether tenants even enjoy the full extent of these rights, for, '...in so personal a matter as the relationship between a landlord and a tenant, the ability of the law to govern actual conduct is severely limited' (Harloe, 1985:266). In-depth studies of the actual private property rights of private renters are few. Harloe comments that

> Given the widespread realisation that the gap between officially sanctioned behaviour and actual practices was often a wide one, it might be thought that a substantial amount of research would have

been carried out into this problem. In fact little information, was available... (1985:266).

This dearth of information on the actual experience of private renting also pertains in Australia where '(p)rivate rental housing compared to home ownership and public housing has been relatively neglected, by both policy makers and academics... (Paris, 1984:9). The general picture of private renting in Australia is somewhat different from the private rental sectors of France, Denmark, Germany, the Netherlands and USA which are all declining in size to become a residual sector for the poor. The Australian private rental sector has maintained a significant share of the Australian housing market of approximately 20–25 per cent of all households (Paris, 1984:10). Some of these households are undoubtedly 'trapped' in private renting, unable to maintain rental payments and save a deposit for house purchase at the same time, yet many households do use private renting as an interim tenure stage between leaving the parental home and house purchase.

In Australia the residual nature of private rental housing stems not from its size but '...primarily from its inherent disadvantages relative to other tenures. Compared to owners, private tenants have limited security or freedom in the use of the dwelling' (Kendig, 1984:67). Whilst this is true for the country as a whole, tenants rights do vary from State to State. In Tasmania, for example, the only law governing tenants rights is the 1935 Landlord and Tenant Act that applies the nineteenth century principles of freedom of contract. In Victoria and South Australia, however, there has been more recent legislation whereby

The Act makes extensive provision on termination, and landlord's recovery of possession; regulates rent increases, 'excessive' rent, and bond money; prescribes a standard form of tenancy agreement containing the new range of rights and obligations which, especially for landlords, exceed the meagre responsibilities and entitlements traditionally supplied by the common law and landlord and tenant legislation; and phases out the rent controls of the Landlord and Tenant Act (1938) (Nicholson and Weeks, 1984:48).

Whilst tenant rights have generally improved throughout the Twentieth Century, although by no means universally, significant security of tenure has only been established in response to cataclysmic circumstances and the most significant rights that tenants enjoy today are largely the skeletal remains of reactions by the state to housing crises.

One of the key reasons why tenants' rights remain so limited is that the rights of home ownership and thus of private property are fundamental to capitalism. A wholesale usurpation of home owners' rights is unlikely and in effect the state's guarantee of private property rights can be taken for granted. Real assurance of the continuation of private property rights most accurately lies with the structures of capitalist formations that reify private ownership of the means of production. This reification provides for an association between the ownership of capital and the ownership of domestic property which is so complete it renders home owners' rights sacrosanct. If the state is to reduce the political inequalities generated through housing tenure it is only tenant rights that provide any room to manoeuvre. The improvement of tenant rights, however, can only take place at the expense of another group of property owners, landlords. It is this dilemma for the state that explains partly why tenant rights have in fact remained severely limited.

Whilst the differing private property rights of home ownership and renting are clear, these political inequalities have not been examined in relation to the formation of social groups through housing tenure. Instead, housing class debaters have focused their attention on what can loosely be termed the political consequences of home ownership; investigating the political activism, voting behaviour and political attitudes of different tenure groups. This indeed focuses on tenure-based action but pays no regard to the inequalities and meanings that inform the action and hence ignores the basis of such social group formation. Nevertheless, it is important that we note how earlier approaches differ from our own and the following three sections examine the relationship between housing tenure and political activism, voting, and political attitudes respectively.

Political Activism

The significance of housing tenure for local political activism is argued to be that home owners are more likely to be active than renters due to a need to defend their private property interests, with property values often seen as the key factor. To the extent that property values are key, home owners can be seen to be becoming politically active due to their economic interests not their political interests. Tenure-based political activism in the pure type as we have defined it, is rather grounded in the political inequalities of differing private property rights such as use and control.

'Political' activism, then, by those of different housing tenures has been examined by Saunders (1979) in Britain and by Agnew (1981), Cox (1982, 1989), Cox and McCarthy (1980, 1982), Davis, J. (1991) Davis, M. (1992) and De Leon (1992) in the United States and Harloe (1985) in comparative perspective.

Saunders' (1979) early work in Croydon, a suburb of London, argues that owner occupiers, acting to defend their property values and housing densities, '...not only constitute a highly articulate and effective political group, but also achieve their successes at the expense of both business and working class interests' (Saunders, 1979, p. 206). The latter group, in the main, consisted of private and public renters.

In a general examination of neighbourhood activism as 'turf politics' and its relation to urban investment patterns in the United States, Cox (1982, 1989) and Cox and McCarthy (1980, 1982) expose the relationship between home ownership and community activism. Cox (1982) and Cox and McCarthy (1982) argue that the home as an investment has little to do with why a home owner may become politically active in the neighbourhood. Rather, the explanation of activism lies with the fact that removal costs are prohibitively expensive and thus it's cheaper to stay and fight. Similar to Saunders, political activism is said to rest with the economic, rather than political interests of home ownership.

More recent studies in the U.S. enable us to consider the activism of home owners in three different cities: Cincinnati (Davis J., 1991); San Francisco (De Leon, 1992); and Los Angeles

(Davis M., 1992). Mike Davis' narrative of home owner opposition to urban development illustrates the empirical interlacing of economic issues (property values) with political issues (neighbourhood control) and how these are cross-cut by an engrained racism (1992, Chapter 3). Whilst Davis does not have our analytical aims and hence does not distinguish the political from the economic, he clearly illustrates the significance of politically generated inequalities grounded in private property rights. Restrictive covenants

> '...both mandated and prohibited certain types of behaviour on the part of the present and future property owner ... Private restrictions, for example, normally included such provision as minimum required costs for home construction, and exclusion of all non-Caucasians (and sometimes non-Christians as well) from occupancy, except as domestic servants.' (Davis M., 1992:161 citing Weiss, 1987:3–4, 11–12.)

De Leon's (1992) study of the urban politics of San Francisco alludes to the significance of home ownership and notes San Franciscan home owners supported urban development in contrast to the home owners of Los Angeles. This difference illustrates the non-determinate nature of home ownership interests specified in Chapter 2 as a key parameter to the analysis of housing tenure.

John Davis' (1991) study of urban protest in Cincinnati more clearly distinguishes the economic and political interests of home ownership (though the cultural dimension remains marginal). For example, 'old' and 'new' home owner activism opposing urban redevelopment is grounded for 'old home owners' in use values, autonomy, security and amenity (in our terms the political), and for 'new home owners' in property values and equity (in our terms the economic) (190).

It is only Agnew's (1981) work in the United States, however, that accurately distinguishes each of the differing aspects of home ownership and causally links them to political activism. Agnew develops a Marxist approach to the understanding of housing tenure, as he phrases it, '...to see how social being and identity are related...and to demonstrate the role of home ownership in the relationship between them' (Agnew, 1981, p. 60). He concludes that the interests associated with home ownership, such as the facilitation of personal autonomy (political interests), the realisation of social esteem (cultural interests) and the maintenance/ enhancement of exchange value (economic interests), are sufficient to require 'community consciousness' on the part of the home owner. The result, he suggests, is greater community activism on the part of the home owner when compared with the renter and importantly we are able to identify what tenure-based interests are being acted upon.

The housing tenure and political activism literature focuses almost exclusively upon home owners. When renters have formed political organisations, they have usually been small scale and '...relatively few have made a significant impact on the more general conditions of private tenants by, for example, successfully promoting changes in the law' (282). Davis' (1991) work in Cincinnati confirms this for '...the tenants of private housing in the West End have exhibited neither a rudimentary political consciousness of their property interest nor a propensity to act collectively in acknowledgement or defense of those interests' (199). The reason for this is that whilst '...tenure may be a vehicle for establishing one's political or social identity ... for the majority of tenants, their status as a tenant is not the way they choose to measure themselves and the politics of their tenancy is a low priority in their lives' (Bounds, 1989, p. 16).

Voting

The relationship between individuals as members of a housing tenure and the state, can also be explored by examining the link between housing tenure and voting behaviour and/or voting intention. In this context the literature argues that housing tenure produces certain types of voter, or generates allegiances to one party rather than another. The conventional wisdom suggests a scenario whereby home owners are associated with the conservative parties and renters the social democratic parties. Again the failing of this literature is that it considers the consequences of housing tenure interests with insufficient regard for the cause of these consequences. That is, it fails to ask what it is about housing tenure that causes such voting patterns.

Dunleavy (1979), based on an analysis of 1974 U.K. Gallup Poll data, notes that home owners are 2.35 times more likely to vote Conservative than council tenants and that '...housing effects are trichotomous, not dichotomous, with private renting having a distinctive effect on political alignment in between those of home ownership and local authority renting' (Dunleavy, 1979, p. 437). These associations between housing tenure and party preference reflect, Dunleavy argues, ideological divisions. He suggests such divisions or cleavages represent the basis for an analysis of consumption sectors, these being '...lines of vertical division in a society, such that certain common interests are shared between social classes in the same sector, while within a social class, sectoral differences reflect a measure of conflict of interests' (Dunleavy, 1979, p. 419).

McAllister (1984) concurs with Dunleavy (1979) that housing tenure has a significant impact upon electoral outcomes in Britain. He also makes the point, however, that the electoral consequences of housing tenure are variable across countries, to the extent that housing tenure appears to have no impact on electoral outcomes in either Australia or the U.S. Explanation of the British case, McAllister argues, lies with the large public housing sector in Britain (approximately 30 per cent of all households at the time of the article) and the traditional Labour party allegiance of its inhabitants. In Australia and the U.S. strong cross-party support for home ownership and for public housing as welfare housing precludes such an alignment.

Williams' (1989) study of voting intention and political attitudes in Aberdeen, Scotland, also concludes that voting intention is statistically related to housing tenure.

> For all classes, the nature of the relationship is the same, with owner occupiers tending to vote Conservative or Alliance, and renters tending to favour the Labour Party. The greatest level of support for the Labour Party is to be found amongst manual workers who are

renters (approximately 60 per cent), whereas the Conservatives draw their strongest support from non-manual owner occupiers (Williams, 1989, p. 120).

However, Williams argues that whilst renters are less likely than owners to hold conservative views, statistical significance cannot be attributed to the relationship between political attitudes and housing tenure, except in reference to skilled non-manual and lower managerial workers. This conclusion also has wider support in the work of Pratt (1986a, 1986b, 1986c, 1986d, 1987, see discussion below). Williams' (1989) overall conclusion, however, is that further work is required to '...unravel the direction of causality between tenure and political variables...' (Williams, 1989, p. 125). This is indeed the case for in fact no one has specified what it is about the nature of differing tenures that results in different voting patterns.

Political Attitudes

The literature examining the link between housing tenure and political attitudes is centred on Canada in a series of articles by Pratt (1986a, 1986b, 1986c, 1986d, 1987). This literature is distinct from that concerned with voting and political activism in that it examines each of these themes as well as political attitudes more generally. The central question addressed in this literature is whether or not housing tenure can be associated with certain political attitudes rather than others.

Drawing upon an urban national sample of 1,941 interviews conducted in 1979 and in-depth interviews carried out in 1983 with 100 home owners and renters, Pratt (1987) argues that amongst skilled white collar workers in urban Canada, home owners have different political values to renters but this is not true amongst skilled blue collar workers. Pratt argues that it is commitment to a production-based organisation such as a trade union that is of key importance in differentiating these two groups. Skilled blue collar workers with strong trade union ties have their attention drawn towards production-based issues rather than consumption-based issues such as housing. Whilst Pratt usefully identifies what it is about production processes that differentiates white and blue collar workers she does not do this for housing tenure. We are therefore unaware of what it is about home ownership, even just for white collar workers, that means they hold different political attitudes to blue collar home owners or white collar renters. Again the consequences of housing tenure are examined without specifying the tenure-related cause.

Pratt, however, does identify housing tenure as a social process, the effects of which will be different for different people. Pratt suggests a more sophisticated conceptualisation of the political significance of housing tenure than the automatic equation of home ownership with political conservatism.

> Self-definition, meaning, and social identity are critical concepts in understanding the political impact of housing tenure ... the different significance of home ownership to the social identities of manual and non-manual workers reflected less the specific meanings attached to home ownership than the priority these meanings were given in the process of self definition...For the manual workers ... pride in home was balanced with a sense of identity developed through the workplace. For non-unionised non-manual workers there was no such identification with a production based group. In absence of this, political solutions through the consumption realm, in this case housing received more support (Pratt, 1986c, p. 378).

Understanding housing tenure as a crucial aspect of self-definition is an important advance clarifying our theorising, and this is developed in this book through examination of the subjective understanding of domestic property rights.

The above literature is important for its focus upon the consequences of housing tenure for social action, be it voting, community activism, or sitting at home watching the television. (See Chapter 4 for definition of social action but note that it can include in-action). There are explanatory weaknesses in this literature in that how housing tenure has been linked to such social action and what it is about housing tenure that causes one course of social action rather than another remain unexamined. This key question was posed as long ago as 1972 by Ineichen:

> Home ownership may affect the willingness of workers to strike; it may lead to new questions being asked in the search for making local political action meaningful ... In our present ignorance of attitudes to buying or renting this is an area where only guess work is possible (Ineichen, 1972, p. 411).

It has also been restated more recently by Pratt (1986d, p. 204–5) and Williams (1989, p. 124–5). Rather than guessing the nature of this relationship the case studies in Part Two examine precisely how housing tenure relates to courses of social action.

CULTURAL INEQUALITIES

Cultural inequalities are the outcome of the ability to secure material and/or ideal advantages that are widely believed to be of high status value. With regard to housing tenure we are concerned with the manner in which the mere fact of home ownership is seen as a conveyor of high status and renting of stigma. Also important is the manner in which home ownership enables the physical structure of the dwelling to become a frame for and container of the trappings of status.

Home Ownership and Status—Renting and Stigma

Commenting on the status considerations of home ownership in the U.S., Perin (1977) attributes much of this status to one's ability to raise credit. (See also Rosow, 1948, p. 751, footnote 6). Perin suggests that entry into home ownership is indicative of a mutually agreeable relationship between the individual and the bank. This portrays permanence and stability unlike the foot-loose tenant whose contractual commitments are temporary and therefore of little social worth (Perin, 1977, p. 74).

Adams (1984) makes a more general point with regard to the symbolism of tenure.

The form of tenure is taken as a primary social sign. Tenure is used to classify and evaluate people in a shorthand way, much as people—unfortunately—are taught to use race, income, and occupation as predictors of other traits. The categories—owner and renter—are real as well as symbolic. The symbolic meanings and the forms they take are what need to be explained (Adams, 1984, p. 523).

As home owners enjoy social status on the basis of their housing tenure, so are renters stigmatised:

As a minority grouping in property-owning Australian society, tenants are often stigmatised: 'In a country where home-ownership is the national dream and home-owners are seen as the paradigm of the model citizen, the status of the tenant inevitably suffers. Tenants are commonly regarded as transitory or as failures, people who have little commitment to property or community.' (Berry, 1977, p. 57, quoting Commission of Inquiry into Poverty, 1975, p. 164.)

However, not only do home owners enjoy status due to the mere fact of being a home owner but the private property rights that they enjoy also enable use of the home as an outward expression of status as well as a container of status symbols.

Home Ownership and the Home as a Status Symbol

As the home owner has full rights of use and control then s/he is free (within the limits of local land-use planning regulations) to exhibit the home as preferred. Display of the home as a status symbol is a social practice that has been observed widely both through time and across space.

In 1950's Britain, Chapman states that 'Status is not only indicated or claimed by possessions in the home, but the dwelling itself, its garden, approaches and location all contribute' (Chapman, 1955, p. 23). Similarly, Young and Willmott (1957) state that 'A house is one bearer of status in any society—it most certainly is in a country where a semi-detached suburban house with a garden has become the signal mark of the middle classes' (Young and Willmott, 1957, p. 155).

More recently Duncan (1981) observes the same social practice in the U.S., that 'The house, its address and its facade, as well as its interior, affirm one's status in the eyes of strangers' (Duncan, 1981, p. 38). In Australia,

> Today the inner urban 'scene' has become an important stage for promoting fashion and new urban life style. The elaboration of consumption techniques is increasingly centred in the private residential and cultural domains, rather than in the public or occupational spheres (Jager, 1986, p. 86).

However, despite the fact that the social practice of using the dwelling as a status symbol appears to be temporally and spatially widespread, it should be remembered that housing tenures are cultural products in a way that grounds them in specific national histories. The significance of such symbolic display must, therefore, be considered of variable importance. For example, Adams (1984) has suggested that home ownership has taken on a particular importance in the U.S., for

> In an immigrant society like the U.S., a society that lacks a visible and established class or caste structure, other markers are introduced to maintain social order and to communicate its meanings. In many ways housing has become one of the central means for serving this function in American society and on the American landscape (Adams, 1984, p. 520).

No doubt parallels between the U.S. and the Australian experience could be drawn on this basis.

However, not only is the historical development of a nation important with regard to the cultural significance of housing tenure but also the role of the state and capital in giving priority to one tenure form over another. In Australia home ownership rather than public or private renting has been the preferred tenure, due to the assumed benefits of social control referred to in Chapter 1. As Agnew (1981) notes in the U.S., few

...would deny that home ownership as a status symbol and source of personal autonomy has required stimulation and has met with resistance. Many writers have noted the importance of government programs and housing industry propaganda in the growth of a 'home ownership ideology' (Agnew, 1981, p. 76).

One of the most prolific writers on the subject of the ideology of home ownership is Kemeny (1977, 1983, 1986), whose work has contributed much to the understanding of housing tenure in Australia.

Kemeny (1983) suggests that the growth of home ownership in Australia has not been a natural event. He argues home ownership has not been a response to an innate desire on the part of Australians but, rather, is the product of government and market mechanisms that have combined to extend home ownership to more and more households by offering larger and larger subsidies while neglecting other tenures. Berry (1988) agrees that a high rate of home ownership is not a natural phenomenon but emphasises the importance of finance market mechanisms over and above housing policy in bringing about such high levels of home ownership.

Cultural inequality is thus constructed through housing tenure as home owners enjoy positive status considerations due to the very fact of being a home owner and due to their ability to use their dwellings as status exhibits. To the contrary renters are stigmatised as they are unable to freely use their dwellings as frames for or containers of the trappings of lifestyle, as they do not enjoy the property rights of full use and control. To assume that all home owners use and see their homes as status symbols is, however, problematic, for the extent to which this is true for different class, ethnic and gender groups requires investigation.

Furthermore, simply establishing that housing tenure is significant in the construction of cultural inequality is to ignore how the meaning of the home as a status symbol has affected different courses of social action. What do householders do to create the status value of their home? How do they react when they perceive it is threatened? This is obviously the area where links between the political and cultural significance of housing tenure can be drawn, although few authors have attempted this (though see Agnew, 1981).

CONCLUSION

This chapter has established the extent of economic, political and cultural inequalities constructed through housing tenure. The links between such data and the theoretical positions in the collectivist and anti-collectivist camps have been detailed. Many criticisms have been raised in relation to the theory, methodology and analysis of each camp.

In reference to the construction of inequality through housing tenure there has been a tendency to emphasise one aspect of inequality, particularly the economic at the cost of serious consideration of other dimensions of inequality. With regard to the dimension of political inequality, commentators have analysed the political consequences of housing tenures with insufficient attention being paid to their cause.

Within the 'economic' and the 'cultural' literature, the misplaced assumption has been that all householders will respond in the same fashion to their perceived economic and/or cultural interests. A concern with the subjective understanding of the material experience of private property rights will avoid such problems by recognising varying responses to these interests due to factors such as gender, ethnicity, age and class.

Due to the widespread spatial and temporal variation of capital gains no firm conclusions as to the nature of their distribution can be arrived at. A concern with the subjective understanding of the material experience of capital gains to establish how home owners act in relation to the knowledge that capital gains are available may well, however, prove more fruitful if we wish to understand the economic significance of home ownership.

Those commentators concerned with the cultural inequalities associated with housing tenure, I have argued, have failed to establish the links between such inequality and courses of social action:

that is, how cultural inequalities are acted out. Similarly those commentators who have attempted to establish the links between housing tenure and political inequalities have been unable to examine the causal nature of such links due to a reliance upon statistical correlation and a failure to examine what it is about the experience of housing tenure that causes one course of social action to occur rather than another.

Three key points can be distilled: first, much of the housing classes debate and associated literature reduces the inequalities constructed through housing tenure to one dimension; economic, political or cultural, rather than recognising that each of these dimensions are constructed concurrently. Second, few attempts have been made to examine the subjective understanding of the construction of inequality through housing tenure. This is important as the subjective understanding and interpretation of housing tenure will affect social action and it cannot be assumed that all householders will interpret and react to tenure-based inequalities in the same manner. Third, those authors concerned with the relationship between housing tenure and social action are unable to specify its causal nature.

A new approach to understanding the social significance of housing tenure must be considered. Chapter 4 details the key aspects of this new approach by outlining the central concepts of a neo-Weberian theory of housing tenure and how these relate to the case studies discussed in Part Two.

Chapter 4

THE SUBJECTIVE UNDERSTANDING OF HOUSING TENURE

Concepts and Research Strategies

Chapter 4 contains three sections, which detail the theoretical concepts and methodological research strategies employed to investigate, respectively: the construction of economic, political and cultural inequalities through housing tenure; the subjective understanding of these inequalities and; how such an under-standing relates causally to courses of social action. These are the three areas which we have identified as weaknesses in the current literature in Chapter 3. The main methodological contribution of this book is formulated in this chapter by examining a range of neo-Weberian concepts that have been applied to the analysis of housing tenure and through critical review reasserting Weber's original concepts of class, status and party as a more appropriate departure point for our research design. Extending existing Weberian analyses of housing tenure, we also draw upon Weber's methodological concepts of *verstehen*, ideal types and causality. In particular, the ideal types of social action and social relationship and the concepts of adequate and accidental causality are included. Towards the end of each section we examine the integration of these concepts into a specific research design. Only points that apply generally to the empirical research are discussed with specific points concerning the individual case studies detailed in Chapters 6, 7 and 8.

It is also hoped that this chapter will engage readers whose prime concerns lie, not with theorising housing tenure, but with methodological issues more generally. In particular, for those grappling with the vexed issue of integrating abstract concepts with empirical research designs, these chapters provide one illustration of how this can be done. Also, the section titled 'Theorising the Subjective Understanding of Private Property Rights' outlines a Weberian understanding of causality which provides an interpretavist alternative to the realist concepts of 'necessary' and 'contingent' causal relations (see Sayer, 1984 for an excellent introduction to realist thought). Weber's concepts of adequate and accidental causality also provide a clear framework for a theorised presentation of both qualitative and quantitative data. How quantitative and qualitative data can be integrated to powerful explanatory affect and perhaps, more usefully, how theoretically informed causal analysis can use qualitative data are illustrated in Chapter 5 and Part Two.

THEORISING THE CONSTRUCTION OF ECONOMIC, POLITICAL AND CULTURAL INEQUALITY THROUGH HOUSING TENURE

The nature of the economic, political and cultural inequalities constructed concurrently through housing tenure have been detailed in Chapter 3. In this section we review how the significance of these inequalities has been theorised in the literature and conclude that Weber's original concepts of class, status group and party will provide a more valuable starting point than the problematic concepts of housing class, domestic property class or consumption sector cleavage. In the second section 'Integrating Class, Political Force and Status Group into a Research Strategy', we examine how these concepts can be incorporated into an empirical research design.

Social Groups and Housing Tenure

Central to Weberian analysis is the notion that economic, political and cultural inequalities are manifest in social life. The interplay of social relations in many different aspects of life, for example religion or education, can produce social inequality. What is more, such inequality need not be of an economic nature but may be either political, cultural or economic in kind and most likely a combination of these aspects. An examination of the current literature has shown how each of these dimensions of inequality are constructed through housing tenure (Chapter 3). Whilst both Pratt (1986a,b,c,d, 1987) and Saunders (1990) tend towards this broader focus in their empirical work, their analyses of social group formation in relation to housing tenure has not encapsulated this plurality and it is the limitations of such theorising that concerns us in this chapter.

Weber (1948) argues that classes, status groups and parties are the social groups that relate to economic, cultural and political power, respectively. Let us examine the defining characteristics of these social groups and how such concepts have been applied to the analysis of housing tenure.

The dimension of economic inequality

In relation to the formation of social groups around economic power,

> In our terminology, 'classes' are not communities; they merely represent possible, and frequent, bases for social action. We may speak of a 'class' when (1) a number of people have in common a specific causal component of their life chances, in so far as (2) this component is represented exclusively by economic interests in the possession of goods and opportunities for income, and (3) is repre-

sented under the conditions of the commodity or labour markets. This is 'class situation' (Weber, 1968, p. 927).

This Weberian definition of class has been used in the analysis of housing tenure, particularly home ownership, by Rex and Moore (1967), Saunders (1979) and Pratt (1982).

Pratt's (1982) critique of Saunders (1979) is the last significant attempt to use the Weberian concept of class in relation to housing tenure. Whilst the particulars of Pratt's (1982) critique are valid, the end point of her conceptualisation is liable to the three criticisms we have discussed in relation to the broader literature and thus is unhelpful in understanding housing tenure as an aspect of class relations. Three points are germane.

First, in her concern with the formation of domestic property classes, Pratt (1982) conflates the construction of economic and political inequalities through home ownership. These two conceptually distinct dimensions of inequality should be analysed in relation to 'class' and 'party', not confused and subsumed within the one concept (Weber, 1948). Despite this, Pratt's (1982) empirical focus upon both economic and political inequality is broader than much previous work although the cultural dimension is over-looked.

Second, Pratt (1982) is concerned solely with the objective conditions of economic and political inequality, not, as is central to a Weberian theory of class, the interaction between the objective conditions of inequality and how they are subjectively understood.

Third, Pratt (1982) addresses the situating of class, not in terms of social action as Weber suggests, ('...class situations emerge only on the basis of communalisation' Weber, 1948, p. 185), but in terms of identifying relations of exploitation between tenants and owners. In doing so Pratt is unable to shake off the fetters of the very fault she charges Saunders (1979) with, by maintaining a Marxist notion of class as a necessarily relational concept. To the contrary Weber argues that 'The differentiation of classes on the basis of property alone is not 'dynamic', that is, it does not necessarily lead to class struggle or class revolutions' (Weber, 1947, p. 425).

To avoid these difficulties in the analysis of the construction of economic inequality through housing tenure, we may recognise home owners and/or renters as a class, when each of the following criteria are fulfilled:

- when economic inequalities of an objective nature can be directly linked with the tenure,
- when home owners and/or renters are understood to attribute a particular set of meanings to their tenure in relation to such inequalities, and
- when particular courses of social action are engaged in as a direct result of the subjective understanding of these inequalities.

These are the criteria that will guide our empirical investigation in Part Two.

The dimension of political inequality

'Party' is the social group that Weber argues forms in relation to political inequality. Though Weber's treatment of party is incomplete 'It would be reasonable to suppose that in including it in the same company as class and status, Weber intended to consider party as a vehicle of power in the distributive set-up' (Parkin, 1972, p. 104).

Weber employed the term party

> ...to designate an associative type of social relationship, membership in which rests on formally free recruitment. The end to which its activity is devoted is to secure power within a corporate group[†] for its leaders in order to attain ideal or material advantages for its active members (Weber, 1947, p. 407).

Weber's concept 'party' has gone virtually unnoticed with regard to the analysis of housing tenure. Only Saunders (1979,

---

† . Weber defined 'corporate group' in the following manner. 'A social relationship which is either closed or limits the admission of outsiders by rules, will be called a 'corporate group' (Weber, 1948, p. 145).

1984) ventures near this concept to identify home owners and renters as political interest groups. Having rejected his domestic property class concept, Saunders (1979) proposes that '...the two major patterns of housing tenure—ownership and renting—are important determinants of the real political divisions which are constituted in housing struggles' (Saunders, 1979, p. 102). Saunders' analysis, however, does not identify the political nature of the cause of such differences between housing tenures but simply identifies the effects or political outcomes, in a general sense, of the inequalities between housing tenures. This tells us nothing about how or why housing tenure relations cause struggle but simply identifies the 'parties' ex post, as they engage in struggle. Due to this *a posteriori* approach, Saunders (1979) has to restrict his analysis to what he terms housing struggles (for example rent strikes), whereas the manner in which housing tenure interests intervene in struggles that are not openly housing struggles (for example industrial strikes) is an equally important and interesting question. In this way we may be able to determine the significance of housing tenure, if any, for broader struggles such as urban social movements (Castells, 1983). This points to another interstices in this book for the reader not centrally concerned with the theorising of housing tenure. The extensive debates on urban social movements, class, gender and/or ethnicity struggles have to date largely ignored housing tenure. Through the later case studies, however, we will explore how housing tenure intersects with other such dimensions of the social structure, to affect the social action of those engaged in struggle.

Returning to Saunders (1979) analysis of home owners and renters as political interest groups, a number of criticisms can be made drawing upon our critique of the literature raised in the conclusion to Chapter 3. First, by identifying all housing struggles as political struggles Saunders devalues the economic and cultural dimensions of inequality constructed through housing tenure. Second, akin to Pratt's (1982) concept of a domestic property class, there is no attempt to reveal the subjective understanding of inequality but, rather, it is assumed that all home owners and all renters will respond to 'their' interests in similar fashion. Third, as there is no examination of the subjective understanding of housing tenure, Saunders is unable to provide a causal analysis of the links between housing tenure and political struggle. These links are assumed to exist rather than being a matter for empirical investigation.

In his latest work Saunders (1990) rejects the Weberian concept of party altogether, not because the criticisms raised above cannot be met but because there is '... no specific home owner party, nor are owners or tenants organised on a permanent basis to pressure or lobby national legislators and civil servants' (p. 332). This assumes that 'parties' will be manifest in direct, overt and observable action (See Lukes, 1974 for an explanation of why this is problematic). Saunders also ignores the notion of political consensus in which home owners' views are such a part of mainstream political thought, that the need for them to defend their domestic property rights is precluded. An altogether surprising position for him to adopt given his insightful analysis of resident action in Croydon (1979). Saunders also ignores the fact that tenure-based parties are more likely to be formed locally, sporadically and for short periods of time, or that tenure-based interests will be struggled for along with many other interests in the guise of parties that are not obviously tenure-based. The fact that tenure-based interests are a part of their agenda is, of course, a fact to be revealed through theoretically informed research.

Furthermore, Saunders fails to recognise the complexity of political motivation and action. There is not just a wide range of reasons across a group as to why they are active but also a wide range of reasons why any one individual will or will not be active. Pure housing tenure-based movements are likely to be the exception rather than the norm. More common will be social action which draws upon a wide range of interests, including job, gender, ethnicity, age and housing tenure. Research must reveal these strands as they relate to different interests and meanings in different social contexts.

In place of the concept 'party' Saunders applies the concept 'consumption sector' (1984, 1986, 1990) to the analysis of housing tenure. This concept derives from the work of Habermas

(1976) and O'Connor (1973) and was first coined by Dunleavy (1979). It grounds the inequalities that exist between housing tenures in the political process of state intervention. Saunders (1986) argues that consumption sectors

> ...are phenomena which have only arisen in the period of advanced capitalism in which the state has intervened directly both in the organisation of production and in consumption. They are products, that is, of the use of state power in civil society and as such they have only appeared in the period since Marx and Weber were writing (p. 156).

Saunders (1986) is correct to assert, following Dunleavy (1979, 1986), that the growth of state intervention has compounded the construction of social inequality. The question remains, however, whether or not 'consumption sector' is the most appropriate concept with which to try and understand this imbroglio. There are some obvious difficulties with the concept in that Saunders and Dunleavy disagree as to the nature of the inequality being analysed. Saunders states,

> The public–private division is not simply ideologically constituted, as Dunleavy suggests, but reflects real and important variations in people's capacity to exert control and autonomy in crucial areas of their everyday lives. The division now opening up between private-sector and public- sector consumers thus has real and far-reaching economic and cultural foundations (Saunders, 1986, p. 155).

Saunders argues consumption sectors have economic and/or cultural foundations, whilst Dunleavy regards them as being of a political origin but ideological nature. The distinction (or lack of distinction) between Dunleavy's and Saunders' definitions is the very root of the weakness of consumption sectors. It is unclear what the actual basis of a consumption sector is. Apparently, it could be cultural, ideological, economic, or political and little clarity or explanation is achieved as long as a consumption sector can be anything from an ideological division to a major economic fault line. Furthermore, the public–private divide of housing tenures sits uncomfortably with the massive state intervention in private housing. As Pratt (1982) states, 'The subsidies directed towards house owners are incorporated in an unclear fashion into the theoretical analysis of consumption sectors and the differences between house owners and non-property owners are left to revolve around ideological issues' (p. 497).

More problems arise with the consumption sector analysis in light of our critique of the literature summarised in the conclusion to Chapter 3. First, whilst the consumption sector analysis of Saunders (1984, 1986) and Dunleavy (1979, 1986) (combined) incorporates economic, cultural and political dimensions of inequality, the manner in which this is done is confusing. The various dimensions of inequality are subsumed under the one concept merely reflecting the confusion of empirical reality. This leaves us with no clear statements about the nature of the causal linkages that should be investigated empirically or about how empirical research should proceed. Second, though Dunleavy dismisses the individual's subjective understanding of housing tenure as ideology, Saunders does stress the importance of the subjective dimension. 'It is this sense of the meaningful experience which people may derive from different modes of consumption which has been lacking hitherto in the debate over consumption sectors' (Saunders, 1986, p. 159). The problem is that Saunders does not adopt the subjective dimension as a central part of a *verstehen* methodology but reduces the subjective understanding of housing tenure to a concern with the cultural aspects of consumption. This not only wrongly equates the subjective with the cultural but also ignores the subjective dimension of economic and political inequality. Third, it is not clear whether consumption sectors are static and un-dynamic or if they can only be situated through social action. In other words, is one in a particular consumption sector on the mere basis of buying a house or does being in a tenure-based consumption sector require some notion of an understanding of one's interests and a commitment to action or inaction upon them?

On the basis of the above critique and in place of the concept consumption sector I propose the concept 'political force'. This concept is a re-working of Weber's notion of party. Re-working is necessary, following Dunleavy (1979) and Saunders (1986) (1990), due to the growth in the role of the state and its part in generating and reproducing inequality. The concept political force adheres to the demand that the analysis of housing tenure take account of the role of state intervention, as political inequality, the dimension around which political forces form, is fundamentally grounded in the notion of state intervention. Political force is coined in place of the term 'party' to mark this change and to avoid confusion with the contemporary notion of a political party.

A political force is the social group that forms in relation to the axis of political inequality. Political inequality can be understood as the result of the ability to secure ideal and/or material advantages that are the prerogative of the state. We are concerned with the manner in which the interests of the home owner or renter are mediated by state intervention in housing tenure. Of primary importance are the essentially different private property rights, experienced through housing tenure, that are guaranteed by the state. At a secondary level exist the effects of state intervention that see home owners consistently benefiting, both economically and culturally, at the expense of renters, but note that such economic and cultural inequalities are driven, primarily, by the relations of market and lifestyle respectively, thus the concepts class and status group are analytically more appropriate.

Political forces are not seen here, as they are by Parkin (1972), as simply a vehicle for the economic and cultural interests of classes and status groups, although they can be such. Rather, they are the social groups that form around the axis of political power and engage in social action directly related to political inequality. That is, they mobilise around inequalities generated and/or perpetuated through state intervention. A political force exists in relation to the construction of political inequality through housing tenure, when all of the following criteria are fulfilled:

• when political inequalities of an objective nature can be linked directly with the tenure,

- when home owners and/or renters are understood to attribute a particular set of meanings to their tenure in relation to such inequalities, and
- when particular courses of social action are engaged in as a direct result of the set of meanings or subjective understanding of these inequalities.

The dimension of cultural inequality

The social group that Weber associates with the axis of cultural power is 'status group':

> ...we wish to designate as status situation every typical component of the life of men (sic) that is determined by a specific, positive or negative, social estimation of honour ... status honour is normally expressed by the fact that above all else a specific style of life is expected from all of those who wish to belong to the circle (Weber, 1968 p. 933, emphasis in original).

Though many authors have noted the cultural significance of housing tenure, very few have theorised this aspect of inequality. As Saunders and Williams state 'What is less often considered is the cultural significance of tenure—the status which is sought and conferred through purchase and the growing stigmatisation of the public rented sector' (1988, p. 86).

Attempts to theorise the cultural significance of housing tenure do exist however. Haddon (1970) was the first to suggest that home owners can be conceptualised as a status group in his critique of Rex and Moore's (1967) analysis of housing access. Haddon suggests that a distinction can be drawn between the housing market, an arena of consumption which gives rise to differences of housing status and the domestic property market, '...which gives rise to genuine class divisions according to the capacity of different groups to realise financial returns from the sale of land and developments' (Saunders, 1979, p. 75).

Haddon (1970) provides a useful Weberian starting point through his separation of the analytically distinct economic and cultural dimensions of inequality and association of the social groups class and status group with each of these dimensions, though little account appears to have been taken of the political dimension. Haddon's (1970) emphasis upon how housing is used also grounds his analysis in the subjective understanding of inequality, yet, how such an understanding translates into wider social action is not included.

The only other author to theorise the cultural significance of housing tenure is Saunders (1986, 1990) in his analysis of consumption sectors. (A critique of consumption sector analysis has already been stated above.) Whilst seeing some value in the concept status group (1990, p. 330), Saunders ultimately rejects the notion that housing tenure groups can be accurately conceptualised as status groups: 'As we have seen, it is not just life-styles, but life chances, which vary with tenure, and if housing is successfully to be integrated into theories of social stratification it is essential that the resulting framework takes account of its economic as well as its social significance' (Saunders, 1990, p. 331).

Saunders is absolutely right that the economic and social (economic and cultural in our terms) significance of housing tenure must be taken into account. However, this does not mean that these different dimensions of inequality have to or indeed can be explained by one theoretical concept. The fact that the concept status group is not concerned with the economic dimension does not mean the concept is of no analytical value in relation to housing tenure. Weber argues that the concept class be used to analyse inequalities of an economic nature, the concept status group used to analyse inequalities of a cultural nature and the concept party (political force) to analyse inequalities of a political nature. Saunders, however, seems reluctant to recognise that housing tenure is the basis for class, status group and political force formation. Saunders, it appears, wants one concept for the one empirical category. To use Weber's concepts as though they are mutually exclusive is to misuse these concepts. Depending upon the tenure-based interests that are being threatened, i.e. whether they are of an economic, cultural or political nature, and the consequent social action, housing tenure groups can be either a class, status group or political force and indeed can be all of these at the same time in the same place.

Building on Haddon's (1970) analysis then, and in the light of the three criticisms raised in relation to the literature, the cultural dimension of inequality must be recognised as only one of the dimensions of inequality constructed through housing tenure. Second, the subjective understanding of cultural inequality is an important aspect of explaining home owners' and renters' heterogeneous experiences of status group formation. Third, the subjective dimension is also crucial to understanding the causal links between tenure and social action.

Cultural inequality should, therefore, be understood as the result of the ability to secure material and/or ideal advantages that are widely believed to be of high status value. Our concern is whether or not home owners or renters are able to and do claim status honour on the basis of their housing tenure and how this affects their social action. Home owners and/or renters may be specified as a status group when the following criteria are fulfilled:

- when it is widely believed that either positive or negative status honour is directly associated with a tenure form;
- when home owners and/or renters are understood to attribute a particular set of meanings to their tenure in relation to such cultural inequalities and;
- when particular courses of social action are engaged in as a direct result of the set of meanings or subjective understanding of these inequalities.

It should also be noted that this conceptualisation of status groups differs from other contemporary Weberian definitions not primarily concerned with housing tenure analysis; notably from Parkin (1972), Giddens (1973) and Turner (1988), in that they define status groups in relation to both 'lifestyle' and 'political entitlement'. Giddens' (1973) argument is perhaps slightly different from that of Parkin (1972) and Turner (1988) in that he argues Weber has confused two separable elements within the status group concept: the formation of consumption groups and the formation of groups around some sort of non-economic value, the former of which Giddens calls 'distributive groupings' (Pratt, 1982, p. 483). However, the arguments of each of these authors are similar enough for a general comment. Whereas the inequalities associated with political entitlement are incorporated by Parkin (1972), Giddens (1973) and Turner (1988) into the concept status group, they are theorised here as a separate dimension of inequality associated with the growth of state intervention and around which forms the social group political force. The definition of status groups employed here, along the lines of lifestyle, is solely concerned with the dimension of cultural inequality and thus is closer to Bourdieu's (1984) understanding of status groups.

This section has detailed the concepts to be employed in the study of economic, political and cultural inequality constructed through housing tenure. It is argued that the social groups that form around each of these dimensions are classes, political forces and status groups respectively. These concepts are derived from Weber's original concepts of class, party and status group. The specification of these concepts rests not only upon a reading of Weber but also on a critique of their recent application to housing tenure.

It is important to note that as each of the economic, political and cultural dimensions of inequality are constructed through housing tenure, so may each of the social groups, class, political force and status group form through housing tenure. These social groups may each be formed through any one instance of social action. However, it is also possible for any one instance of social action to be subjectively meaningful in terms of only one of the dimensions of inequality. If, for example, the social action is only subjectively meaningful in an economic sense, then the social action can only be interpreted as class action. What is more, housing tenure is only one aspect of the formation of such social groups. We may also anticipate the formation of classes, political forces and status groups through many other aspects of social life such as employment and welfare.

The term 'social group' is used generically to encompass class, political force and status group. The term 'social group consciousness' thus refers to an individual's understanding of their position within the overall social structure, i.e. the extent of economic, political and cultural power one holds in relation to others. It also suggests a degree of understanding as to why one is in that position. It can be expected that to the varying degree that different instances of social action are economically, politically or culturally meaningful, then the social group consciousness (re)constructed will reflect a greater or lesser understanding of the economic, political or cultural dimensions of the social structure.

The next section details how the concepts of class, political force and status group can be employed methodologically to assist in the empirical study of housing tenure, economic, political and cultural inequality and social action.

Integrating Class, Status Group and Political Force into a Research Strategy

Drawing upon the literature reviewed in Chapter 3 where the objective interests of housing tenures were detailed, we may identify a range of hypothetical scenarios in which the economic, political and cultural interests of home owners could come under threat. For example, the building of an airport could represent a threat to a home owner's economic interest in his/her property value. The noise and air pollution from such an airport would make the area less desirable to live in and therefore devalue the properties. Directly connected to such a loss of desirability could be a loss of status for the neighbourhood, hence a threat to the cultural interests of home owners. Third, if land needs to be purchased to build such an airport the politically guaranteed interests of home owning could come under threat through compulsory purchase by the state.

In order to identify scenarios such as the one above in Melbourne, a search of local weekly newspapers 1986–1987 and an interview with the urban affairs reporter at 'The Age', a major Melbourne daily newspaper, were conducted. Three case studies were eventually chosen on the basis of this search which hypothetically would allow for the study of economic, cultural and political tenure-based interests. These were: a Neighbourhood Watch scheme; the Brunswick–Richmond powerline dispute and; the Victorian nurses strike, 1986.

A Neighbourhood Watch scheme, a community-based crime prevention program aimed at preventing burglaries, was chosen as the first case study. Here it was hypothesised that burglary would represent a threat to the economic, cultural and political interests of home owners. Economic interests are threatened by damage to the property and a declining house price if the neighbourhood becomes known as a 'bad' area for burglaries. The political interests of control and security are threatened by the invasion that burglary represents and the cultural interests associated with neighbourhood status are threatened by a locally escalating crime rate. These threats, it was anticipated, would result in greater levels of participation by home owners (attending more NW meetings, undertaking further security measures) when compared with renters. This case study is detailed in Chapter 6.

The Brunswick–Richmond powerline dispute was selected for study as the proposed construction of a high-voltage overhead powerline represented an environmental, aesthetic and health threat to the economic, political and cultural interests of nearby home owners. As a long running dispute moving towards its zenith, the dispute offered the opportunity of participant observation in/of the social action in the neighbourhood. It was anticipated that home owners would be more active in this dispute than renters as a consequence of the perceived threat to their tenure-based interests. This case study is detailed in Chapter 7.

The Victorian nurses strike, 1986, one of the most protracted recent industrial disputes in Melbourne, was selected as a case study to examine the interaction of economic interests in the job and housing markets. It was hypothesised that the economic interests of home owning and renting would come to the fore in this situation as householders evaluated their commitment to going out or remaining on strike against their need to maintain their housing payments. This case study is detailed in Chapter 8.

THEORISING THE SUBJECTIVE UNDERSTANDING OF PRIVATE PROPERTY RIGHTS

This section details the Weberian concepts and ensuing research strategies devised to examine the subjective understanding of the material experience of private property rights. The second major criticism of the literature raised in conclusion to Chapter 3, was that this has previously received scant attention.

The *Verstehen* Approach and Ideal Types

Central to Weberian theory is the concept of *verstehen*. This concept is drawn from the German philosophic tradition of hermeneutics. The *verstehen* approach used here is based on Weber's (1948) concept of 'social action' as subjectively meaningful action and includes '...the paradoxical fact that the results of interactions are by no means always identical with what the actor intended to do.' (Gerth and Mills 1948:58), or what Giddens (1982) labels, a concern for the unintended consequences of such action. Following Gadamer (1976), the concept of *verstehen* can be located squarely in language, language being a medium in which understanding is fundamental to human life, as opposed to Dilthey's (1961) psychological conceptualisation of 're-living' or 're-experiencing' the mental states of those whose activities or creations are to be interpreted. The logical consequence of this is that we may employ the 'interview' as a faithful mode of inquiry.

Included within the *verstehen* approach, I employ the double hermeneutic interpretation of social life which '...depends upon the social scientific observer accurately understanding the concepts whereby actors' conduct is oriented' (Giddens, 1982, p. 13), and in a dialogical relationship '...that the 'findings' of the social sciences can be taken up by those to whose behaviour they refer...' (Giddens, 1982, p. 14). Finally, following Giddens' post-positivist reformulation of social theory as structuration theory, neither agent nor structure is seen as primary, rather, 'Each is constituted in and through recurrent practices' (Giddens, 1982, p. 8).

Bearing in mind the comprehensive use of Weberian theory in relation to the conceptualising of housing tenure, it is in fact surprising that 'What has been almost completely neglected is the Weberian legacy of *verstehende* which focuses upon individuals and the situations in which they think, talk and act' (Kemeny, 1988, p. 212). This may be due to the fact that *verstehen* is not an easy term to narrow to a precise definition. However, *verstehen* is understood here as '...the observation and theoretical interpretation of the subjective 'states of mind' of actors' (Editorial comment by Parsons in Weber, 1947, p. 87). However, any social science that is interested in explaining social phenomena cannot remain at the level of individual subjective meanings. A process of generalisation has to be undertaken through which our understanding moves toward a more objective (in rational terms) basis; this is the role of ideal types.

To understand the importance of ideal types, in Weberian theory, it is necessary to situate them within Weber's frame of reasoning through ontology to methodology. Weber's ontological position, after Kant (1978) and Rickert (1962), is that 'reality' is an infinity of which our knowledge can only ever be partial and subjective. As the character of that reality is subjective, Weber's epistemological stance is to demand from the social scientist a declaration of that subjectivity through the construction of ideal types. These are the methodological tools that Weber devised for social science research through which the researcher is able to declare his/her subjectivity or 'value orientation'.

Ideal types represent the extremes of a continuum, pure, idealised, abstractions of phenomena against which empirical data can be measured. Ideal types are a research tool, heuristic devices constructed (in reference to social action) on the basis of purely rational courses of action. They are used as a yardstick against which the action of individuals can be measured to discover the extent to which the phenomena under study are based on rational or irrational action. (Not all ideal types are constructed in relation to social action, for example, see Weber's well known essay 'The

City', 1958.) The extent to which any particular set of meanings may or may not conform to an ideal type is, then, indicative of their rational nature.

The methodological value of ideal types rests with the extent to which they clarify the complexities of 'reality'. The value of the ideal types used here can only be judged in light of the explanations provided for the social action under examination. One of the drawbacks with using such constructs lies with the pitfalls of predetermining the nature of the data to be collected and the interpretations to be considered. Although advances in computer aided data analysis, of qualitative data in particular, allowing the researcher to rapidly explore many different lines of interpretation and analysis, have significantly lessened these dangers.

Integrating *Verstehen* and Ideal Types into a Research Strategy

The *verstehen* method was operationalised as a research strategy in the following manner. A qualitative research method was adopted in order '...to understand the point of view and experiences of other persons' (Patton, 1980, p. 36). As 'Data are qualitative ... in so far as they are subjectively meaningful...' (Halfpenny, 1979, p. 803), qualitative methods are well suited to a *verstehen* approach and enable the study of the subjective understanding of the material experience of private property rights.

Qualitative methods incorporate a wide range of different techniques but for our purposes it was decided to use the case study approach. 'As a working definition we may characterise a case study as a detailed examination of an event (or series of related events which the analyst believes exhibits (or exhibit) the operation of some identified general theoretical principle.' (Clyde-Mitchell, 1983, p. 192). The case study method, thus, provides the means of studying key conjunctures ('a series of related events') in which householders' interests are in some way being threatened. The overall point being to investigate the theoretical principle of housing tenure being one aspect of the formation of social groups.

Following Gadamer's (1976) situating of language within the *verstehen* approach, in each case study it was decided that a series of interviews would provide the most appropriate means to examine subjective understanding. This research strategy was selected to generate data on meanings, feelings, thoughts, intentions, actions that took place at another time, or situations that preclude the presence of an observer. It was proposed to carry out approximately thirty interviews in each of the three case studies to enable a thorough examination of the causal role of housing tenure. A narrow focus on housing tenure across a wide range of interviews was preferred to an all-encompassing strategy with very few participants. (The latter strategy would have enabled examination of the relative significance of housing tenure in causing social action, *vis-a-vis* other social factors. This was not undertaken, however, as the preferred focus was upon the causal role of housing tenure per se). The analysis of approximately ninety interviews, it was thought, would provide a data base capable of generating abstract generalisations in the form of ideal types.

Also open to the qualitative researcher is a range of interviewing styles. What is termed a 'general interview guide approach' (Patton, 1980, p. 197) was selected for these case studies, as within each case study and across the case studies it was assumed there would exist a body of common information that should be obtained from each participant. This method of interviewing ensures that each participant is asked a full and similar range of questions, whilst also enabling the researcher to adapt the wording and sequence of the questions to the specific respondent in the context of the actual interview. This structured but flexible interview style was decided upon as it would yield common information across and within the case studies for the purposes of comparison and allow the flow of the interview to be moulded by the participant. The latter point is important to permit discussion of matters often considered quite personal.

Within any one interview or series of interviews a further decision has to be made as to the form and wording of the questions. As far as was possible it was decided to use open-ended questions that were neutral and singular. This would provide the best opportunity of obtaining high quality data. The interview schedules (see Appendix 1) were piloted and re-written several times to meet the above requirements. (For details of the piloting see Chapters 6, 7 and 8.)

The second methodological concept employed to aid the study of the subjective understanding of the material experience of private property rights, is that of the ideal type. 'Its function is the comparison with empirical reality in order to establish its divergences or similarities, to describe them with the most unambiguously intelligible concepts, and to understand and explain them causally.' (Weber, 1949, p. 43). Whilst ideal types may be used for the generation of hypotheses prior to empirical research and as declarations of ones' value orientation, their primary function, in this work, is as an analytical device to assist the abstracting and generalising of data to a conceptual level. Chapter 5 and Part Two demonstrate how ideal types are used in the data analysis to define meanings that can be associated with particular tenure forms and to relate those meanings to an understanding of specific courses of social action. Two sets of ideal types are used in the research design; Weber's ideal types of social action and social relationship which are discussed in the following section.

CAUSALITY IN THE SUBJECTIVE UNDERSTANDING OF PRIVATE PROPERTY RIGHTS AND COURSES OF SOCIAL ACTION

The third criticism of the literature that arose in Chapter 3, was that those authors concerned with the relationship between housing tenure and social action have been unable to specify its causal nature. Though links have been drawn between housing tenure and various forms of social action, commentators have been unable to specify how and why housing tenure may cause a particular course of social action at a particular time, in a particular place. This stems from a lack of concern for the subjective understanding of housing tenure and from the conceptualisation of 'activity' as behaviour rather than social action. It is through

Weber's concepts of social action and his methodological under-standing of causality that we hope to overcome these short falls.

Social Action and Causality

Weber defines social action, which includes both action and inaction, as subjectively meaningful action. Subjectively mean-ingful action can be understood as the acting individual taking account of the behaviour of others and as such represents the corner-stone of Weber's *verstehen* approach. Social action can be differentiated from behaviour as

> Not every type of contact of human beings has a social character; this is rather confined to cases where the actor's behaviour is mean-ingfully oriented to that of others. For example, a mere collision of two cyclists may be compared to a natural event. On the other hand, their attempt to avoid hitting each other, or whatever insults, blows, or friendly discussion might follow the collision, would constitute 'social action' (Weber, 1947, p. 113).

As any one instance of social action will obviously have many different meanings attributed to it, the problem for the social scientist becomes one of disentangling which meanings are directly relevant to the observed social action and which are not. Our concern is with whether or not the meanings that occupants attribute to their housing tenure are directly relevant to any observed social action (herein the case studies), or whether they are merely coincidental. In other words, are the meanings attrib-uted to housing tenures related causally to the observed social action or not? To assist this form of analysis Weber suggests differ-entiating between adequate and accidental causality. To establish adequate causality, in the Weberian view, first, it is necessary to ascertain whether a certain event would have been likely to occur in essentially the same manner in which it did, if one or more of the factors had been lacking (Weber, 1948; Weber, 1949). The problem we face can be stated as a brief question: Are the meanings associated with housing tenure essential to the social action investigated? If this is not the case then housing tenure is deemed to be an accidental causal factor; if this is the case, then housing tenure is potentially an adequate causal factor. The qualification 'potentially' is required because adequate causality for Weber needs to be established at two levels: at the level of meaning in that the identified meanings are essential to the observed social action and at the level of typical probability, in that the relationship between meaning and action is likely to occur again and again.

In Chapter 5 and Part Two qualitative data from the three case studies are used to establish causality at the level of meaning and quantitative data, from primary and secondary sources, causality at the level of typical probability. Causality at the level of meaning cannot be represented through the frequency of an occurrence, only through the establishment of the essential relations to such an occurrence. Hence, one should not equate the frequency with which meanings are documented with the strength or weakness of this type of causal relationship. The fact that more or less quotes are reported from the case studies (below) in reference to any one meaning, simply reflects the frequency with which such a meaning was clearly stated. The likelihood of this relationship being reproduced frequently is examined only with the quantitative data. Particular quotes may also be used more than once to illustrate different points. This is not problematic as it is simply indicative of the ontological inter-twining of the meanings of tenure that the theoretical framework employed here separates conceptually.

With the aim of more accurately interpreting and understanding the confusion of events in each of the case studies, two sets of ideal types, specified by Weber, were also included in the research design: social action and social relationship. The case studies were selected to enable study of a range of different types of social action and social relationship. The manner in which this occurred is detailed in the following section on research strategy.

Weber proposed four ideal types of social action:

- *zweckrational,* social action that calculates a certain means to achieve a certain end or ends. The emphasis here is upon rationality and pragmatism;

- *wertrational,* social action oriented towards absolute or ultimate ends. The emphasis here is upon values;
- *affectual,* social action based on emotion, and;
- *traditional,* social action based on tradition or habit.

A variant of these four ideal types of social action is the ideal type of economic action. *Wirtschaften* or '(e)conomic action is a peaceful use of the actor's control over resources, which is primarily economically oriented' (Weber, 1947, p. 158). Economic action is identified separately as it is not necessarily social action, although it can be, as not all economic action takes account of the actions of somebody else, e.g. the actions of a miser hoarding money for the mere sake of it.

Whilst there is no guarantee that one will ever find these pure types of social action in empirical research, they offer the researcher a tool that helps to understand the social action under examination. As Weber states,

> ...this classification of the modes of orientation of action is in no sense meant to exhaust the possibilities of the field, but only to formulate in conceptually pure form certain sociologically important types, to which actual action is more or less closely approximated or, in much the more common case, which constitute the elements combining to make it up. The usefulness of the classification for the purposes of this investigation can only be judged in terms of its results (Weber, 1947, p. 118).

Weber's ideal type of social relationships is akin to Tonnies' (1955) differentiation of *gemeinschaft* and *gesellschaft,* commonly translated as community and society respectively. Weber (1947) differentiates between communal relations, which are '...based on a subjective feeling of the parties...that they belong together' (Weber, 1947, p. 136), and associative relations, which are based '...on a rationally motivated adjustment of interests or a similarly motivated agreement, whether the basis of rational judgment be absolute value or reasons of expediency' (Weber, 1947, p. 136). The term 'social relationship' can thus be understood to refer to the '...behaviour of a plurality of actors in so far as, in its meaningful content, the action of each takes account of that of the others and is oriented in these terms' (Weber, 1947, p. 118).

Again, it is not to be expected that empirical investigation will produce mirror images of these pure types of social relationship. However, understanding the types of social relationship that home owners and renters enter into in specific cases of social action will allow for greater explication of the action in question. Now we examine how these concepts and ideal types have influenced the research design.

RESEARCH STRATEGY

The ideal types of social action were incorporated into the research design by selecting case studies that would enable the study of various types of action. In the case study of a Neighbourhood Watch scheme it was hypothesised that social action of an 'absolute or ultimate ends' type (*wertrational*) would appear. The ultimate value that active 'neighbourhood watchers' would be defending in preventing the invasion of burglary, is the sanctity of the home. Through the case study of the Brunswick–Richmond powerline dispute it was hoped to study social action that was of a 'calculated means to achieve a certain ends' type of action (*zweckrational*). The certain or pragmatic end was to prevent construction of the overhead powerline and the calculated means, the negotiated process of community activism. In the case study of the Victorian nurses strike, 1986, it was hypothesised that it would be possible to study economic action (*wirtschaften*). That is, nurses would fall into two main categories: either strikers out on strike to obtain higher wages, or non-strikers remaining at work to maintain their income, with the links between this decision and housing costs being of prime interest. Both of these courses of social action would represent examples of economic action.

The two types of social relationship, communal and associative, were included in the research design by selecting case studies that would enable the study of both ideal types. Whilst strong hypotheses about which social relationships would predominate in any one of the case studies could not be broached, it was felt that each of the case studies offered the potential of studying either type of social relationship.

The case studies were, thus, designed to allow for the examination of different types of social action and different types of social relationship. A further dimension built into their design and not yet commented on, was that of spatiality (Soja, 1989). Each of the case studies was designed to take account of social action that was occurring in a different locale, to examine the spatial command of housing tenure-based meanings and to assess the impact of locale upon the causal processes. The Neighbourhood Watch scheme case study was centred on social action, primarily at the level of the home but also potentially at the level of the neighbourhood, to examine the tension between individualist and collectivist forms of social action. The Brunswick–Richmond powerline dispute case study focused upon social action at the level of the neighbourhood. The Victorian nurses strike case study allowed for the study of the interaction of social action between the home and place of employment.

The concept of causality was incorporated as part of the research strategy through a particular research method, that of analytic induction. Analytic induction is '...intended to maintain faithfulness to the empirical data while abstracting and generalising from a relatively small number of cases' (Bulmer, 1979, p. 661). It is the process of logical or causal abstraction from the data that allows the researcher to generalise. As Znaniecki states, analytic induction '...abstracts from the given concrete case characters that are essential to it and generalises them, presuming that in so far as essential, they must be similar in many cases' (Znaniecki, 1934, p. 251). The notion that abstractions should be based upon essential characteristics as opposed to general characteristics suggests the suitability of this method to the Weberian conceptualisation of causality being employed, identifying as it does adequate or essential causal factors.

A qualitative data analysis package, Non-Numerical Unstructured Data Indexing Searching and Theorising (NUDIST) based upon formal logic, was used to analyse the data aiding the process of logical, causal abstraction (see Appendix 2 for further details).

CONCLUSION

Chapter 4 has developed the methodological implications of the three criticisms of the literature raised in Chapter 3. In particular we have examined the implications of these criticisms in terms of the concepts and research strategy adopted. A critical reading of the existing literature, informed by Weberian theory, has provided the backbone of the re-conceptualisation of housing tenure suggested above. One of the key elements of this re-conceptualisation is that the subjective understanding of housing tenure should be central to any analysis of housing tenure. This is the nub of the second criticism raised in Chapter 3.

Moving on to Chapter 5, the contours of the subjective understanding of housing tenure are our key concern. Both qualitative and quantitative data are examined in order to establish the essential and the general characteristics of the subjective understanding of housing tenure. Primary data is drawn on to establish causality at the level of meaning between the experience of housing tenure and particular meanings and then secondary data to establish causality at the level of typical probability.

Chapter 5

THE MEANINGS OF
HOUSING TENURE

Chapter 5 is primarily concerned with revealing how home owners and renters subjectively understand their housing tenure. Three sections detail the economic, political and cultural meanings of housing tenures respectively. The case studies in Part Two examine whether this subjective understanding of the economic, political and cultural inequalities constructed concurrently through housing tenure leads to the formation of housing tenure-based social groups.

Chapter 5 presents both qualitative and quantitative data on the meanings of home owning and renting. The qualitative data are used to carry out an analysis of causality at the level of meaning drawing upon the in-depth interview data. The quantitative data are used to carry out an analysis of causality at the level of typical probability, drawing upon secondary data from a range of periods and countries. On the basis of these two sets of data, it is argued that the meanings associated with housing tenure can be generalised, not only in terms of their essential characteristics but also in terms of their common characteristics.

Theoretically, the construction of the meanings or subjective understanding of housing tenure is seen here as the result of interaction between a structure (housing tenure) and an agent/s (household member/s). This interaction is understood here in the light of Giddens' post-positivist reformulation of social theory as structuration theory, in which neither agent nor structure is seen as primary. Rather 'Each is constituted in and through recurrent practices' (Giddens, 1982, p. 8). It is, however, the agent's interpretation of structure that is dealt with here. Structures, as part of an immediate and local social context, following Lockwood (1966), are seen to be an important influence upon the formation of social groups. The experience of housing tenure as a social structure is the experience of the immediate and local. How individuals interpret that experience is reported in this chapter. How that interpretation may then lead to the formation of social groups through social action is the subject of Part Two. The manner in which the state and civil society combine to affect structures within the immediate social context is not our primary focus, instead, we are concerned with the agents' interpretation and attribution of meaning to the immediate social context, with respect to the constitution of housing tenure relations.

HOUSING TENURE, MEANINGS AND CAUSAL ADEQUACY

Analysis of the interview data reveals a wide range of housing tenure-based meanings. These meanings represent the subjective understanding of housing tenure. Examples of the range of tenure-based meanings emerging from the data include 'financial security', 'making money', 'control', 'legal security', 'status' and 'attachment'. Distinctions between the meanings can be identified in terms of their varying economic, political and cultural nature. Meanings such as 'financial security' or 'making money' relate to the economic dimension of inequality as they are primarily monetarily oriented. Meanings such as 'control' and 'legal security' relate to the political dimension of inequality as they are primarily concerned with ideal and/or material advantages secured from the state. Meanings such as 'status' and 'attachment' relate to the cultural dimension of inequality as they relate primarily to phenomena that are widely believed to be of high status value. It should be noted that whilst for analytical purposes distinct economic, political and cultural meanings have been identified, the actual expression of these meanings is often one whereby these dimensions are intertwined.

Analysis of secondary, quantitative data will examine the typical probability or likelihood of the causal relationship at the level of meaning being reproduced in other socio-spatial-temporal contexts. For example, do home owners and renters interpret their experiences of housing tenure in similar terms in countries such as the U.S. or Britain? This movement from the particular to the general, from the particular Australian interviews to other general social instances, is central to the method of analytic induction being employed. This method also incorporates a change of focus from the essential relations of housing tenure to the general or common characteristics of housing tenure. A strength of this quantitative information is that it enables an examination of variation in the meanings associated with housing tenure in relation to other social factors such as gender, age, ethnicity occupation, etc.

The sections below, in documenting the meanings of housing tenures, are structured to examine, in turn, the economic, political and cultural nature of these meanings and draw primarily on data from Australia, North America and Britain. These countries, it appears, have commanded most research attention in the same way that more material is available on home ownership than renting, either private or public.

ECONOMIC MEANINGS AND CAUSALITY AT THE LEVEL OF MEANING

How then are the economic inequalities constructed through housing tenure subjectively understood by home owners and renters? First, amongst Australian home owners a range of different economic meanings can be identified. These meanings are economic as they are primarily monetarily oriented and include:

'financial security',

Q. What do you think the advantages of owning your own house are, if any, today?

A. Security.

Q. In what sense?

A. Financial.

Q. And what does that security mean to you?

A. Having something that's your own or financially that you've got something for your rent, for all the time that you've been working you've got something to show for it.

(owner/female/30s/couple no children/occ 3)

(See Appendix 3 for explanation of abbreviations)

'investment',

Q. Given complete freedom of choice what is your preferred housing option, owning or renting?

A. Owning.

Q. Why?

A. Because it's ours, it's an investment in the future. ...

(owner/female/42/couple with children/occ 3)

'making money',

Q. Do you think buying a house has been a good investment decision?

A. I think we've, well I think we've made money. If we sold this house we would have made money.

(owner/female/34/couple with children/occ 2)

'saving money',

Q. Do you think buying a house has been a good investment decision?

A.   Yes.

Q.   In what way?

A.   Well it's compulsory saving and it's not wasted money.

(owner/female/33/single no children/occ 2)

and 'leaving something for the children',

Q.   So in what way do you think buying a house has been a good investment?

A.   Just as a future investment for the children really.

(owner female/39/couple with children/occ 3)

The economic meanings of home ownership are important as a potential basis to home owners' tenure related economic action. As such they represent home owners' interpretations and understanding of the property market which, of course, are not necessarily accurate reflections of current property market trends. However, the manner in which any one property value is inextricably related to the local housing market broadens the spatial basis of the home owner's economic interests to, at the very least, the neighbourhood level. This means that most threats to property value and associated economic action occur at the neighbourhood level rather than at the level of the individual house.

Whilst many of the economic meanings of home ownership assume a property market in which values are generally rising, some meanings do not. Meanings such as 'making money via sweat equity', 'saving money via forced savings' and the 'devaluation of mortgage repayments by inflation' are attributed outside the assumption that property values are generally rising. The significance of this is that, regardless of both property market trends and the inevitable inaccurate interpretation of such trends, meanings are still attributed that will impact upon economic action. This sub-set of economic meanings, that does not rest on the assumption of generally rising property values, suggests that home owners' interpretation of their economic interests has a degree of independence from the vagaries of the property market. To the extent that this is the case the value of research that

continues to try and establish actual rates of capital gain, the variability of which has often been used to undermine the theoretical
significance of home ownership (see Thorns, 1981; Edel *et al.*,
1984), may well be overstated.

If we turn to renting, the economic meanings are strongly influenced by an individual's understanding of home ownership. It is
very difficult for Australian renters to be at all positive about their
tenure, in an economic sense, when the economic advantages of
home ownership are so celebrated and consistently supported.
The economic meanings of renting include:

'financial insecurity',

A.   I suppose with owning you've got this idea eventually that
     you'll own the house... with rental you don't know how much
     things are going to go up, you don't know how much your
     income is going to go up or down so there is insecurity with
     renting, with owning you can say at least one day you won't
     have to pay rent to anybody.

     (renter/male/33/couple no children/occ 6)

'dead money',

Q.   What do you think the disadvantages of renting are?

A.   Dead money. Just goes to someone else whereas if you're
     paying off a mortgage at least you're getting something.

     (renter/female/24/single no children/occ 3)

and 'unable to save',

A.   Well you couldn't save anything, it was very hard to save
     unless you lived at home with your parents. So if you were
     living (renting) in a house you couldn't save any money and
     that's all there was to it.

     (renter/female/20s/single no children/occ 3)

The comparison with home ownership, however, did lead to
some positive statements about renting, for example, that it was
less of a financial responsibility than owning,

Q.   What do you think the advantages of renting are?

A. That I don't have to make any huge decisions and I don't have to have any huge financial outlays.

(renter/female/30s/single no children/occ 3)

The economic disadvantages of renting are well documented and nigh uncontested, most significantly that rental payments rise with inflation. As renters do not gain economic power through their housing market position they have attracted less theoretical attention than home owners. This, of course, ignores the theoretical significance of the subjective understanding of renting and the consequences of this for tenure-based social action. As is demonstrated below there is a causal relationship between the experience of renting and specific meanings. Renters are equally aware of their tenure-based interests (and the negative nature of them) and engage in social action accordingly (see Part Two). The section below compares some of the economic meanings of home owners and renters. It should be noted that whilst home ownership generally entails positive economic meanings, renting entails negative ones. The following pages look at each of these meanings in more detail.

Home owners from the interview sample attributed financial security to home ownership.

Q. Given complete freedom of choice what is your preferred housing option, owning or renting?

A. Owning.

Q. Why?

A. (sardonically) Oh I'm an Australian, we all like to own our own home.

Q. Not good enough, try again.

A. I think that the greatest asset an individual will ever own in their life, if we look at the thing economically and I think that's a lot to do with it, economic merit and security are why people like to own homes. I spent most of my early childhood in Housing Commission accommodation and thereafter in a home that my mother was purchasing and my early childhood had a profound impact upon me. Not a needed impact but a profound impact all the same. I was certainly concerned with security and I think that that's a very strong reason why Australia's home ownership rate is pretty high, it's probably where, 75 per cent or some such, and I think that security is an important feature.

(owner/male/30s/couple with children/occ 1)

The financial security of home owning was also interpreted as security for later life.

Q. Given complete freedom of choice what is your preferred housing option?

A. Owning. To have a roof over my head when I'm retired so that as long as I can pay the rates off nobody can tip me out. I mean on a pension and I haven't a big super(annuation) or anything like that, one can manage to save a little. Cost and mental security or the illusion of mental security is every bit as important. If you own you have an asset value that should you be unfortunately retrenched early or can't find a job, or you're very ill, you can then either realise that asset and live off that or you can borrow against that asset value and still maintain a standard of living and you can't do that with renting.

(owner/female/50s/single no children/occ 1)

The financial security of home owning was also seen to extend beyond people's own lives to their children's.

A. I was in a flat for a year or 18 months after my marriage broke up and I realised that the rent was just money going down the drain and I felt I needed some security for my retirement, or for my old age or to pass down to my children or whatever and that became quite important to me.

(owner/female/53/single no dependents/occ 3)

The financial security gained from home ownership also stemmed from a greater degree of control over the level of repayments and the fact that they would be devalued by inflation over time.

Q. So mainly financial?

A. Yes, and security I think it leads to. Because eventually you own it and you have a lot more options, for example, when you are paying $400 a month rent, that locks you into having to work for a living, whereas if you own something and it is only, say going to cost you $200 to maintain it with rates and everything, probably doesn't even cost that much.

(owner/female/30s/couple no children/occ 3)

Financial security can also flow very directly from the fact of rising property values.

Q. Do you feel sufficiently secure in your own home?

A. Financially I suppose so because it has doubled in value so it is easier now to spend money on fixing it up because it has gone up so much so we are not going to lose on it that way.

(owner/female/30s/couple with children/occ 2)

The significance of the meaning 'financial security' is heightened in the context of an Australian capitalist society in which the other major tenure form, private renting, is distinctly insecure financially. In stark contrast to the financial security that home owners spoke of, renters complained of financial insecurity in relation to their tenure form.

Q. Can you explain to me what those feelings of insecurity mean to you?

A. Not in one word—insecure financially in that we know that the person who owns this house is going to invade and put it all back into one and we'll have nowhere to live, so that's the first one. Financially it costs too much and we could get kicked out at any time...

(renter/female/26/single with children/home duties)

Whilst the above quote refers to a financial insecurity stemming from the uncertain action of the landlord the quote below refers to the uncertain action of one's fellow tenants.

A.   Yeah that's the only thing that I find a bit worrying in that I'm a bit at the mercy of the person I live with, in that if the person I'm living with wants to move out then I have to go and find someone else to live with me or shift out altogether or pay extra rent, double rent, and so that's a bit of a concern.

(renter/female/24/single no children/occ 3)

Finally, the financial insecurity of renting is all too readily brought home by an unavoidable awareness of the financial security of home ownership.

Q.   Given complete freedom of choice what is your preferred housing option, owning or renting?

A.   Owning, I think it is more secure...I think from that point of view even if you're paying off for a very large portion of your life you have got the house owned. It's probably going to give you that extra security, you're not worried that rents might treble, specially with the ability now for foreign ownership.

(renter/female/30s/couple with children/occ 2)

A second meaning of an economic nature that home owners associated with their tenure is that of the home as an investment.

Q.   What advantages did you see in home ownership when you bought your first house?

A.   Security, a good bank book, a good investment.

(owner/female/20s/couple no children/occ 3)

Q.   What advantages did you see in home ownership when you bought your first house?

A.   Well it was a financial one I suppose and having an investment that would increase in value hopefully.

(owner/female/53/single no dependents/occ 3)

Investment and security are obviously closely related and are spoken of together in relation to the future.

Q.   Why did you decide to buy your own house?

A. Looking to the future, eventually it's some security and also it's an investment.

(owner/female/42/couple with children/occ 3)

Some home owners used the term asset rather than investment. The distinction is perhaps not very significant but this meaning again indicates how home owners view their tenure form as a rational economic choice.

Q. What advantages did you see in home ownership when you bought your first house?

A. I suppose it's your chief asset in life and renting to us was money down the drain.

(owner/female/40s/couple with children/occ 3)

The advantage of making an economically rational choice is of course that the likelihood of realising monetary gains is increased.

Q. Given complete freedom of choice what is your preferred housing option, owning or renting?

A. Owning.

Q. Why is that?

A. Only because I feel it's an asset, something that you can call your own, something that you can work towards improving, you know with gains for yourself.

(owner/female/23/couple no children/occ 3)

Whilst home owners interpret their homes as an asset or an investment, some recognise that this equity is in many ways unrealisable as disposable income. For these home owners their homes represent 'building wealth' rather than income.

Q. Do you feel you have actually made money?

A. Oh I have, but I'll never see it. Because, when I mean I'll never see it, if I sell this I've got to replace it and everything else has gone up accordingly, so it's equity more than it is actually making money at the minute. If I did sell it I would have to replace it in an area like this or similar and they've all gone up accordingly.

(owner/female/38/single no children/occ 6)

Whilst some home owners recognise that their wealth is unrealisable in terms of readily disposable income others think that home ownership is the best form of investment available.

Q. Do you think you have actually made money?

A. Oh I think so yes, I mean if I were to sell this house—yes on any grounds. I mean maybe if you had the same amount of money invested in the stock market you might, if you got out before the crash, you might have done as well. I don't know, these complex financial calculations have got to be taken into account—the cost of rental accommodation. But at the normal grass roots level, the way most people work these things out, we are much better off financially now than when we bought this place simply because we could now sell it. Yes we could now sell it and clear all debts and yes, we can work it out. I think you'd be hard pressed not to make money selling a house that you had bought 8 years ago.

(owner/male/37/couple with children/occ 2)

'Making money' was also seen to be dependent upon the event of selling the house.

Q. Do you think buying has been a good investment decision?

A. Personally it has yes. As people say, a house isn't much use unless you liquidate it, but it is nice to know that the money you've put into it has been growing at a healthy rate, that in the event of you wanting to liquidate it then you've made a profit from it and haven't lost any money on the way either.

(owner/female/29/single no children/occ 3)

Q. Do you think buying a house has been a good investment decision?

A. Undoubtedly.

Q. In what sort of way, do you feel you have actually made money?

A. I won't make money on it until I sell, but when I do sell I am sure that I will make money on it.

(owner/male/25/couple no children/occ 2)

The notion that one can make money through home ownership is reinforced by an awareness of the alternative that renting offers—'dead money'.

Q. Given complete freedom of choice what is your preferred housing option, owning or renting?

A. Owning.

Q. Why?

A. Well because you've got security and it makes money. You make money on it and renting is just dead money.

(owner/female/30s/couple with children/occ 3)

Renters themselves are also well aware that they are not going to make money through renting but on the contrary that renting represents 'dead money', 'empty money' or the 'paying off of someone else's mortgage'.

Q. Given complete freedom of choice what is your preferred housing option?

A. Owning, renting is dead money. I prefer to be owning and working on my own house than renting so I suppose it is financial really.

(renter/female/25/couple no children//occ 5)

Q. What do you think the disadvantages of renting are?

A. I mean you're paying off someone else's mortgage basically. It would be great to be able to buy a house and let someone else pay off the mortgage. I don't think there are any advantages to renting.

(renter/female/20s/single no children/occ 3)

It is also thought, by renters, that as rental payments are about the same as mortgage repayments the rent they are paying should really go towards their own mortgage.

Q. Given complete freedom of choice what is your preferred housing option, owning or renting?

A. Owning.

Q. Why?

A. For the reason that the money you're putting towards your rent you could be putting to paying off a mortgage and in the end you're achieving something. In three years I don't know how much money I've spent in rent, it would've been a lot and it would have been a lot of money toward paying off a housing loan. If you could do that it'd be ideal.

(renter/female/20s/single no children/occ 3)

Q. Given complete freedom of choice what is your preferred housing option, owning or renting?

A. Owning. I may as well be paying off my own as someone else's. Purely from the financial viewpoint—I find it a little bit difficult to justify spending all the money I do without getting anything tangible in return. I pay enough to be paying off a mortgage, so it's purely financial.

(renter/female/26/single no children/occ 2)

Whilst renters think that they are squandering money, owners are not only making money but also 'saving money'. Home owners see this as being forced to save money.

Q. Do you think buying a house has been a good investment decision?

A. Oh yes, I mean it forces you to save…it is not just an easy way of saving money, but in my case it probably has been. I'd never have saved money by putting it in the bank as fast as I can save it through the loan, if you know what I mean.

(owner/female/25/single no children/occ 3)

Q. Do you think buying a house has been a good investment decision?

A. Oh yes.

Q. In what way?

A. We would never save money otherwise, we don't save it now.
    It forces us to save in that we are paying a mortgage and the
    house has doubled in value, so it has been good that way. We'd
    never have made as much by saving as we've done now, plus
    trying to save at the same time, which we wouldn't have done.

    (owner/female/30s/couple with children/occ 2)

Again in contrast renters speak of being 'unable to save money'
whilst paying rent.

Q. Have you ever had to postpone or rethink any particular deci-
    sions due to the level of your housing costs?

A. Yes I have. The reason I moved home was because I'm buying
    a house and I'm saving, so yes, I couldn't do it while I was
    living out of home.

    (renter + no tenure status/female/single no children/occ 3)

Finally, in terms of economic meanings, the economic disadvantages of home ownership are rarely stated, relatively minor or
only felt temporarily.

Q. Given complete freedom of choice what is your preferred
    housing option, owning or renting?

A. Owning. Renting is a waste of money. There are disadvan-
    tages, however, in owning a house, in terms of upkeep.

    (owner/female/45–55/single no children/occ 1)

A. I mean buying your first house is hard, after that it is relatively
    easy to get loans ...

    (owner/female/34/couple with children/occ 2)

Q. Could you describe to me your feelings when you bought
    your first home?

A. Horror really. I thought 'oh hell, what have I done here'. When
    I bought my first home it cost $9,000 in North Melbourne
    and I can remember before going to the auction that we
    decided we could only afford $8,500 or something like that
    and we were absolutely horrified that we'd gone over that and

it just seemed like this was loss of freedom for life having taken on this responsibility.

(owner/female/40s/single/with children/occ 1)

Similarly the economic advantages of renting are rarely stated. Renters feel there are no advantages in renting, though some recognise that renting might be cheaper than owning and that as a renter one isn't responsible for repairs and maintenance costs. That renting might have the economic edge over owning, however, is rarely if ever proposed.

Q.   What do you think the advantages of renting are?

A.   I suppose you don't have to worry about the maintenance of the house. It's too expensive, it's just dead money.

(renter/female/24/single no children/occ 3)

The above list of economic meanings is not exhaustive. 'Losing money' does not appear in the list of meanings ventured by the home owners interviewed, which if the property market were in a down-phase of its boom-slump cycle, it probably would. However, the fact that this list is not exhaustive does not detract from the fact that there is a causal relationship, at the level of meaning, between the experience of private property rights and specific meanings. The causal relationship is grounded in the fact that the experience of specific domestic property rights is essential to the attribution of particular meanings.

ECONOMIC MEANINGS OF HOME OWNERSHIP AND TYPICAL PROBABILITY

To what extent, however, are these meanings being attributed to home ownership in other socio-spatial-temporal contexts? Is there a typical probability that these meanings will recur due to the experience of home ownership?

In a study of family life in suburban Australia, home owners were asked 'why do you want to own?' and (coding up to three responses for each interview), a third of 305 responses fell into the 'financial investment/security' bracket. What is more, financial investment/security responses represented over half of all first responses (Richards, 1990).

In the U.S. an examination of the attitudes of 120 blue-collar home owners revealed that,

> For these men residential property is the most important way of saving, accumulating, and inheriting wealth...the regular mortgage payments are an important form of saving, and a house is a solid asset whose value, in these men's experience, is prone to rise. If their parents owned houses, they were almost always the most valuable pieces of property they had to pass on to their children (Halle, 1984 pp. 11–12).

It is the close affinity between the words Halle uses to describe the attitudes of his interviewees and those used by the interviewees in the case studies that is significant. Economic meanings such as 'saving, accumulating and inheriting wealth' that directly relate to the experience of home ownership in the U.S. echo the meanings of home owners interviewed in Australia.

Whilst cross-national similarities are apparent there is also some evidence to suggest that the meanings associated with the experience of home ownership have been consistent over time. Thirty-odd years prior to Halle's study in the U.S. it is reported that the financial complex of home ownership motives '...involved some form of economic security ... rent payments become a type of 'savings' ... a liquid asset in case of necessity ... a form of old-age insurance, purchased in a life stage of higher earning capacity and enjoyed afterwards during lower earning power' (Rosow, 1948 pp. 754–755). Again in the U.S. but thirty years later Rakoff (1977) states similarly that, '...for many people the house was a commodity or an investment opportunity, something to be bought and sold with an eye to profit as well as use' (p. 92). The phrases 'economic security', 'savings', 'liquid asset', 'old-age insurance', investment opportunity' are all resonant of the economic meanings identified in the case studies.

Remaining in the U.S.,

A consequence of home ownership ... is its role as an investment ...informants held two concepts of investment. The first of these was 'making a profit' and the second was 'protecting the equity' (Agnew, 1981 pp. 80–81).

These are again similar economic meanings to those identified in the case studies. Agnew (1981) goes on to suggest, however, that economic meanings, such as 'investment' and 'making a profit', do not hold for British home owners. Whereas 73 per cent of a sample of home owners in the U.S. thought that the profit motive was an important factor in their decision to purchase their houses, 86 per cent of the British sample thought the profit motive was unimportant. Saunders (1990) finds these results difficult to accept and contends on the basis of his study of three towns in the North (Burnley), Midlands (Derby), and South (Slough) of England,

...that 29 per cent of owners bought in order to 'get something in return' for what they were paying out, and 20 per cent of them made explicit reference to home ownership as an investment. ...15 per cent said that it provided something for their money, and 38 per cent went further and replied that home ownership gave them an appreciating asset. ... Pressed further on whether they thought that they had made money out of owning a house, 34 per cent ... replied unequivocally that they had, while only 11 per cent ... thought they had not... (p. 198).

In another British study it is reported that 43 per cent of newly married couples saw the major benefits of owner occupation as financial with 24 per cent of them mentioning asset value or investment potential (Madge and Brown, 1981). Research on home owners in inner Birmingham found that 23 per cent of home owners bought their homes primarily as an investment (Karn, Kemeny and Williams, 1985).

Importantly the phrases are always similar to those of the Australian case studies. The wide extent to which these phrases appear to be used by other home owners in other socio-spatial-temporal contexts implies a degree of consistency in the attribution of meanings to home ownership. It should be noted, however, that whilst similar phrases appear to be associated with the experience of home ownership across cultures, space and time, this is not to say that these phrases mean the same thing in each of these contexts. For example, home ownership as old-age security means something very different in a country where there is no welfare support for the aged in comparison with one where there is.

Bearing this point in mind, whilst there does appear to be a strong degree of replication of the economic meanings of home ownership, we must ask, do all home owners hold the same subjective understanding of their housing tenure or can we expect some differentiation in the meanings of housing tenure according to variables such as gender and ethnicity? What, then, are the key dimensions of variation in the economic meanings of home ownership?

When Australian home owners answered the question 'Why do you want to own your own home?'

> Women were more likely than men to give reasons to do with the haven of home—privacy, stability—but these soft answers were only a minority of responses. So too were reasons about status. The gender differences fade beside the fact that both men and women were far more likely to give answers coded in the apparently hard categories: investment, security of tenure, or 'you can do what you want with it' (Richards, 1990 p. 129).

The fact that there are gender differences in the meanings of privacy and stability, what are understood here as political meanings, is important and is discussed below. This heterogeneity though does not differentiate, according to Richards (1990), the economic meanings of home ownership. In other Australian data, however, the financial advantages of home ownership were given particular emphasis by 23.8 per cent of women who were part of a couple compared with only 11.3 per cent of men and 11 per cent of female single parents (CAPIL, undated).

Another line of variation in the economic meanings of home ownership amongst Australians is birthplace. Asian born home owners were largely disinterested in the financial advantages of home ownership with only 2.9 per cent of them emphasising it in comparison with 16 per cent for Australian born, 15.6 per cent for British/Irish born and 15.7 per cent for European born. Instead Asian born home owners emphasised 'security' (38.6 per cent) and 'pride in ownership' (34.3 per cent) (CAPIL, undated). This trend is also supported by studies of home ownership in Britain where Asian home owners were found to stress the principles of ownership (Karn, Kemeny and Williams, 1985, p. 56; quoted in Saunders, 1990, p. 116) and to value independence and autonomy (Davies, 1972, p. 39; quoted in Saunders, 1990, p. 116) over and above the financial advantages of home owner-ship. Saunders (1990), when discussing the 29 Asian home owners in his sample, states that, 'Financial motives did not seem particularly important—only four said that they wanted some-thing for their money, and three spoke of housing as an invest-ment' (p. 117).

This ethnic-based heterogeneity amongst home owners in Australia and Britain is a further reminder of the cultural specifi-city of home ownership. As such it is an important counter to over extension of the meanings of home ownership and a further warning of the dangers of tenure fetishisation (see Ball, 1986, Gray, 1982, Hayward, 1986, Sullivan, 1989, Barlow and Duncan, 1988, Pratt, 1989). Note though that these data do not question the notion of a relationship between the experience of home ownership and particular meanings, simply the specific emphasis within the range of meanings of that relationship.

Other lines of variation in the economic meanings of home ownership include life cycle, class, location and length of resi-dence. Agnew (1981), drawing on Deverson and Lindsay (1975), '....found contrasting attitudes towards the house as an invest-ment between the younger, lower-middle-class heavily mortgaged interviewees living in the 'newer' suburban areas and the older, upper-middle-class ones living in the 'older' area they surveyed' (Agnew, 1981, p. 83). This study also suggests there may well be regional differences amongst home owners in terms of interest in the house as an investment, with London home owners being more attuned to this meaning. The same has been found amongst

Australian home owners with 23.5 per cent of non-metropolitan home owners emphasising the financial advantages of home ownership compared with only 8.7 per cent of inner city home owners (CAPIL, undated). Finally, returning to the U.S., Cox (1982) suggests that length of residence may well be of significance in relation to investment orientation. 'With length of residence...the memory of the investor role fades and the house as a provider of use values rather than as a repository of exchange values becomes more salient.' (p. 121.)

In terms then of the heterogeneity of the economic meanings of home ownership variation occurs along the lines of birthplace, family type, location, employment, 'class' and length of residence, with birthplace apparently the most significant. These dimensions of difference are interesting and important in explaining the different emphasis placed upon different aspects of home ownership by different elements of the population. Importantly, however, at no stage does the relationship between the experience of home ownership and particular meanings break down altogether. If economic meanings are less important to a certain group, they are replaced by an emphasis upon either cultural or political meanings. The relationship between the experience of home ownership and particular meanings continues to exist in some form, it does not dissipate altogether.

ECONOMIC MEANINGS OF RENTING AND TYPICAL PROBABILITY

The economic meanings that relate causally to the experience of renting include: 'financial insecurity', 'dead money', and 'unable to save'. Other studies that attempt to elicit the subjective understanding of renting are few. Hence, there are only vague hints regarding the typical probability of a wider association between the experience of renting and the economic meanings stated above.

Public renting in Britain '...was seen as a waste of money (Saunders, 1990, p. 92). In the U.S. private renting was seen as 'just keeping afloat, using up all monthly income' and 'not saving' (Perin, 1977, p. 34). In Canada home owners (not renters) had wanted to buy '...because they felt that they were 'throwing money away' while renting' (Pratt, 1989, p. 299). Finally, Australian home owners (again not renters)

> ...repeatedly described renting as 'wasted money', 'dead money', 'money in another person's pocket', or 'down the drain'. (Each of these phrases occurs in one or another of the overseas studies— these are international key-words!) (Richards, 1990, p. 120 original emphasis.)

As there is little discussion of the subjective understanding of renting by renters so is there even less exploration of the differences amongst renters in that understanding. There is little, if any, evidence to suggest anything but that these phrases are common to the experience of renting. Perhaps the economic interpretation of renting would be different in countries where home ownership is not so prevalent such as France. One distinction that can perhaps be suggested is that between the trapped-permanent and temporary-mobile renter. The duration for which one is likely to have to experience renting will affect whether or not one can see light at the end of the tunnel, which will in turn lead to different interpretations of what the tunnel is actually like.

POLITICAL MEANINGS AND CAUSALITY AT THE LEVEL OF MEANING

The meanings home owners' and renters' derive from the political inequalities constructed through housing tenure include control, as in autonomy and privacy, and security as in legal security of tenure. For example,

Q. Given complete freedom of choice what is your preferred housing option?

A. Owning.

Q. Why?

A.   ...the ability to hang pictures where you like is important, the ability to do what you want is important and the ability to not do what you want to do...

(owner/male/30s/couple with children/occ 2)

Q.   Given complete freedom of choice what is your preferred housing option?

A.   Owning.

Q.   Why would that be?

A.   Oh I guess the security of owning something...I like shutting the door and knowing it's my space and no one is going to turf me out.

(owner/female/31/single no children/occ 2)

These meanings are labelled political as they are the essential outcomes of the private property rights enjoyed by home owners which are guaranteed by the politico-legal structures of Australian society. As such it is only through politico-legal avenues that private property rights can be legitimately challenged, for example through compulsory purchase orders.

The political meanings of renting again refer to the guarantee of private property rights, however, in this case the rights of the landlord are upheld at the cost of the tenant. As a consequence the political meanings of renting are a 'lack of control' and 'legal insecurity'.

Q.   Do you think owning as opposed to renting is an important part of those notions of home, security and control?

A.   Definitely, renting you don't have much control at all in the way the house is arranged or how you dispose of everything in the house or how you use the house ... Of course I'm renting, which means I don't feel as secure as if I owned it. I have the lease for a year and we'd be interested in buying the house but not sure of what the owners would do so it is reasonably insecure because they may want to move back in.

(renter/female/30s/couple with children/occ 2)

For both home owners and renters control is simply synonymous with home ownership.

Q.   Do you feel you have sufficient control over what happens in and around your home?

A.   Yes.

Q.   And what does that control mean to you?

A.   I think it is just there, something that I expect, it is not something that I think about in great detail.

Q.   Is there anything in particular about your own housing situation that contributes to those feelings of control?

A.   I guess being a home owner as opposed to being a tenant contributes to that and having a voice, I mean the body corporate here, that gives you a slightly increased voice.

(owner/female/25/single no children/occ 3)

A.   Yes definitely, if you own a house you have more control over what you want to do with the house. Like security doors, they don't look like much but they are effective. Also too this house doesn't have any window locks, I would put window locks on even if you don't mind drilling a hole through the frame of the window up top—you know—and then you put a great big nail through and they can't get them up that way. I mean it doesn't look much but it's effective, much cheaper than window locks. Also too I think that you—if anything needs fixing you'd fix it and make sure that your home is as secure as possible.

(renter/female/31/single no children/occ 5)

The political meaning of control in fact contains multiple meanings. For home owners control can refer to a feeling of autonomy.

Q.   Can you explain to me what that control means to you?

A.   It's a tenuous thing really. You are not at the mercy of someone else, again that comes back to owning and renting I suppose. If something is broken you can fix it, if something needs doing you can do it, you haven't got to worry about waiting for someone to come.

(owner/female/30s/couple with children/occ 2)

Q. Could you describe to me your feelings when you bought your first home?

A. It was really good, this is it, yeah, it's a great feeling. Even though you've got a big mortgage you feel, sort of, freer.

Q. Why freer?

A. It's yours you can do what you want with it, you can knock down a wall if you want to and you don't have to worry about putting marks on the walls and losing bonds...

(owner/female/28/couple no children/occ 3)

Renters on the other hand stated that autonomy was something they simply do not have.

Q. Given complete freedom of choice what is your preferred housing option, owning or renting?

A. Owning.

Q. Why is that?

A. Autonomy.

Q. In terms of control?

A. Yes, control over my own environment.

Q. Which you don't have at the moment?

A. No. For instance, the other day I received a letter at 5 o'clock in the afternoon saying that the next morning at 9.30 they'd be doing a maintenance inspection. That really annoyed me because either they just hadn't taken into consideration how convenient it might be at 12 hours notice or else they did it deliberately so they could do a spot check and it was in my own interests to let them do it that way anyway so I didn't jump up and down about it. But I don't like that sort of thing, I don't like other people having that sort of power over my own space.

Q. What other advantages would you say there are to owning?

A.   Being able to do things just as I like without having to think about how is this going to affect the owners or whatever. That is I'd like to give Alice complete freedom in her bedroom, let her do whatever she wanted in terms of writing on the walls or painting the walls or anything like that but I can't. And also I suppose basically they can ask me to leave at any time.

(renter/female/38/single with children/occ 5/pilot interview)

Another interpretation of 'control' is the ability to carry out physical changes to the house and garden.

A.   That I'm free to do what I like in my own home, if I want to knock out a wall and put in a bloody arch or whatever I can do, which I've done and which you can't do in a rented home.

(owner/male/50/single no children/occ 7)

Q.   Given complete freedom of choice what is your preferred housing option?

A.   Owning. You can change things you don't like. I've lived in so many houses with revolting carpets, revolting lights, revolting things, you knock them down and throw them away. We've got this (carpet) I mean it is ugly but at least we can get rid of it when we want to, if you are renting you are stuck with it.

(owner/female/30s/couple with children/occ 2)

Renters, however, feel that they can't carry out such changes, or that it isn't worth their while to carry out such changes either in terms of effort or money.

A.   ...when you rent all your life, you know all your working life, since I've been in Melbourne I've rented some absolute dumps, real dumps, but you obviously don't do anything to them because you don't own and if the owners think it's okay to let you live in a dump like that then really its a catch-22 situation. Why should you be bothered to paint it for them when they won't even be bothered fixing up the heater so you don't freeze to death in the winter?

(renter/female/31/single no children/occ 5)

One notable exception to renters' expressions of a lack of control is suggested in the following quote whereby control over the dwelling in terms of physical changes is gained at the expense of losing one's bond.

Q. So do you feel you have sufficient control?

A. Yes to a large extent I do. For instance I don't think the owners or the agents would have liked me putting up all these pictures and I'll probably have a certain amount taken off my bond, but in order to make it home I decided to do it anyway. So yes I have control but I'll probably have to pay for some of that control when I leave.

(active/female/38/single with children/occ 5)

For home owners, however, the ability to make physical changes is an essential part of home ownership and of creating a home.

A. Well obviously control and homeliness is much easier to manage if you own the house because part of the homeliness is putting your own stamp on it, and putting your own stamp on it means spending money on it. One is naturally reluctant to spend money on someone else's house and that somebody else would object to you making radical changes. For example, the place next door is actually the same as this but it's a rental house and it hasn't changed and we have built the back of this, therefore this has a much nicer feel about it than the one next door...

(owner/male/37/couple with children/occ 2)

And renters recognise this as well.

Q. Again with complete freedom of choice which tenure, owning or renting, would be the most likely in which you would establish a home?

A. Owning.

Q. For what sorts of reasons?

A. I think if you own a place you are more likely to put more time into making it a place that you really like. If you're renting you really haven't got much choice in what you've got. You really can't do any alterations or knock down a wall, add something here, because it is just not on.

(female/23/single no children/tertiary/occ 3)

One renter even saw control as essential to not only 'the home' but also 'the family'.

Q. With complete freedom of choice what is your preferred housing option, owning or renting?

A. I'd rather own.

Q. Why?

A. Don't know. For the same reason that it's yours and you can do what you like to it. I suppose a home to me does mean a family. You can improve it or do what you like to it. Doesn't matter if someone smashes a wall, you don't have to go and tell—there's no one sort of looking over you to make sure you're looking after the place, it's yours.

(renter/female/24/single no children/occ 3)

For other home owners, being able to carry out physical changes to the home reinforces their notions of ownership, of it being theirs.

Q. Given complete freedom of choice what is your preferred housing option, owning or renting?

A. Owning.

Q. Why would that be?

A. Oh I guess security of owning something, it's a good way to make money, I think it's a good investment, a good way of forced saving. I suppose I like it too because I like it being mine so I can do what I like to it. If I want to pull things out of the garden I can do so, if I want to knock a wall down with council approval I can do so. Those sorts of things I think are important, that feeling of control and being able to—and I guess I really like that, I like shutting the door and knowing it's my space and no one's going to turf me out.

(owner/female/31/single no children/occ 2)

Q. Do you think ownership of a house as opposed to renting is an important part of those notions of home, security and control?

A. To some extent I think so yes.

Q. In what sense?

A. It is the overall psychology of it being a home that you own. I think the actual physical surrounding gives you a feeling of greater security in a number of ways rather than just the financial side of being secure, of being in control. Physically being able to make modifications to the house without worrying about going through the landlord and things like that, knowing the house, quirks and sounds in the house and feeling comfortable in it. I think you get a greater feeling of that than if you're renting.

(owner/male/25/couple no children/occ 2)

And again renters recognise this interpretation.

Q. Do you feel you have sufficient control over what happens in and around your home?

A. Yes.

Q. And what does that control mean to you?

A. We've got control outside the rent part, the agent's part that sort of thing. Because you live here, you do whatever you want to do within reason. You can have parties or whatever.

Q. Do you think ownership of a house as opposed to renting is an important part of those notions of home, control and security?

A. Yes, they add to it.

Q. How?

A. Because it's yours.

Q. What difference does that make?

A. It emphasises everything else. When you're renting it's always temporary, you don't know how long, I mean they can come along and—in the back of your mind it's only temporary. It's not really yours even if you pretend it is.

Q. And does that affect how you relate to your home?

A. Yes, I think it does.

Q. In what ways?

A. Just silly little things like putting up hooks and stuff. You can't do it without thinking 'will they mind', you bump a wall, 'oh, what are they going to say'—you know. 'How are we going to hide it?' Things like that. If it was your own you wouldn't worry.

(renter/female/23/single no children/occ 3)

Security and control or security stemming from control are sometimes linked by home owners.

Q. Do you feel you have sufficient control over what happens in and around your house?

A. Yeah I think so.

Q. Can you explain to me what those feelings of control mean to you?

A. I suppose they add to the feeling of security and the feeling that you can prevent things from being spoiled...

(owner/male/41/couple with children/occ 2)

Again in contrast, it is insecurity stemming from a lack of control that is mentioned by renters.

Q. Given complete freedom of choice what is your preferred housing option, owning or renting?

A. Owning.

Q. And why is that?

A. Because you have more control.

Q. To do?

A. Not only to do things but in terms of, if you are renting from someone and the landlord decides to sell a place, you have to

move, there is nothing else you can do, which can be very
inconvenient and expensive.

Q. Do you think owning a house as opposed to renting one is an
    important part of those notions of home, security and
    control?

A. Yes I do.

Q. What sort of (interruption)?

A. Well particularly with the control issue, more with security
    too. I mean we are not going to be asked to move anywhere if
    we own a place.

    (renter/female/35/couple with children/occ 2)

The control gained from home ownership is not restricted to
control over the physical dwelling but also includes control over
other people who may want to enter your property.

Q. Can you explain to me what those feelings of control mean to
    you?

A. Oh, just to me it would mean being able to do what I want to
    do to my home or to the area around it and to choose who I
    wish to be there or not be there.

Q. Is there anything particular about your own situation that
    contributes to those feelings of/lack of control?

A. No I think just because it's my house.

Q. So owning is important?

A. Yeah.

    (owner/female/single no children/occ 2)

Home ownership involves control over your life.

Q. Can you explain to me what those feelings of control mean to
    you?

A. I suppose control would really be, is part of, control over your
    life, you can determine things about your life and obviously if
    you're living in a situation that you like you are going to be
    happier than in a situation which you don't like and possibly
    don't feel you can control.

(owner/female/30/single no children/occ 3)

The other major political meaning of housing tenure is security. As with 'control' the overall picture is one whereby home owners enjoy security and renters endure a lack of security.

Q.   Given complete freedom of choice what is your preferred housing option, owning or renting?

A.   Owning.

Q.   Why would that be?

A.   Oh just because you don't get forced out of it and you can do what you like to it. It gives you security.

(owner/female/28/single/no children/occ 2)

A.   As for security, we had a one year lease last year and that was much more secure. At the moment we don't, we only have it month to month, and like I said I don't feel totally secure in knowing that I'm going to be living here for a whole year. That's not something that I like, I'd like to sign another lease for another year.

(renter/female/24/single no children/occ 3)

Q.   And why would you prefer to own in the long term?

A.   It's the Great Australian Dream to own your own home. You have to conform to these things. Oh no, of course it would just be like owning your own car, it's just something that you own and it's a security and you can do with it what you like, it's just something of your own.

(renter/female/20s/single no children/occ 3)

Home ownership also relates to personal security.

Q.   Do you feel sufficiently secure here?

A.   Not terribly secure here in terms of problems with theft and burglary. There seems to be quite a high incidence in this suburb. I wouldn't like to have to put bars on my doors and windows on the other hand. Of course, I'm renting which means I don't feel as secure as if I owned it. I have the lease for a year and we'd be interested in buying the house but not sure of what the owners would do, so it is reasonably insecure because they may want to move back in...

(renter/female/30s/couple with children/occ 2)

The meaning 'security' also hides many other minor meanings. This man gave the stereotypical response of the home as haven.

Q. Can you explain what those feelings of security actually mean to you?

A. It's like going into my own little cave, I can shut off from the world, I can relax, I can meditate without people intruding into my lifestyle, I can lick my wounds and calm my nerves from the day out in the jungle and feel safe that I'm not going to be attacked and I can gather my strength to go out and fight again.

(owner/male/50/single no dependents/occ 7)

Others express their relative security by highlighting the insecurity of renting.

Q. And what does that word 'home' mean to you?

A. It is just a sense of security I think, it is part of me, it has my personality because I came to it and furnished it and things like that. It is an extension of myself I suppose.

Q. Do you feel sufficiently secure in your own home?

A. Yes.

Q. And can you explain what those feelings of security mean to you?

A. I think, I guess it is freedom from concerns as to whether I'm going to have a roof over my head and things like that.

(owner/female/25/single no children/occ 3)

Home owners also express their security in terms of permanency.

Q. Can you explain to me what those feelings of security mean to you?

A.   ...I guess I've always taken it for granted. So I suppose it's a constant in my life, ... perhaps it's a basic from which I work ... You know I've got a permanent place where I live, where I can go, I can sleep and eat and always be there and I don't have to think about shelter, so I can concern myself with a whole lot of other activities because I know that this very basic need is thoroughly catered for.

(owner/male/41/couple with children/occ 2)

A permanency that leads to stability which is essential to family life.

Q.   Do you think ownership of a house as opposed to renting is an important part of those notions of home, security and control?

A.   I think so yeah.

Q.   Why?

A.   Well if you're owning your own home you've got control over how long you're going to stay there and because you know what you're doing and when you're doing it, you're not going to be told to move on at any particular time, or you're not going to have to look for alternative accommodation all the time unless you want to. Could be unsettling, I think, shifting all the time.

Q.   And what does that control mean to you?

A.   I think it's important to the family unity, to keep the family together and make sure everyone is going along the straight and narrow. To influence the kids for the good.

(owner/female/37/couple with children/occ 3)

In contrast, renters complain of feeling insecure due to a lack of permanency or a feeling of temporariness.

Q.   Given complete freedom of choice what is your preferred housing option, owning or renting?

A.   Owning.

Q.   Why is that?

A. It's secure, you don't have to keep moving, you can do what you want.

Q. More secure in what sense, money wise or?

A. No, in that you don't have to keep moving around, you don't have to waste a lot of money on that, the children you don't have to bring them up—going to school they don't like being moved around that much.

(renter/female/26/single with children/home duties)

Q. Again with complete freedom of choice which tenure, owning or renting, would be the most likely in which you would establish a home?

A. Owning. A home could be a rented flat but a home really equals something permanent, something you've settled down to, feels more secure. I think people here are very conscious of that sort of stuff. If somebody asked where is home, I wouldn't say Clifton Hill.

(renter/female/24/single no children/occ 3)

For some renters the temporary nature of their residency means that their homes do not reflect them as individuals.

A. I suppose it basically means from both points of view, from the personal and rental safety security aspect something quite vague about being able to put down roots and say this is me, not this is mine so much but that this space that I'm occupying, says something about me ...You see this rented space at the moment says I'm very temporary about being here I guess, the furniture is makeshift, one room is almost empty because I haven't quite worked out what to do with it yet ... it is not worth renting it, having someone else to live in because the house isn't big enough and the baby currently sleeps in the same room as I do. So if we were to stay here for 5 years then it would be her room but for the moment it is the room, you know, so that says something too, that I'm not using the whole of the space, I guess, so there's a tentative feeling about it.

(renter/female/34/single with children/pensioner)

Though renters can feel relatively secure within the context that renting, as a structure, sets.

A.   No, I have a lease so legally I'm secure for the rest of the year then probably you know another 'x' number of months, but I couldn't contemplate living in the same rented house for years on end, that idea is quite alien to me. I assume that landlords ask you to leave after a couple of years and that has been my experience. My experience hasn't in fact been with many people being asked to leave, just that in the homes I've lived in people have tended to move after 2 or 3 years.

Q.   Do you feel sufficiently secure in your own home?

A.   Well I mean renting you're never secure because you don't have security of tenure. But, given that I've lived in other places where housing has been much more difficult comparatively, I suppose, I worry about it less.

(renter/male/31/single no children/unemployed)

As is the case with the list of economic meanings discussed previously, this list of the range of political meanings is by no means exhaustive but it is indicative of the breadth of the subject under investigation.

It is clear though that a causal relationship exists between the experience of different housing tenures and certain political meanings. These political meanings are argued to be control as in autonomy and privacy, and security as in the legal security of tenure. Home owners enjoy the positive aspects of such meanings and renters endure the negative. To what extent, then, are these meanings being attributed to home ownership and renting in other socio-spatial-temporal contexts? These are the respective concerns of the following two sections.

POLITICAL MEANINGS OF HOME OWNERSHIP AND TYPICAL PROBABILITY

In a study of new suburban home owners in Australia two themes to the meaning 'control' were apparent. First 'no one can put you out' (p. 124), which is akin to the meaning we have labelled 'security' and second 'you can make it yours' (p. 124), closer to our meaning 'control' (Richards, 1990).

Home owners in Britain have talked about '...the sense of independence and autonomy which ownership confers—the freedom from control and surveillance by a landlord and the ability to personalise the property according to one's tastes' (Saunders, 1990, p. 84). Saunders' study also found differentiation between the reasons for first house purchase. The 'desire to own', 'security' and 'autonomy, independence' were ranked third, seventh and eighth in terms of importance by 18, 8 and 7 per cent of home owners respectively. The perceived advantages of home ownership, where 'can do what you like' and 'security of tenure' were ranked first and fourth by 39 and 13 per cent of home owners respectively (Saunders, 1990, pp. 85 and 87). This is due to the fact that '...in the daily round of living in a house, as opposed to the special occasion of moving into or out of it, it is the 'use value' rather than the 'exchange value' which is likely to be of greatest concern' (Saunders, 1990, p. 88).

In other British studies 17 per cent of newly married couples saw home ownership '...in terms of values such as independence, freedom of action, privacy and choice' (Madge and Brown, 1981, p. 84). In the 1977 National Economic Development Office (NEDO) national study 23 per cent of respondents identified a desire for independence as the main reason for owning, 22 per cent the freedom to decorate and 17 per cent a feeling of security (Saunders, 1990, p. 84 and also quoted in Jones, 1982, p. 126). Similarly, home owners in Glasgow favoured home ownership for reasons of 'choice, mobility, freedom and autonomy' (Madigan, 1988, p. 38, quoted in Saunders, 1990, p. 84). Finally in Britain, 30 per cent of home owners in Bath valued ownership mainly for autonomy and independence (Couper and Brindley, 1975, p. 572).

Turning to the U.S., '...there is something of a consensus among researchers in the United States concerning the strong association between owning and designations of the house as a ... source of personal autonomy' (Agnew, 1981, p. 76). Rakoff (1977) states,

> ...a third aspect of the house's meanings revolved around the sense of permanence and security one could experience in his or her own house...The house, particularly the owner-occupied house, seemed to be a powerful symbol of order, continuity, physical safety, and a sense of place or physical belonging (p. 94).

Forty years prior a 1937 article referred to 'the feeling of owner-ship and independence' and 'like to fix up to suit self' (Rosow, 1948, p. 751). Rosow himself states,

> The individualism-independence factors appeared in several connections, but almost invariably included freedom from landlord caprice and its uncertainties. Individualism involved ownership chiefly as a 'success' index and also for security of residence. It further constituted an incentive to home improvements on the one hand, and on the other, protected such improvements, which was important if they were felt to be highly personalised (p. 75).

Again, across a range of socio-spatial-temporal contexts the political meanings of control and security attributed to home ownership appear remarkably consistent. The potentially different underlying significance of these meanings, however, must be borne in mind.

The political meanings of home ownership seem to vary little according to other social factors. It is worth noting that the British data of Couper and Brindley (1975) and Saunders (1990) make no reference to any variation. Rakoff (1977) when discussing political meanings in the U.S. states that all respondents used these metaphors (p. 94). The only avenue of difference appears to be gender. Seeley et al. (1956) found,

...there was a widely accepted conception of the home as an emotional refuge in a cold and competitive society. This was particularly apparent among the women, who, although attached to the home as a means of enhancing personal autonomy, were less inclined than the men to see the house in terms of status and achievement (in Agnew, 1981, pp. 77–8).

Some Australian data support this in as much as 'Women were more likely to give reasons to do with the haven of home—privacy, stability...' (Richards, 1990, p. 129), however, such responses were few in number and the gender difference evaporates when considering the more frequently stated economic meanings.

POLITICAL MEANINGS OF RENTING AND TYPICAL PROBABILITY

The political meanings identified in the case studies as related causally to the experience of private renting are 'lack of control' and 'legal insecurity'. Our knowledge of the extent to which such meanings are attributed to renting elsewhere is limited due to a dearth of research.

Evidence from Britain centres on the experience of public renters, the dominant rental tenure. Twenty-four per cent of Saunders' sample mentioned 'lack of personal control' making it the most often stated disadvantage of public renting (1990, p. 89). The 1977 NEDO survey found the major disadvantages of council housing to be '...that you never own your own property (20 per cent), lack of choice (15 per cent) and the lack of freedom to decorate (14 per cent)' (Jones, 1982, p. 126).

On the experience of private renting in the U.S. Rakoff (1977) states that,

Even renters agreed that ownership made real and possible the control, the security, the status, the family life that all of these people were seeking in and through their houses. This centrality of ownership was usually expressed in terms of freedom (p. 94).

Finally, Ineichen's (1972) droll comment is very apt, 'Things happen to the tenants, rather than their going out and changing the world' (p. 406).

The variation in these political meanings amongst renters is again un-researched. One logical distinction that can be made, however, is that between public and private renters. Public renters do enjoy security of tenure which private renters do not, though these rights will vary bureaucracy to bureaucracy.

In mapping the meanings of housing tenure through this chapter, so far we have examined a range of economic and political meanings. There are clear differences in the nature of these meanings between home ownership and renting. Home owners tend to enjoy positive aspects and renters negative. This variation in meaning is clear through the qualitative data of the case studies and has been supported by secondary quantitative data over significant periods of time and a range of countries. This difference in the meanings of housing tenure at the level of meaning and at the level of typical probability, is suggestive of a causally adequate relationship between housing tenure and particular subjective understandings of the home. The final section of Chapter 5 moves on to consider whether such variation also exists in the cultural meanings of housing tenures.

CULTURAL MEANINGS AND CAUSALITY AT THE LEVEL OF MEANING

The cultural meanings of home ownership include 'status', in terms of respect and lifestyle and 'attachment' to both the home and neighbourhood. As an example of 'status'.

A. Home owner or not, I think you feel a bit more proud, you've got a bit more status. You feel, especially in a block of units like this, they're only renting and I'm an owner. That's a fact, you feel it, it's not a snobbish sort of thing but it's a fact and I think you feel you've got a bit of status.

(owner/female/53/single no dependents/occ 3)

A.   People who own houses, I think, have more respect for other people who own houses. People who rent houses don't give a stuff, you know, and probably have a bit of envy or don't particularly like it if people own houses because they can't afford it themselves.

(renter/male/27/single no children/occ 2)

And examples of 'attachment'.

Q.   Would you call where you now live home?

A.   Yes.

Q.   And what does that word home mean to you?

A.   This is my little bit of land and house.

(owner/female/couple with children/occ 3)

Q.   Would you call where you now live home?

A.   No.

Q.   Where is home?

A.   I haven't got one yet, no.

Q.   Do you feel you'll get one when you buy a house?

A.   Yes.

(renter/female/26/single with children/home duties)

These meanings are a part of the process whereby home owners are the ones who have 'made it', they have climbed the ladder of social expectation and bought their 'quarter-acre block'. It is the same process whereby renters, both private and public, although especially public, are heavily stigmatised. The status or standing that is enjoyed by home owners and the stigma endured by renters is a lived experience not just an end point of inequality or social distinction. The packaging of this social distinction is 'lifestyle'. Home ownership has, for many years now, been a pivot for specific lifestyles. From the 1950s on; the suburban ideal, the quarter-acre block, the Hills clothes hoist, single income family life—all have been synonymous with home ownership in Australia. 'New' life-styles are today emerging alongside the suburban ideal but in a different spatial setting. Gentrified inner-city living, renovated

Victorian terraces with picket fences and dual income professional life all represent a lifestyle of the 1970s and 1980s, which is again synonymous with home ownership in Australia.

The cultural meanings of housing tenure to an extent operate at two different spatial levels; the home and the neighbourhood. One of the major reasons for this is that the lifestyle market is a public market. Whilst lifestyle can be privately consumed it needs to be publicly demonstrated that one is privately consuming for this to be a 'successful' aspect of cultural action. Furthermore, this demonstration of lifestyle is taken beyond the bounds of the property as the status of an individual dwelling is intimately related to the status and character of a neighbourhood. The following quote illustrates the inter-connectedness of home and neighbourhood status.

A. When you live in a neighbourhood like this where you've got all these prestigious houses around you I suppose we need to make it look like it's more part of the area. If we cheapskate on things and don't do the place to a certain standard we'll be letting down the area. We bought a reasonably cheap house in a reasonably expensive area and we need to keep up the appearance of the place so that it doesn't bring down the whole area. Like one of the selling points for this house when we were buying it was the fact of where it was and the same thing if we sell it one of the selling points will be where it is and how it looks. As I said this is the smallest house with the lowest roof, it's the only place that doesn't have a garage or anything like that so you've got to make it look special. Like we've got big plans for the garden and we're not going to just concrete all the driveway we're going to save for a more expensive pattern paving because we feel like we don't want this house to look really cheap as opposed to—when you've got a two storey place there, two storey place there, four storey across the road, this one they're building over here is going to be two storey at least and this is the only single storey, you've got to make it sort of live up to the area I think.

    (owner/female/26/couple no children/occ 3)

As with many of the other meanings considered above, 'status' hides many sub-meanings. The first aspect to consider, which is voiced by both home owners and renters, is that home owners actually gain status from the simple fact of being a home owner.

Q. Given complete freedom of choice what is your preferred housing option, owning or renting?

A. Owning.

Q. And why would that be?

A. I think I feel that I've achieved something by owning a house...

Q. Do you think people respect home owners more than those who don't own their own homes?

A. I don't think they respect them more but are sometimes amazed if you're young and you own your house and they think, 'God, how did you do it'. Or older people, like my boss and others, have been very proud of the fact that I was young and had a house, and it made him think about his own kids and what they could achieve as people on their own.

Q. Could you describe to me your feelings when you bought your first home?

A. Very happy. I felt really very proud that I had something that was mine... I was proud that I got it for the price that I did and for the value that's on it and was pleased to be able to send photos and things like that (of the house) and I really felt proud of it.

(owner/female/31/single no children/occ 2)

Q. Could you describe to me your feelings when you bought your first home?

A. That was a long time ago. I think we were elated, just the fact that it was ours and we'd finally made it.

(owner/female/37/couple with children/occ 3)

Renters also recognise this tenure-based distinction.

A. ...I think people do respect you more if you own your own house, they see you as someone who has got a little more behind you maybe—I don't know about standing—but a bit better off probably.

(renter/female/31/single no children/occ 5)

Q. Do you feel people respect home owners more than those who don't own their homes?

A. I would say yes.

Q. Why do you think that is?

A. I suppose people who own homes, people think they are hard workers, they put enough money away to have bought their own house, they are steady, dependable, all that sort of hoo haa. And renting—people that rent, I suppose people think well you know they haven't enough money they are not staying, that sort of thing, that's the general idea...

(renter/female/23/single no children/occ 3)

The second aspect of the meaning 'status' to consider, is that home owners gain status from the appearance of their homes and gardens. This is enabled by the meaning of control which consequently frustrates renters' attempts to gain the same advantage.

Q. Is the appearance both external and internal of your home of importance to you?

A. Very much so, why do you think I have all those tubs of plants sitting out there, yes of course it's important. For a block of flats, only a few of which are owner occupied, I think this one looks very good.

(owner/female/50s/single no children/occ 1)

A. Home owner or not, I think there's only one rented place in the street and it stands out like a sore thumb because a lot of them couldn't care less.

(owner/female/couple with children/occ 3)

Q. What factors do you believe are the most important in shaping your views about your home?

A. Pride. I don't have one of the best houses on the street but just want it to be pleasant to the eye...Being a home owner is important. Obviously if you own you are going to take more pride in how it looks.

(owner/female/35/single no children/occ 3)

Accordingly renters are largely unconcerned about status in terms of appearance.

Q. Is the appearance (external and internal) of your house of importance to you?

A. Not really. Certainly if I owned it would be, but when I rent, no. I think it would be lovely if it looked nice, if it was really quaint and all those sorts of things, but no. But we hate this house, so, I mean...

Q. Is the appearance of your garden of importance to you?

A. Not at all. Except the grape vine makes good vino. Not at all, not an issue.

Q. Is it important to you that your house should be seen to blend with the rest of the neighbourhood?

A. No...

Q. What factors do you think are important in shaping other people's views about their homes?

A. I think fairly simply, they own a house, they've worked hard to save the money to buy a house in the neighbourhood therefore they are probably spending a lot of time on maintenance, building improvements, looking after the garden, planting trees and shrubs. So, therefore, a sense of pride in what they've achieved and the effort expended in making the house nice or just how they like it.

(renter/female/30s/couple with children/occ 2)

Q. Is the appearance of your home, both external and internal, of importance to you?

A.   Only internal yes, because I don't own it and I don't have any control over the outside of it.

(renter/female/25/couple no children/occ 5)

One of the important outcomes of the economic, political and cultural meanings of home ownership is 'attachment' to both the home and the neighbourhood. This notion of attachment, whilst being an outcome of the combined meanings of home ownership, most accurately sits under the 'cultural umbrella'. Developing a community conscience, close ties with neighbours and the neighbourhood and most particularly self-identification with the home are all fundamental values, if not aspects, of contemporary lifestyles.

Home owners state very enthusiastically how attached they feel to their homes.

A.   I feel comfortable in my own home because as I've said I've renovated it myself, I've decorated it myself, it's strictly my personality in this house and so I'm in harmony with it, it's pleasing to me, whatever I look at is pleasing because I've put it there and nobody else's character is there.

(owner/male/50/single no children/occ 7)

A.   It's always been difficult for me because home always used to be where Mum and Dad were so I'd say only within the last year or so I'd call this home. I now start to say Mum and Dad's place rather than home as it's where I used to live. I think where we used to rent I didn't consider that home, that was that sort of feeling that was a rented place, that was a means to an end but it wasn't where we were going in the future. So that was really a house to me, that wasn't a home.

(owner/female/23/couple no children/occ 3)

A.   Home means it's here, it's ours, it's permanent, this is where we stay. We saved so long for something that was going to be right for us that now this is everything I wanted really.

(owner/female/26/couple no children/occ 3)

Renters, however, whilst recognising that home ownership may enable feelings of attachment feel indifferent to their homes. Again this is related to the meanings of control and security.

A. I suppose also if I owned the place I'd want to make it look nice and feel nice and things like that. When you rent, and I have been renting different places for years, there is very little attachment to the house, you tend to pass through and forget about it...

A. Yes, having a home that's owned would, I think, make me (feel) quite strongly that I could put down those roots to sort of explore myself a bit more.

(renter/female/34/single with children/pensioner)

A. The mere meaning of the word owning has more permanency about it and permanency equals a home. This doesn't have to be a home, it is just a place to put my head, to hang my clothes when I shower in the morning. It doesn't really matter if I don't get attached to it. It's fine, it's comfy and everything else but I could set up somewhere else and I'd be fine. I equate owning with certainly a far better chance of being a home and permanent.

Q. Is this home?

A. Quite obviously it is my home but no, not really. This isn't even my official address or anything, so no. ...these four walls I don't own but everything else in here I do and I could move everything else to somewhere else and that will be my home... Because I don't own it basically. If you want it directly related to me, as I don't own it I don't really care, it doesn't really bother me. I care about my own personal rights and in that sense I am secure, very secure. This is my little home and I'm not trying to say it is not and it makes me happy but I could be equally happy somewhere else. I'm just not attached to it...

(renter/female/26/single no children/occ 2)

As stated above, the manner in which the status of the home is intimately related to the status of the neighbourhood means that we can also examine the extension of these tenure-based meanings into the neighbourhood.

For example:

neighbourhood status,

A.   If we cheapskate on things and don't do the place to a certain standard we'll be letting down the area.

(owner/female/26/couple no children/occ 3)

Q.   Is it important to you that your home should be seen to blend with the rest of the neighbourhood?

A.   Yes, well it does. It is not that important because again we don't own it. It does blend very nicely because they have done a nice job on the front, so I think it does.

(renter/female/23/single no children/occ 3)

And neighbourhood attachment,

Q.   How would you describe your attachment to this neighbourhood?

A.   Oh very close attachment to the neighbourhood, it's a terrific place to live. It's close to the inner city, it's small, it's relatively quiet and it's got tremendous virtue.

(owner/male/30s/couple with children/occ 1)

Q.   How would you describe your attachment to this neighbourhood?

A.   Temporary.

(renter/male/27/single no children/occ 7)

The following comments from owners regarding neighbourhood status, relate particularly to the associations people make between a certain tenure form, public renting, and the sorts of people, they think, live in public housing.

Q. If the ministry of housing announced plans to build some houses in this street or to put tenants in some of the houses along this street how would you feel?

A. Like Housing Commission homes you mean?

Q. Yes.

A. [long pause] I don't think I'd be very pleased about it, but I suppose I'm more thinking of the sort of people that go into Housing Commission—I'm not meaning to degrade them or anything but I just wonder whether it might just bring down the standard of the area.

(owner/female/32/couple with children/occ 2)

Q. If the ministry of housing announced plans to build some houses in this street or to put tenants in some of the houses along this street how would you feel?

A. I'd be outraged because the type of people that they attract are, they are no-hopers. People have this really abominable opinion about things that are not their own and they just don't care for them and that would really annoy me. Because you just need to go through some of the areas—I often go to Northland and you drive through very large housing commission areas there. Some of the places, honestly, there are weeds up to the window sills and the flywire screens hanging off the hinges, people just don't care. They've got all their old bombs parked in the yard and just don't have any respect for something that is not theirs. They probably wouldn't have the respect if it was theirs either but the thing is they tend to be dirty type of people which doesn't appeal to me.

(owner/female/29/single no children/occ 3)

Sometimes oblique references are made to private renters and neighbourhood status.

Q. What is it do you think that contributes to the standing or status of this neighbourhood?

A. It's so established with many of the older neighbours being here for many years, whereas these days you tend to get your more transient population, particularly Box Hill is very transient.

(owner/female/couple with children/occ 3)

Or not so oblique.

A.   ...there's a few houses in this street that are rented and every time I drive past them they always looks so revolting. There's one house where Fiona always used to be out in the garden looking after it and it's been rented for 4 years now and the gate is falling off its hinges and the fence is falling down. You know those sorts of things and I sometimes think, 'God this street looks a nightmare. If only those people renting those houses would mow the lawns it would look nice and tidy', I sometimes think that, I'm conscious of that.

(owner/female/30s/couple with children/occ 3)

Even some renters react to the stigma of having renters in the neighbourhood.

A.   Don't necessarily think I'd live in the inner city if I got married and had kids say. I wouldn't live right out either, but sort of middle of the road. I wouldn't want lots of people renting, we'd want people around us who owned their houses.

(renter/female/24/single no children/occ 3)

Some renters point out that as they are renters this impacts on their interpretation of the neighbourhood.

Q.   Is it important to you that your house should be seen to blend with the rest of the neighbourhood?

A.   Oh no that doesn't matter, not when I'm renting.

Q.   It would be if you were owning?

A.   Yes.

Q.   Why?

A.   Because I like things to look nice and if I owned—when you rent—I guess it's my feeling that this isn't permanent, it doesn't really matter. But I like it to look nice, a nice house out the front and, sort of, inside. I think if I was owning a house

I'd like it all to look, I'd pick something that looked nice in the neighbourhood as well, matched with everyone else.

(renter/female/24/single no children/occ 3)

Not all renters, however, are as negative about their neighbour-hoods. Many of them have quite positive feelings about their neighbourhoods. This may indicate that distinct tenure-based meanings are at their strongest within the home or private sphere and are generally weaker when we move into the neighbourhood or public realm. However, having said that, renters' comments about neighbourhood status are less enthusiastic than owners' and often referred to in a less personal manner with the use of words such as 'they' rather than 'our'. Overall though the differences between owners and renters with regard to neighbourhood status are far less marked than for any other meaning.

Q. What do you think actually contributes to the standing of this neighbourhood?

A. I think they have a pretty active council. The Council is fairly concerned about the welfare of its residents. I mean all facil-ities that I've mentioned are pretty good here.

(renter/female/23/single no children/occ 3)

Q. What is it that contributes to the standing or status of this neighbourhood?

A. I think it is cut off by the freeway, Hoddle St and Heidelberg Rd so it tends to isolate this area a little bit. It makes it diffi-cult for cars to travel straight through it so it tends to make it a little bit quieter. The park and the Merri Creek contribute significantly to the neighbourhood and the people in this area seem to be quite friendly. There are a lot of migrants still living here which makes it a little more interesting — well it doesn't seem to be a conservative neighbourhood.

(renter/female/27/couple no children/occ 3)

Moving on to look at neighbourhood attachment, home owners are positive about their neighbourhood and generally feel very attached to it.

Q. How would you describe your attachment to this neighbour-hood?

A. Well I'm not actively involved at a community level but I'm very attached to it, I mean I feel the intent to settle here and stay for a long time. I'm very fond of this neighbourhood.

(owner/female/25/single no children/occ 3)

A. One of the reasons why one buys a house next to a park is to enjoy that amenity. I mean we've got no yard of our own but the council comes and mows our front garden twice a week in summer, it goes forever. And I suppose in there lies... and I don't think I'm the only one in this street who has a very parochial, no, not parochial, what's the word, personal ownership of the park in front. When the drug addicts come and shoot up in the cars across the road I take it as a personal affront that they're using my park to come and shoot up and I'd prefer it if they went elsewhere. I suppose that's irrational but that protective attitude towards the park is important. ...

A. Home owners tend to identify with their area more greatly, both with an area and with a residence to a greater level than renters. It usually can be identified by the amount of effort they put into the garden or something like that and I—in a sense it's not their castle.

(owner/male/30s/couple with children/occ 2)

A. The feeling is good in the neighbourhood

Q. What is that feeling?

A. Well it's a comfortable sort of feeling, people are friendly, especially in this side of Clifton Hill, they call it the village and it is, we can walk around and know where everyone we see in the street lives, just about, and so there's that nice feel about it, the environment is nice I mean it's lovely here with the park across the road, there's a fair bit of community involvement over here, there's a lot of involvement with schools and kindergartens and those sorts of things so people get to know one another.

(owner/female/34/couple with children/occ 2)

Renters on the other hand are far less enthusiastic about their attachment to the neighbourhood.

Q. How would you describe your attachment to this neighbourhood?

A. I just enjoy living here, I'm not particularly attached to the people around me or anything, or the community.

(renter/female/25/couple no children/occ 5)

Q. Have you generally speaking been concerned about local issues in the past?

A. ...No I've had a fairly transient lifestyle over the last ten years. I haven't really settled into a particular community.

Q. How would you describe your attachment to this neighbourhood?

A. It is not a close attachment. I like the area, it is pleasant to live in, however, I will be leaving soon.

(renter/male/33/couple no children/occ 2)

Q. How would you describe your attachment to this neighbourhood?

A. Practical, not really any emotional attachment. We chose here because it was close to the house (that they're renovating), it's close to the children's schools. ...

A. I think home owners on the whole feel more part of a neighbourhood because they own the home, they are a rate payer, they feel like a permanent resident and for that reason they tend, perhaps, to be more active in local issues.

(renter/female/40/couple with children/occ 3)

Though some renters do have positive feelings about their neighbourhoods, again indicating that tenure-based meanings are at their strongest in the private realm and become weaker as we move into the public realm.

Q. How would you describe your attachment to this neighbourhood?

A. We really like it. I could live in any other house in this street almost. I think the neighbourhood here is great, people are really friendly and I like the way it is only a small street. You don't have loads of traffic, Holden St was always really busy and you used to just about have a heart attack every time you tried to park. So I think this neighbourhood is really good and I would certainly look at living in a smaller neighbourhood again.

(renter/female/20s/single no children/occ 3)

CULTURAL MEANINGS OF HOME OWNERSHIP AND TYPICAL PROBABILITY

The cultural meanings of home ownership include 'status', 'respect', 'lifestyle' and 'attachment'. The extent to which these are reproduced in other contexts again appears widespread.

A study of home owners in Britain found that,

> Sixty-four per cent of owner occupiers said that they did feel attached to the house they lived in compared with only 40 per cent of tenants. Similarly, only 28 per cent of owners denied any such feelings of attachment, yet 46 per cent of tenants did so. Furthermore, '...when asked whether owners and tenants 'feel differently' about their homes, 32 per cent of home owners (and 44 per cent of council house purchasers) spoke of the pride which came with ownership and 37 per cent suggested that owners look after their homes more assiduously (Saunders, 1989, pp. 187–188).

British council house purchasers, stated that,

> ...the majority of buyers were prepared to say that after the change of tenure they did feel differently about the house which they had lived in for many years. The tendency was even more marked for

later buyers, who were twice as likely to report that they felt the house was 'more mine, somehow' or that they felt more secure (Stubbs, 1988, p. 153).

In the U.S. 'status-prestige' was found to be the second most important motive for home ownership (Rosow, 1948). In one of the classic studies of suburban life in North America Seeley *et al.* (1956) states that,

> Property is an essential component of status in Crestwood Heights. The Crestwooder who owns an adequate house has become a substantial member of the community and, as such, is respected and admired by his (sic) peers. The house and its furnishings; the street and the street number; the location in Crestwood—all are acquired items which make up the total property complex of the house (p. 46).

Perin's (1977) work in the U.S., some twenty years later, also identifies a similar range of meanings. Key phrases from owners include: 'home owners' ethic means a very high value on you'; 'a step up the ladder of social as well as economic standing'; 'great deal of pride even in the ownership of very modest dwellings'; 'people display the fact that they own that house even though it may not be much of a house'; 'predominant thing in people's minds as being a mark of quality of the person'; 'more safe, non-transient in nature', and; 'can function better' (pp. 34–5). Perin also makes the point that home owners gain status through being vetted by the bank manager as able to service a long-term debt.

Canadian home owners also recognise these status differences and advocate that these cultural distinctions should be reflected materially through public policy.

> Some felt that home ownership should be more heavily subsidised than the rental sector because, in the words of one respondent 'people are making an effort...' Some maintained that tenants should have restricted political rights at the local level... (Pratt, 1989, p. 301).

In terms of the variation in the cultural meanings of home ownership, *vis-à-vis* other social factors, Rosow (1948) found that whilst holding socio-economic class constant 'businessmen with a mean high school education and a largely *nouveau riche* orientation' were more likely to identify with meanings such as status or prestige in the U.S. On the other hand, 'professional people with a mean college education and diversified interest areas' stressed the 'living activities' associated with home ownership (p. 754). Deverson and Lindsay's (1975) results, that different middle class communities place differing amounts of stress upon status, support the non-class based nature of these cultural meanings (quoted in Agnew, 1981, p. 78). Finally, referring to attachment to the home, Saunders (1990) points out that age may be a significant variable as less than half of those under 35 felt attached to their homes compared with 80 per cent of those past retirement age (p. 295).

CULTURAL MEANINGS OF RENTING AND TYPICAL PROBABILITY

The cultural meanings of renting identified through the case studies include 'stigma' and 'lack of attachment'. Perin (1977) found similar meanings amongst U.S. renters. Key phrases referring to renters (though not always the words of renters) include 'in the South particularly you're just not the best type person if you're a renter', 'we're in a transition stage in adopting the renter as being the full-fledged citizen', 'not truly indigenous to the neighbourhood', 'not as likely to maintain property' and 'could be gone tomorrow' (p. 34).

Home owners in Canada also voiced similar opinions about renters.

> In general people who rent don't maintain their property. Their general living habits are lower. Their attitudes are different. You have to look at why they're renting. They're either kids or lower income people who don't care about their living surroundings. ... If

you don't have something to look after you tend to spend your money on alcohol or cars or trips (Pratt, 1989, p. 300).

In Britain the concern is more often with public than private tenants but the sentiments are the same—'Council tenants are labelled as of low status' (Holme, 1985, p. 161). Council tenants in Britain are also less attached to their homes than home owners. Saunders again reports that only 40 per cent of council tenants had a strong feeling of attachment to their home compared with 64 per cent of home owners. What is more 46 per cent of council tenants compared with only 28 per cent of home owners had no strong feeling of attachment to their home (1990, p. 295).

Once again then there is evidence to suggest that the meanings attributed to renting in the case studies, are replicated in other socio-temporal-spatial contexts. Whether or not the significance of these meanings is the same is, however, another matter and one that needs to be addressed through comparative research.

CONCLUSION

Chapter 5 argues that causality at the level of meaning and causality at the level of typical probability have been established in the attribution of particular meanings to the experience of housing tenure. This constitutes a causally adequate relationship between the experience of housing tenure and particular meanings or interpretations of the home.

In Chapter 4 three criteria that would need to be met to sustain the argument that housing tenures are significant in the formation of social groups were noted. The first criterion was that economic, political and cultural inequalities of an objective nature be linked directly with housing tenures—this was met through the secondary data reviewed in Chapter 3. The second criterion stipulated as essential to the identification of housing tenure-based social groups such as classes, political forces and status groups, was that home owners and renters attribute particular sets of meanings in relation to the economic, political and cultural inequalities constructed through housing tenures. These meanings have been detailed in this chapter and a causally adequate link between housing tenure and particular meanings established. The third criterion, that particular courses of social action are engaged in as a direct result of the subjective understanding of the objective inequalities is the subject of Part Two—the case studies.

In Part Two we examine the wider significance of the causally adequate relationship between housing tenure and particular meanings of the home by exploring the extent to which such meanings relate to different courses of social action. Does the fact that home owners and renters interpret their homes differently affect their social action in any way? The relationship between housing tenure, meanings and social action is investigated through three case studies, examining the social action of home owners and renters in three different locales, the home (Chapter 6), neighbourhood (Chapter 7) and place of employment (Chapter 8).

HOUSING TENURE AND SOCIAL ACTION: THE CASE STUDIES

Part Two focuses upon the relationship between housing tenure and social action in the home, neighbourhood and place of employment. Three distinct case studies are drawn upon: participation in a community-based crime prevention scheme, in local community activism and an industrial strike, respectively. Chapters 6, 7 and 8 detail each of the case studies, situating them historically, outlining how the study areas were selected, how the interview samples were constructed and then the data analysis.

The data analysis for each case study seeks to establish a causal relationship between housing tenure and particular courses of action, a task that has proved difficult for earlier housing class debaters. In doing so these chapters attempt to extend the adequate causal relationship established in Chapter 5 between the experience of housing tenure and particular meanings, to examine whether those meanings relate causally to social action. Moving between the ideal types of social action (*wertrational, zweckrational,* etc.) and the data from the case studies, we are able to examine the role of housing tenure relations in causing particular courses of social action. The data analysis thus examines the third of our criteria in relation to the formation of housing tenure-based classes, political forces and status groups; that particular courses of social action are engaged in as a direct result of tenure-based meanings.

Going beyond simply establishing whether or not there is a causal relationship, however, we will also examine the nature of the social group consciousness being (re)constructed through the interrelationship of housing tenure relations and social action by drawing upon the ideal types of social relationship (communal, associative, etc.). This enables investigation of the relationship between housing tenure and social change. Does home ownership necessarily cause politically conservative social action and construct a social consciousness of the 'respectable pillars' variety as has been assumed in the past?

Chapter 6

SOCIAL ACTION
IN THE HOME

Neighbourhood Watch (NW) is the community-based crime prevention scheme that operates in the state of Victoria, Australia. The case study focuses upon one NW Area and is concerned with participation (social action) in the scheme by resident households. The study offers the opportunity to trace the links between housing tenure, meaning and participation in NW and the opportunity to investigate the nature of that social action. For example, on the one hand, NW may represent an extension of state police powers and a dispersal of monitoring and surveillance processes incorporating the civilian population into an institutionalised spy network. On the other hand, NW may represent a social form with the potential for creating a democratically responsive and responsible police force (O'Malley, 1989). As Wilson states,

> While the official scheme (NW) has positive aspects in increasing the possibility of citizen interaction as well as communication between the police and residents, the scheme also has certain negative and divisive features. Under its rhetoric of 'community' and 'neighbourhood' there exist very real contradictions (1986, page 68).

It is this ambiguity with regard to the nature of social action within NW, that makes it particularly interesting as a case study of the relationship between housing tenure and social group consciousness. In particular, it permits inquiry into whether home ownership causes social action that is inherently conservative, as is suggested in the literature.

The case study focuses upon social action that was predominantly home-centred and that rarely extended into the neighbourhood. This was due to the lack of a public hall that could be hired for larger public meetings of NW participants. So, whilst a study of participation in NW could have provided opportunity for study of both individuals' social action in the home and their engagement in wider social relations through collective action in the neighbourhood, the study, in fact, focused upon non-group social action.

NEIGHBOURHOOD WATCH—A COMMUNITY-BASED CRIME PREVENTION SCHEME

> Neighbourhood Watch is a community based crime prevention programme. It is aimed at minimising the incidence of preventable crime, especially burglary, within a defined area (Victoria Police, 1983, p. 1).

Neighbourhood Watch is a crime prevention scheme of recent origin in Australia and was first piloted in an outlying suburb of metropolitan Melbourne in 1983. The scheme was adapted from the U.S. Crimewatch program and was implemented throughout Victoria in March 1984, as traditional policing methods for combating burglaries had failed. The number of burglaries committed in Victoria had risen to one every seven minutes in 1983 (Victoria Police, 1983).

The stated objectives of NW are as follows:

1. To minimise the incidence of preventable crime in the NW Area.
2. To increase the incidence and quality of reporting of crime and suspicious activity within the NW Area.

3. To improve the degree of personal and household security in the NW Area through an education programme and operation identification.
4. To reduce fear of crime in the NW Area.
5. To deter criminal activity in the NW Area by increasing the probability of apprehension.
6. To ensure effective maintenance of the programme by planning, monitoring and evaluation.
(Neighbourhood Watch Manual, Victoria Police, 1983, p. 5.)

NW programs are implemented in defined areas of approximately 600 households with a significant crime rate (especially burglaries) and a demonstrated community interest. Once the police are satisfied that these criteria have been met an initial meeting is called to which all residents in the proposed Area are invited. At this meeting an Area Co-ordinator is elected from volunteers, who is then responsible for liaison and information exchange between the police and residents. Each NW Area is divided into zones of approximately 30 homes. Zone leaders are then selected from volunteers who are responsible for fostering co-operation between residents of their zone, the administration of committees and liaison with the Area Co-ordinator and Police Co-ordinator. Participation in NW has proved very popular and the scheme has a major presence in Victoria through a variety of mediums. NW produces its own publication 'The Watch' and the NW logo of citizen average merging into a policeman is now evident on street-signs throughout Melbourne's suburbs and many parts of rural Victoria. A wide range of pamphlets and stickers have been produced to give NW a high profile. Each NW Area produces a newsletter keeping residents up to date with local NW happenings and detailing the recent crime in their area.

In terms of its effectiveness the scheme appears to have had a significant impact upon the burglary rate within NW Areas. Table 6.1 shows significant reductions in the burglary rate in some of these areas, though these statistics tell us nothing about the burglary rate in suburbs without NW. This of course raises the issue of whether schemes such as NW actually reduce the overall burglary rate or simply displace it from one suburb to another. The

Table 6.1 Percentage increase/decrease in residential burglaries for Neighbourhood Watch Areas 1984–1990[a]. Source: Victoria Police (1986, 1988, 1989, 1990).

	1984–86	1987–88	1988–89	1989–90
A	–39.74	– 4.51	– 2.88	–15.03
B	– 8.35	–25.03	– 5.76	+10.82
C	+ 0.57	+ 6.15	+17.14	+ 1.02
D	–54.54	–51.61	– 2.71	–19.76
G	–75.86	–63.16	–20.31	+ 4.17
H	–29.19	+ 2.45	– 6.58	– 5.96
I	–25.97	+12.65	–29.27	–17.46
J	– 0.20	– 2.01	+ 7.23	–15.55
M	– 9.40	–13.21	–21.36	– 4.07
P	–56.64	–15.25	+13.28	
Q	– 6.22	– 7.19	–14.21	–20.00
S	– 9.35	–38.51	– 5.17	
U	–22.48	+17.10	– 3.08	
V	–28.01	– 8.42	–17.41	
Y	–29.57	– 0.82	–15.16	
Z	–20.68	–17.45	– 1.44	

a. The number of NW Areas within a district changed over the time period. The districts also appear to have been renamed in 1989-90, hence the blank cells. Whether their boundaries were re-drawn is unknown.

displacement of crime is, however, becoming increasingly difficult as by late 1989 there were 801 NW Areas covering 1.8 million people or approximately 600,000 homes in Victoria (i.e half the State's population). Interestingly, as NW has grown so has the focus broadened, so that today, in evaluating the success of NW the Police are not only concerned with the crime rate but also whether or not it leads to an improvement in neighbouring relations.

THE CASE STUDY AREA AND CONSTRUCTION OF THE INTERVIEW SAMPLE

The case study area lies within Clifton Hill, an inner-urban suburb of the City of Collingwood in metropolitan Melbourne. It is an old working class area with pockets of older working class families still resident but they are increasingly being replaced by young single professionals and young professional married couples with either very young or no children. The housing stock of single storey Victorian and Edwardian terraces occupies narrow streets which are laid out in a grid pattern.

There are two NW Areas within the suburb of Clifton Hill. The Southern Clifton Hill NW Area was selected for the case study as the Area Co-ordinator was willing to assist in the research and this co-operation enabled the processes of sampling and pilot interviewing. Founded on September 5th 1984, this NW Area includes 577 households in fourteen zones with eighteen zone leaders. Since that time the Area Co-ordinator has been a retired woman, who was recently awarded a plaque for her services to NW by the Victoria Police. The zone leaders of the Area meet every two months in the home of the Area Co-ordinator as the hiring of a public hall is difficult. This in turn makes it difficult for any residents, other than the zone leaders, to attend NW meetings.

This particular NW scheme has had a limited impact on the crime rate within the Area over its six years of operation (see Table 6.2). However, the Victoria Police do not consider the crime rate of the area to be high in comparison with other inner-city suburbs (pers. comm.).

Sampling interviews were carried out with 120 households (50 per cent of the households in the census district, though far more

Table 6.2 Percentage increase/decrease in residential burglaries for Clifton Hill, 1984–1990[a]. Source: Victoria Police 1986, 1988, 1989, 1990.

1984–86	1987–88	1988–89	1989–90[a]
+15.54	–5.17	+14.55	+1.92

a. 1989–90 figure relates to changed NW boundaries.

than 120 doors were knocked on!) to give a sampling population of 76 owners and 44 renters (see Table 6.3), from which approximately thirty would be chosen to carry out in-depth interviews.

The key characteristics of the thirty in-depth interviewees are detailed in Table 6.4.

A further four interviews were also carried out with 'key actors' for the views of those who 'manage' NW and to provide important

Table 6.3 Neighbourhood Watch sample.

	owners	*renters*	*total*
h/h's in c.d.	166	73	239[a]
sample	76 (46%)	44 (60%)	120 (50%)
active[b]	29 (38%)	4 (9%)	33 (27%)
inactive	47 (62%)	40 (91%)	87 (73%)

a. when the research was carried out in 1988, there were thirteen households less than the 1986 Census figure.
b. An individual was considered active in this sample if he or she had attended at least one NW meeting and/or borrowed an inscriber or ultra-violet pen from his or her Zone Leader with which to mark personal property. This definition of activity involves a degree of deliberation on the part of the participant, considerably more than, for example, displaying a NW sign, most of which were originally delivered to households. The definition also embraces both social action within the home and collective action within the neighbourhood. However, attendance at NW meetings, was restricted in this particular NW Area as noted above.
(Yates corrected chi-square value = 10.396, d.f.= 1, p = 0.001.)

Table 6.4 Key characteristics of interview sample.

	active	*inactive*	*male*	*female*	*age 31-40*	*single*	*total*
renter	3	10	5	8	8	11	13
owner	9	8	7	10	9	11	17

contextual information. These interviewees included the current and former state wide co-ordinators of Neighbourhood Watch for the Victoria Police, the Police-Community Liaison Officer for Clifton Hill and the Area Co-ordinator for the NW Area studied.

Whilst it is clear from Table 6.3 that, within the study area, home owners are far more active in NW than renters, the intensive interviews were designed to establish why this should be so and to examine the role of housing tenure in that participation.

THE MEANINGS OF HOUSING TENURE AND PARTICIPATION IN NEIGHBOURHOOD WATCH

To explain the causal nature of the statistical relationship between housing tenure and participation in NW (see Table 6.3) we must now consider the qualitative data of the case study. The data analysis examines the proposition that being a home owner or a renter affects, causally, one's home-oriented participation in NW. For example, are home owners more active in NW because they want to reduce the crime rate due to its negative impact upon property values? The data needed to support such a proposition are home owners and renters linking tenure-based meanings to their activity or inactivity in NW. We examine three different forms of participation in NW: First, general involvement; second, the marking of valuable possessions; third, securing the dwelling. As the different forms of participation are detailed so is the nature of the causal relationship with housing tenure revealed.

This section examines, in general terms, why home owners are more active in NW than renters. Contrary to expectations home owners' heightened activity does not relate to the more obvious propositions regarding the relationship between a concern for property values and a concern about crime rates, for two reasons.

First, home owners tend to think that the crime rate does not affect property values.

A.   ...I don't think people take much notice of (the) crime rate when they are looking at properties. Clifton Hill has the highest crime rate and appears great in property values at the moment so...

(owner/active/female/single)

(See Appendix 3 for explanation of abbreviations).

Second, home owners do not think that NW can improve their house values.

A. ...if you're living in a NW area people say that's good but it doesn't do anything either way for house values or whatever.

(owner/inactive/female/couple)

A. I don't think it has anything to do with house values in Clifton Hill. I think Clifton Hill is a bit of a boom area anyway and there are a whole lot of factors related to that. Clearly the fact that it is inner city is related to that more than the fact that it's in a NW area.

(owner/inactive/female/single)

However, this does not mean that the heightened activity of home owners is not grounded in their tenure-based experiences. For example, the tenure-based political meaning of security and the cultural meaning of attachment appear particularly important.

Home owners felt that being involved in NW was worth their while as the legal security that they enjoy enables them to reap the longer term rewards of becoming involved.

Q. Do you think home owners support NW for different reasons than renters?

A. Well I think they probably would because they're more permanently in the area, they see themselves as being permanent in the area so they probably would be a strong supporter of it.

(owner/active/male/couple with children)

Yet, renters are in a legally insecure position and are consequently only temporary residents in the neighbourhood.

A.   ...people who are renting their places wouldn't worry about getting involved in it as regards putting up the signs and things like that.

Q.   Why do you think that is?

A.   ...you know, they're just renting a place so they don't worry about it, a lot of people, younger people move around a lot anyway so...

(renter/inactive/female/couple with children)

Renters also felt that home owners were more likely to be involved in NW due to the threat of loss of security and attachment consequent upon a burglary being greater for owners than for renters.

A.   I am sure if you owned your own house you would be more likely to be involved in and support NW. I think you have more to lose...they must have more to lose in the security and peace of mind.

(renter/active/female/single)

A further aspect to the greater involvement of home owners in NW is that home owners appear to have a greater neighbourhood attachment or community conscience than renters, reflecting the different cultural meanings of the tenures.

A.   I think home owners would be more inclined to support NW. I think they'd probably have, not only for themselves but if they've got any sort of community conscience at all they're helping themselves and helping other people who may be in their own neighbourhood, whereas I don't think people who are renting necessarily have that affinity with their own community or locality.

(owner/inactive/female/single)

Q.   Would you describe yourself as a supporter of NW?

A.   Yes, but not a radical one, in other words I don't go to their meetings and I'm not helping them at the moment but maybe if I buy a house in the area I'll help them, but you know at the moment I suppose you'd call me an inactive supporter .

(renter/active/female/single)

Q. Do you think any particular sort of person may tend to become involved in NW?

A. I suppose more community minded people, people with families or people with obvious assets, own their own homes, things like that, people with things to protect.

(renter/inactive/female/single)

In considering the generally higher levels of involvement of home owners in NW, it is possible to trace how tenure-based meanings have led to this situation. If we consider particular aspects of participation within NW, rather than general involvement, this illuminates the relationship between housing tenure and NW activity further. There were two main aspects to NW participation; first, the marking of valuables and second, securing the dwelling.

With the marking of valuables for identification purposes the politically based legal insecurity of renting is significant. Renters are often forced to be mobile, working against the accumulation of goods of value and generally contributing to less involvement in NW.

Q. Do you think home owners support NW for different reasons than renters?

A. Well renting to me is such a transient life you don't think of things like that, you don't normally have that many possessions. Over the five years that I've lived (owned) here I've got things that I would hate to have stolen, whereas before (when renting) I had one stereo that came from Queensland to here. You don't have things that you care about probably and you feel that you could be burgled, probably more chance of being burgled when you're renting because there are more people coming and going.

(owner/inactive/female/single)

The second aspect to participation in NW, securing the dwelling in a physical sense, includes the displaying of NW stickers and signs and is readily engaged in by owners but less so renters. The political meaning of control and economic meanings related to maintenance are of particular importance. First, some comments from renters:

A. Yes, definitely, if you own a house you have more control over what you can do with the house, like security doors, they don't look like much but they are effective, also this house doesn't have any window locks, I would put window locks on … I mean that back door, it's only got, what do you call it, one night latch on it and it's all complete glass, so all you have to do is break the glass, put that little thing down and open it. So if I lived (owned) here I'd have a different back door to the house … Well security, security is having no fears, no worries but I don't really like it here…you think about that back door, because that back door has dropped you hear them coming in because it scrapes across the floor…

(renter/active/female/single)

Q. How involved would you say you have become in NW?

A. Oh not very involved as far as marking any of our things, not that we've got anything of very great value, … it doesn't affect us that way and we can't display any signs because it's not our house, we're only renting it.

(renter/inactive/female/couple with children)

The comparison with owners again provides a stark contrast:

A. It is the overall psychology of it being a home that you own. I think actually the physical surrounding gives you a feeling of greater security in a number of ways rather than just the financial side of being secure, of being in control, physically being able to make modifications to the house without worrying about going through the landlord and things like that, knowing the house, quirks and sounds in the house and feeling comfortable in it, I think you get a greater feeling of that than if you're renting.

(owner/inactive/male/couple)

The economic meanings of home ownership relate to securing the dwelling, as a form of home oriented social action, in that home owners desire to minimise the cost of physical damage to the house that occurs through 'breaking and entering'. Renters, however, have little economic interest in the dwelling and thus care little about the cost of physical damage to the house incurred during a burglary. Renters see little economic reason for participating in NW yet recognise that this is a factor for owners.

Q.   Do you think home owners support NW for different reasons than renters?

A.   I guess again because they own their houses they are probably more worried about the physical house getting damaged as well as what's in it.

(renter/inactive/female/single with children)

Owners, on the other hand, are very aware of this. It is perhaps somewhat ironic, then, that as home owners improve the security of their dwellings more damage is done by burglars in gaining entry. It would seem that a typical mode of entry for burglars into houses with dead-locks is to simply use a sledge hammer on the front door and take it off its hinges!

Q.   Do you think home owners support NW for different reasons than renters?

A.   Yes I'd agree with that one in that rental people tend not to have as vested an interest in the property as, say, the owner of the property. I mean if somebody's house is burgled and it's rented, it's not so much about the smashed window on the yard, it's not the actual house itself, it's more the personal contents, whereas if you're an owner you're concerned about the whole lot of it.

(owner/inactive/female/couple)

Three aspects of participation in NW have been identified. These include: general involvement, marking valuables and securing the dwelling. We have seen how various economic, cultural and political meanings of housing tenures relate to these activities. Suffice it to say that the meanings of home ownership encourage participation whilst the meanings of renting encourage non-participation.

The data presented thus far specify a relationship at the level of typical probability (statistical association, see Table 6.3) and a relationship at the level of meaning between housing tenure and participation in NW within the case study area. In Weberian terms, this represents a relationship of causal adequacy between housing tenure and participation in this NW scheme. The test-case for such a statement is whether NW would be essentially different without the presence of home owners.

IS THE PARTICIPATION OF HOME OWNERS ESSENTIAL TO NEIGHBOURHOOD WATCH?

Let us imagine that home owners were not present in the NW Area studied and thus that the Area was occupied solely by renters. Would the participation in NW be essentially different if this was the case? The answer is 'yes' for, as is clearly shown above, the experience of renting generates a series of meanings that constrain participation in NW. If the area were to consist solely of renters, the participation would be essentially different in that the scale and hence effectiveness of NW would be reduced severely. There is also evidence to suggest that a NW scheme consisting solely of renters would have more of a focus on personal crime than property crime. The Australian Bureau of Statistics Crime and Crime Prevention Survey, 1987 suggests that renters are more concerned about personal crime than home owners and less concerned about property crimes such as burglary (see Tables 6.5 and 6.6).

What is more, renters in Inner Melbourne, the region of the case study, feel less safe when alone at home at night (see Table 6.7). Using this as a crude indicator of 'fear of crime' we can postulate that 'fear of crime' is not a major motive for participating

Table 6.5 Persons perceiving that major crime problems exist in Victoria: tenure by perceived crime or public nuisance problems in local area. Pearson chi-square value = 21.985, d.f. = 1, p = 0.000. Source: Australian Bureau of Statistics, Crime and Crime Prevention Survey, 1987.

Victoria	owners	renters	total
assault (yes)	33 (0.0005%)	24 (4%)	57
assault (no)	2596 (99%)	565 (96%)	3161
total	2629	589	3218

Table 6.6 Persons perceiving that major crime problems exist in Victoria: tenure by crime or public nuisance problem in local area of most concern to persons. Pearson chi-square value = 8.833, d.f.= 1, p = 0.003. Source: Australian Bureau of Statistics, Crime and Crime Prevention Survey, 1987.

Victoria	owners	renters	total
burglary	266 (94%)	63 (83%)	329
assault	18 (6%)	13 (17%)	31
total	284	76	360

in NW as renters have lower participation rates than home owners (see Table 6.8).

Home owners are also not only more likely to be active but less likely to be inactive than renters in NW schemes, both within Inner Melbourne and throughout Victoria. One important reason for this greater participation on the part of home owners lies with the meanings of housing tenures, detailed above.

Two of the 'key actors' interviewed also confirmed the heightened activism of home owners. First, a Victoria Police state-wide co-ordinator of NW stated that,

> ...home owners are more likely to be involved. People renting homes often say 'I'm only renting it, it's not my house' and you have to point out to them that burglars don't steal houses (author's field notes).

Table 6.7 Tenure by feeling of safety when alone at home at night.   Pearson chi-square value = 2.815, d.f. = 1, p = 0.093.   Source: Australian Bureau of Statistics, Crime and Crime Prevention Survey, 1987.

Inner Melbourne	owners	renters	total
very safe	74 (97%)	48 (91%)	122
very unsafe	2 (3%)	5 (9%)	7
total	76	53	129

Table 6.8 Participation in Neighbourhood Watch.   Inner Melbourne chi-square value = 0.610, d.f. = 1, p = 0.435.   Victoria chi-square value = 3.363, d.f. = 1, p = 0.067.   Source: Australian Bureau of Statistics, Crime and Crime Prevention Survey, 1987.

	h/h's in NW	h/h's covered by NW	h/h's covered h/h's in[a]
Inner Melbourne			
Owners	30	19	63%
Renters	27	12	44%
Victoria			
Owners	474	369	78%
Renters	114	65	57%

a. The measure appearing in the final column of Table 6.8 is not necessarily a true measure of participation, as 'in NW' was established on the basis of the respondent's opinion as to whether or not his/her house lay within the boundary of a NW area and some households may have wrongly believed that they were in or out of such an area. Furthermore, the Australian Bureau of Statistics are unclear as to the precise meaning of the category 'covered by NW' and so it is unknown what sort of participation in NW this was measuring! It is also worth noting that when controlling for length of residence, a variable often associated with housing tenure, the disparity between owners' and renters' participation remains significant.

This viewpoint was also corroborated by an earlier Victoria Police state co-ordinator of NW, who pointed out that suburbs which have a high percentage of renter households are characterised by low levels of participation in NW and largely unsuccessful schemes.

This pattern of owners' greater participation in NW is also replicated internationally. A United States Bureau of Justice Survey of 11,198 households, carried out in 1984, revealed that 20% of all U.S. households live in areas with a NW or equivalent program and that within program areas 38% of households were actively participating. This participation varied with income and housing tenure so that 44% of households with incomes greater than U.S.$25,000 were participating and home owners were twice as likely to participate as renters (*New Spirit*, 1986). However, in considering an international case it is important to remember that housing tenures are social constructs both spatially and temporally bound. The typical meanings of housing tenures that relate to participation in NW within Australia, may have little relevance in a different national context.

The evidence does suggest, however, a typical probability of home owners being more active than renters in community-based crime prevention programs. The extent to which this is due to the meanings of home ownership specified above, is an empirical question. The case study evidence above suggests that the relationship is more than one of statistical association but is of a causally adequate nature due to the relationship between the meanings of housing tenures and participation in NW. On the basis of this evidence the actions of these home owners and renters can be interpreted as the actions of tenure-based classes, political forces and status groups. For example, if active home owners drew upon tenure-based economic meanings, their actions can be interpreted as tenure-based class action. In so far as inactive renters were inactive due to the political meanings of renting their social action can be interpreted as tenure-based political force action.

In sum, the meanings of home ownership relate causally to higher levels of participation in NW and there is a typical probability of this occurring repeatedly. This, however, says nothing about the actual type or nature of the NW participation that has been observed. By identifying the nature of the social action that housing tenure is causally related to, some clues are given as to the nature of the social group consciousness being (re)constructed through housing tenure relations and therefore of the relationship between housing tenure and social change. The problem, then, that we now need to address is does home ownership enable or constrain certain courses of action rather than others?

THEORISING THE SIGNIFICANCE OF HOME OWNERS' PARTICIPATION IN NEIGHBOURHOOD WATCH

Within the case study area two particular types of activity were being carried out as specific forms of participation in NW, predominantly by home owners. These were: physically securing the dwelling (a defence of private property) and marking possessions (a defence of one's own possessions). (This excludes the more general term 'involvement'.) Using the Weberian concepts detailed in Chapter 4, the *wertrational* aspects of these forms of social action are that 'physically securing the dwelling' aims to defend the sanctity of the home, an absolute end and the marking of possessions aims to maintain the absolute value of the sanctity of private property. Yet, there are also *zweckrational* elements in both of these forms of social action, that is pragmatic action to achieve a pragmatic end, with the aim simply being to prevent burglary in the first instance and to dissuade theft and/or enable the recovery of goods in the second.

If we examine the social relationships that characterise these forms of participation, we may gain further insights to the nature of NW tenure-based social action. The social interaction that takes place through the marking of possessions or the securing of the property is pragmatic and rational, rather than based on a feeling of commonality. Contact with a zone leader is made for a very particular purpose—in order to borrow an engraver or invisible marker so that one can mark one's possessions. This exchange does not take place 'by the by', it is not something that happens in passing whilst at some sort of social function, it is a calculated rational exchange. The social relationships that characterise these forms of participation are generally associative, that is they are based on a rational motivation.

So, what can we say about the nature of the social group consciousness (re)constructed or reinforced on the basis of such forms of participation? Neither of the forms of participation in NW display any of the potentially progressive aspects of NW such as increasing citizen interaction or creating a democratically responsive and responsible police force, yet, nor are they typical of the fears of some that participation in NW amounts to incorporation of the civilian population into an institutionalised spy network. Whether one sees these forms of social action as achieving absolute (*wertrational*) or pragmatic (*zweckrational*) ends, they represent little more than the maintenance of the status quo: those who 'have' defending what they have. There is nothing about these forms of participation that is in any way radical, quite the reverse in fact and much of this may relate to the home-centred nature of the reported social action.

It appears less likely that social action carried out in and for the private realm is going to be of a radical nature. In this sense the locale of social action may be an important aspect to understanding the nature of social group consciousness. Home-centred social action appears more likely to be either rational and thus oriented towards the monopolisation of market position, or based on absolute ends to suit the private realm that are inherently conservative. It is in these ways that home ownership can cause the (re)construction of a conservative social group consciousness. This very much supports the widely held view of home ownership being a social process that includes and incorporates people into dominant social relations. This is not a passive acceptance of the status quo but an active reinforcement of it for housing tenure causally relates to these particular courses of social action.

In specifying a causal relationship between housing tenure and social action, albeit conservative and oriented to maintenance of the status quo, we are identifying tenure-based class, political force and status group action. The detail of this causal relationship lies with the manner in which home owners and renters link tenure-based economic, political and cultural meanings to their actions. Thus, to the extent that home owners and or renters draw upon economic tenure-based meanings their actions can be interpreted as tenure-based class action, similarly with political meanings and political force action and cultural meanings and status group action.

CONCLUSION

The aim of this chapter has been to examine the causal nature of the relationship between housing tenure and courses of home-oriented social action, a relationship that has not been specified previously by the literature. This causal relationship has been detailed through an analysis of a case study of participation in a crime prevention scheme. The analysis demonstrates a relationship between the meanings of housing tenures and participation in NW by home owners and non-participation in NW by renters. On the basis of these data it is argued that causality at the level of meaning is established between housing tenure and particular types of social action in NW. A relationship of typical probability was also established between housing tenure and participation in community-based crime prevention schemes at four different spatial scales: the case study area, Inner Melbourne, Victoria and the U.S. The combination of these data sets, it is argued, is sufficient to indicate an adequate causal relationship between housing tenure and participation in a community-based crime prevention scheme. These aspects of tenure-based social action can be identified as tenure-based class, political force and status group action to the differing extent that tenure-based economic, political and cultural meanings were drawn upon.

The nature of the social group consciousness being (re)constructed through these forms of social action is inherently conservative. This appears due to the home-centred nature of the social action being carried out in the particular NW scheme studied. That the social action did not extend into the neighbourhood is less to do with housing tenure than the simple lack of a public hall in the area. The contribution of this chapter to our inquiry is that the causal relationship between housing tenure and home-oriented social action has been specified, affording a greater understanding of the significance of housing tenure and the extent of community participation. Chapter 7 builds on this to examine the relationship between housing tenure and collective action in the neighbourhood.

Chapter 7

SOCIAL ACTION IN THE NEIGHBOURHOOD

This chapter provides background and methodological information and the data analysis for a case study of community-based political activism by residents, in an inner Melbourne suburb, opposing a proposed overhead, high voltage powerline. The dispute began in the early 1970s and involved, on one side, the State Electricity Commission of Victoria (SECV) and the Victorian State Government, and on the other, residents along the route of the proposed powerline, their local councils, environmental groups and coalitions thereof.

This particular instance of community activism was selected as a case study as it contained the two major elements necessary to examine the relationship between housing tenure and collective social action. The issue had an explicit tenure component, in the form of the threat to property values, and collective action was evident in the form of public meetings.

A BRIEF HISTORY OF THE
BRUNSWICK–RICHMOND POWERLINE

The SECV proposed construction of this powerline to ensure a secure electricity supply to the Central Business District (CBD) of Melbourne. This involved an overhead cable connecting two terminal stations via a route that passed through residential streets and the linear park of the Merri Creek and Yarra River valleys. Opponents of the powerline originally pointed to the likely environmental and aesthetic damage to the parkland should it be built. In 1984 they widened their case drawing on evidence that demonstrated a link between electromagnetic radiation (EMR) emitted by powerlines, and leukaemia in young children. The adopted position of the opponents was that to reduce the health risks and environmental/aesthetic damage, the powerline should be put underground, away from residential and environmentally sensitive areas.

The potential for this issue to become a major political controversy lay with its long history. Public opposition to the SECV proposal began in the early 1970s, some fifteen years prior to this case study being conducted. The roots of the dispute lie in the 1950s and 1960s and our account of it through to 1990 is guided by the Powerline Review Panel Report, 1989, press-cuttings and participant observation field notes.

As increasing demand for electricity took effect in Melbourne, particularly through the continuing development of high-rise office buildings in the CBD, the SECV converted the metropolitan transmission system from 132kV to 220kV. The SECV argued that the construction of a link between Brunswick and Richmond terminal stations, via a proposed terminal station at Clifton Hill, would secure the supply of this 220kV network to the central city. The existing easement for the link, through which ran a 66kV line would, the SECV believed, provide for this 'simple up-grading' and would not raise any difficulties.

However, the rumblings of public discontent soon began. Between 1974 and 1976 both Fitzroy and Kew Councils expressed concern at the widening of the easement necessary for the upgrade from 66kV to 220kV. In March 1976, the Studley Park Progress Association, a local residents group, requested the State Premier, Sir Rupert Hamer, to intervene by requiring the SECV to find a more suitable route or to use an underground cable. However, as construction appeared to be only a long-term possibility, the opposition was minimal and the easement was widened.

By 1978 the proposals were firmer as the General Manager of the SECV approved in principle construction of the line, still anticipating minimal public opposition. This view was endorsed by the Victorian State Government's Ministry of Conservation which exempted the proposal from the need for an Environmental Effects Statement (EES). It was not until May 1982, when the plans for the powerline were released, that public opposition began to mount. Local residents and councils sought the intervention of the responsible ministers and the Merri Creek Co-ordinating Committee and Conservation Council of Victoria called for the preparation of an EES. On June 4 1982 these demands were met when the Minister for Planning and Conservation stated that an EES and public inquiry would take place.

The newly constituted Natural Resources and Environment Committee (NREC) headed the inquiry. In mid-1983, the Committee endorsed construction of the powerline with only minor modifications to the original plans. The post inquiry debate was largely condemnatory, centring on (ab)use of the Yarra River, Melbourne's main waterway, which flows through the middle of the city. Such was the public pressure that the Minister for Minerals and Energy was compelled to announce a further twelve month period of public consultation in March 1984.

In April 1984, local newspaper and television reports highlighted recent U.S. research in which the occurrence of leukaemia, particularly in young children, was linked with the electromagnetic fields produced by powerlines. This health issue became the focus of community and trade union opposition to the powerline, surpassing the environmental concerns and the opponents' aim of undergrounding the powerline thus gained further support as this would reduce the levels of EMR and thus reduce the health threat.

After the consultation period, on June 13 1985, the Minister for Industry, Technology and Resources, Robert Fordham, announced the Government's acceptance of the NREC recommendation, that the powerline be built subject to minor modifications.

The Environmental Effects Statement (EES) released by the SECV in 1985, attracted 179 submissions. Of these, 159 addressed the health issue and 71 the environmental/aesthetic issue. Over seventy per cent of the submissions (115) were received from people living in the vicinity of the proposed alternative underground cable route through Clifton Hill.

On 11 August 1986 the Minister for Industry, Technology and Resources and the Minister for Health (in an attempt to assuage health related fears) jointly announced the Government's intention to construct the line in accordance with the NREC recommendations. However, a Supplementary EES would assess alternative overhead and underground options along the route. This Supplementary EES received 185 submissions. Again seventy percent of these submissions were from opponents living near the proposed route in Clifton Hill.

The 8.5 km proposed route, down the Merri Creek and Yarra River valleys, both of which act as municipal boundaries, directly affected the residents and Councils of seven municipalities: Brunswick, Northcote, Fitzroy, Collingwood, Kew, Hawthorn, and Richmond. The fact that the river valleys are important linear parks for the wider populous and are well used recreation areas, plus the fact that the Yarra River is a 'Melbourne symbol', resulted in widespread condemnation of the proposals. In an attempt to co-ordinate this widespread opposition the Powerline Action Group (PAG) was formed as an 'umbrella' organisation in November 1987.

Opponents of the powerline were by this stage, after nearly ten years of struggle, 'hardened' political campaigners. Realising the dilemma that faced the Government if they accepted the health related arguments (i.e. that all powerlines would have to be placed underground, as this reduced levels of electromagnetic radiation), the PAG emphasised the environmental/aesthetic objections in the hope that this would provide the necessary let-out clause for the Government.

To present a coherent position to both the Government and the media and to co-ordinate the activities of the various opposition groups, a campaign officer was employed. The costs of $100/day, which were met for several months through donations, testifies to the commitment of powerline opponents.

The union members of the Australian Workers Union, Federated Ironworkers Association, Electrical Trades Union, Federated Engine Drivers and the Municipal Officers Association (SEC branch), who would construct the line, became key players in the dispute in January 1988. Despite representations by the PAG, the Trades Hall Council agreed to commence work on the powerline from 7 January 1988. The PAG moved into a phase of co-ordinated and well organised non-violent direct protest action. The 51 pole-sites were the focus of this action. Work progress was interrupted as protesters occupied these sites, carrying out ceremonial tree plantings and powerline burials. After many months of trying, powerline opponents finally had the media eye. The unions responded to the growing public profile on the 14 January 1988, by placing a health related work-ban on a section of the powerline that would pass through the grounds of Richmond High School. On 21 January members of the PAG attempted to occupy the office of the Minister for Industry, Technology and Resources, gaining widespread media coverage. Though not prepared to open his door the Minister, Robert Fordham, agreed to speak with a deputation.

In the run up to a State by-election in Kew, in which the powerline was a key issue, pole-site demonstrations that effectively stopped work on the powerline became weekly occurrences. News coverage was daily. The SECV hired work crews from Queensland, negotiated a wage deal outside of the Arbitration Commission far in excess of its standards and carried out work at week-ends in an attempt to get back on schedule. Yet, workers downed tools as soon as either demonstrators or police were on-site and the police still made no arrests despite the threats of trespass. The SECV attempted to counter the adverse media coverage it was receiving by placing double-page advertisements in Melbourne's three daily newspapers. Premier Cain was forced to ban the advertisements under Opposition pressure that they interfered with the political process of the nearing Kew by-election.

By March 1988 the unions had placed health-related work-bans on forty percent of the powerline route. The community groups now occupied a precarious position between on the one hand the SECV and Victorian State Government, acting in the interests of those active in the CBD property market, and the representatives of labour, the Trades Hall Council (THC). Whilst it is easy to establish the State Government and the SECV as the opponents of the PAG, the latter's relationship with the THC is far less clear. The moratorium on construction of the powerline, which both the THC and the PAG were fighting for, suggests a unity between the PAG and the THC which was at all times fragile. Moreover, the unity of the PAG was at times threatened, for a number of reasons.

First, opponents of the powerline were spread across a wide range of suburbs characterised by vastly different socio-economic backgrounds. Apart from their opposition to the powerline there was little in common between those from high on the east banks of the Yarra in Kew and their lowland comrades in Richmond and Collingwood. Tensions within the PAG and between the PAG and the THC were never more apparent than during the Kew by-election.

The safe Liberal seat of Kew had become vacant and two issues dominated the campaign to fill it. In the wake of the Hoddle St massacre and the Queen St killings (mass-murders committed by individuals who had an apparent fascination with and easy access to guns), gun law reform had become a state wide issue. Locally the powerline controversy dominated events. The PAG faced a conundrum. Should they support the Australian Democrat candidate, a locally active powerline opponent of many years, who if she were to win the seat and this was not thought to be impossible, would give them a strong voice in the State Parliament? Or should they put their weight behind the Labor Party in order to avoid offending the THC, a result that PAG had been informed by the THC was likely if they supported any other candidate? The major problem with supporting the Labor candidate, however, was that it was a Labor State Government who was supporting construction of the powerline and in fact the Labor candidate refused to make any commitment to a position opposing the powerline as it would go against State party policy. The further fear about supporting Labor was that the powerful PAG supporters of Kew would be alienated by the decision. The third option was to back the Liberal candidate who had declared her firm opposition to the powerline. Many PAG committee members, however, could not bring themselves to support a Liberal candidate whose party was currently opposing the passage of the State Government's new gun law reforms. As the PAG committees worked on attaining a consensus for any of their decisions, this particular issue took up many hours of meetings, attracted the largest numbers of participants and the most heated discussion. It was at this time that the essential differences amongst the residents became most stark. As soon as discussion moved beyond the single cause, the differences amongst them broke through.

Ultimately, the PAG decided not to support any one candidate but simply to outline the positions of the various candidates on the powerline issue and to let voters decide for themselves who would best represent their interests. On the day of the by-election many PAG members made individual decisions to offer voluntary help to the Democrat candidate. So many, in fact, that the delicately balanced diplomatic position of the PAG, that had taken so long to reach, toppled. The THC interpreted these individual actions as tacit support for the Democrats by the PAG, thus straining the good relationship that had been developing with the THC.

The result of the by-election, however, was a significant victory for powerline opponents. Seventy percent of voters in the four polling booths closest to the route registered a protest vote, against the powerline by placing a yellow sticker on the corner of their ballot paper, (this method of protest still allowed the formal vote to be counted). Fifteen percent of voters at polling booths where no 'stick-on campaign' was conducted registered a protest by writing on their ballot papers, thus discounting their vote (*The Age*, Monday 21 March, 1988, p. 10). Though a safe Liberal seat, the Democrats (Australia's third political party), for whom a vocal powerline opponent was standing, 'came within a whisker of polling better than Labor' (*The Age*, Monday 21 March, 1988, p. 10), the Government party. The Labor Party's primary vote in fact dropped nineteen percent whilst the Democrats polled better than they ever had in Victoria.

Arrests were made of powerline opponents for the very first time at a demonstration the day after the by-election. A political interpretation of the timing of this event is almost unavoidable. However, as pressure within the Parliamentary Labor Party grew the Government finally conceded a moratorium on construction of the powerline and established a Panel of Inquiry on 31 March 1988. Despite the fact that the Panel's terms of reference did not allow full investigation of the health issue, the Brunswick to Richmond Powerline Review Panel's Final Report of July 1989 recommended that the powerline be built underground following the route of a main road, not overhead down the river valleys and these recommendations have now been carried out. The powerline opponents had won!

THE CASE STUDY AREA

Interviews for the case study were conducted in a street of double fronted Edwardian style detached houses, on large blocks of land, situated in the middle of the proposed powerline route. The detached houses are interspersed with three blocks of 'shoe-box' flats built in the 1970s. The dwellings occupy only one side of this tree-lined street facing onto parkland through which flows the Merri Creek. This street lies within Clifton Hill, a suburb of the City of Collingwood, which is the second oldest municipality in metropolitan Melbourne, dating from 1855.

Prior to selecting this area, sampling interviews were conducted in six of the municipalities along the proposed route. These included Northcote, Fitzroy, Kew, Collingwood, Hawthorn and Richmond. An area in Clifton Hill, part of the City of Collingwood, was finally selected as the study area in which to carry out the in-depth interviews for reasons that relate to the population of this suburb, rather than anything particular about the suburb per se. First, seventy percent of the submissions to each of the EES came from the residents of this suburb. Second, the sampling interviews demonstrated that the area contained a mix of both owners and renters who were both active and inactive in the dispute. Third, the active powerline opponents in this area were to a large degree involved in collective action such as meetings and direct action. This was not the case in many other localities where opponents were apparently content to send letters of protest. Fourth, by concentrating the interviews in a spatially confined area, analysis of the data could focus on those social factors of greatest concern (tenure and participation), rather than trying to take account of factors such as spatial variation.

THE CASE STUDY POPULATION

The general characteristics of the population of Clifton Hill and of the population in the actual study area within Clifton Hill, are as follows. In 1986, 29% of households in Clifton Hill were outright owners, 28% were purchaser owners, 31% were private tenants and 4% were public tenants. The housing stock has recently been upgraded as a growing number of tertiary educated singles and couples in well paid jobs have moved into the area. The 25–39 year age group was the only one to increase its numbers within the City of Collingwood between 1981 and 1986 and most of this growth took place in Clifton Hill (City of Collingwood, 1989, p. 1). This process of gentrification has boosted house prices in the area and at the time of the interviews the local housing market was at the height of a boom, perhaps increasing property value oriented sensibilities in relation to the proposed powerline.

The population of the study area from which the in-depth inter-viewees were selected consists primarily of professional, tertiary educated, married couples in their mid–late 30's with young children, living in owner occupied housing. Beyond this group exists a wide range of household types including elderly couples, single mothers, and group households. Of the 89 dwellings on the street there are 52 flats and 37 houses. Most of the flats are rented, as are only two of the houses; thus, the street consists approximately of equal numbers of owners and renters. On the basis of those households willing to conduct a sampling interview, there are 31 owner households and 26 renter households in the street, with 32 'no replies' (see Table 7.1).

CONSTRUCTION OF THE INTERVIEW SAMPLE

Sampling interviews were carried out at 57 of the 89 dwellings (see Table 7.1). These were designed to establish the extent of participation amongst home owners and renters and to obtain data on household characteristics for a sample population from whom

Table 7.1   Owners and renters by participation in the powerline issue, from sampling interviews.[a]

	owners	renters	total
active[b]	21	7	28
inactive	10	19	29
total	31	26	57

a. Out of 89 dwellings in the street 26 of the 52 flats and 31 of the 37 houses were sampled, i.e. 64 per cent of dwellings in the street.
b. Definition of 'active': participants were asked in the sampling interviews whether or not they considered themselves to be actively involved in the power-line dispute. This opinion was then corroborated through participant observation and during the follow up interviews. A person was considered to be active if s/he had carried out any of the following activities in relation to the dispute which appear in ascending order of levels of activism:
• signed a petition
• written letters or made telephone calls
• donated money
• attended meetings.
All of the above forms of political activism occurred during the dispute. 'Attending meetings' and 'direct action', forms of collective action, are the central concerns of this chapter.
(Pearson chi-square test, value = 9.427, d.f. = 1, p = 0.002.)

approximately thirty would be chosen for in-depth interviews (see Appendix 1 for copy of sampling interview schedule). The data gathered from the sampling interviews demonstrate that home owners were more actively involved in the community activism than renters (Table 7.1). Inactive owner households proved as difficult to find as active renter households. This was an important early indication of the significance of tenure in relation to the community activism, an indication that the in-depth interviews were designed to explore further. It is also worth noting that this statistical relationship between housing tenure and participation has been replicated in both the NW and powerline case studies.

This variation in the extent of activism between home owners and renters, showing home owners to be more active in the community-based political activism than renters, concurs with the findings of Cox (1982) but contradicts those of Pratt (1986d). As Pratt (1986d) points out, however, such discrepancies do not necessarily reflect upon the findings of the other studies other than to highlight national and/or local differences in tenure structure, planning laws, social values, etc. This sample, however, does indicate higher rates of activism amongst both owners and renters than either Cox or Pratt discovered. This may be a result of this case study being carried out in the midst of a particular political struggle and not retrospectively as was the case for both Cox and Pratt. Any further explanation of these discrepancies is made more difficult as neither Cox (1982) nor Pratt (1986d) provide sufficient detail about the nature of the neighbourhood activism they investigated. Without knowing the content or subject of such activism it is impossible to evaluate accurately whether higher rates of activism amongst either home owners, renters or both can be expected. For example, a threat to property values in a particular neighbourhood is likely to concern many resident home owners but for renters property values are unlikely to be of any direct concern, unless they are attempting to enter home ownership in which case a fall in property values may well be to their advantage. Similarly, a threat to close a local school may concern many households with school-age children whilst not those without children. On this basis, different sorts of neighbourhood issue are likely to attract different types of activist, hence, political activism can only be understood in detailed reference to the context in which it is situated. On this point it is worth noting that the powerline issue was being contested along many different axes (health, environment, aesthetics, property values, etc.). Opposition, therefore, was not restricted to narrow sections of the population.

From the sampling interviews sixteen owners and fifteen renters were selected for follow-up interviews. The final interview sample emphasised the key variables of housing tenure and participation in neighbourhood-based collective action. Thirty-one interviews were carried out in order to see if the adequate causal relationship between housing tenure and home-oriented social action, revealed in the NW case study, extended into the neighbourhood and to explore whether the statistical relationship established through the sampling interviews would also hold at the level of meaning.

The significance of this case study is that it enables examination of the manner in which home-centred meanings, grounded in the experience of housing tenure, extend beyond the home into the neighbourhood and how this structures social action and in turn affects the nature of social group consciousness. This allows for further exploration of the third criterion specified in relation to the formation of housing tenure-based classes, political forces and status groups; that particular courses of social action are engaged in as a direct result of tenure-based meanings. Our exploration is structured in three sections that investigate in turn: the relationship between the meanings of housing tenure and neighbourhood activism; whether or not home ownership is essential to the observed social action, and finally; the theoretical significance of any housing tenure-based social action.

THE MEANINGS OF HOUSING TENURE AND PARTICIPATION IN NEIGHBOURHOOD ACTIVISM

The results of the sampling interviews demonstrate that home owners were more active than renters in this instance of community activism (Table 7.1). This section examines the role of housing tenure in this collective action through the responses of active owners and inactive renters, as these were the two groups for whom the sampling interviews indicated housing tenure was important.

One aspect of the explanation of owners' greater levels of participation in the dispute relates to economic meanings in the form of concerns about property values. For example,

Q. Would you leave the neighbourhood if the powerline was built?

A. I wouldn't be prepared to move and lose a lot of money or be financially disadvantaged because of the powerline. I took this action to try and prevent them from going ahead so that I wouldn't be financially disadvantaged. To me that is one of the major concerns. I can see that, instead of staying on the steady incline that it has been experiencing ever since I came here, the area will experience a sort of levelling off, nothing ever goes back, but the steady sort of healthy growth would level off because of the powerline, because of the value, you know.

(owner/active/female/single)

(See Appendix 3 for explanation of abbreviations.)

Q. Please state whether you agree or disagree with the following statement. Home owners involved in this campaign have different reasons for participating than the renters involved.

A. Yes I agree with that ... Yes I think that's very basic, but I think people were worried about their property values and that's—we were—if they'd put it up we'd have moved and we would have basically carried our losses and gone I think. We got involved to the point where we just couldn't countenance living here with the powerline across the road. They say people vote with their wallets and I believe that and I think that—I don't think that was the main reason we were involved, but it was definitely a reason and I think it was a reason why a lot of other people were involved.

(owner/active/female/couple with children)

Q. Are those concerns any part of your opposition to the power-line?

A. Once again I'd have to be very honest with you and say yes they are. I'd be annoyed as hell if the SEC slammed a power-line just on the other side of the street and if that affected the value of my property, I'd be extremely annoyed.

(owner/active/male/couple with children)

However, it is wrong to assume that property value concerns were the major reason amongst home owners for opposing the powerline. None of the active home owners ranked property value as their major concern and most opponents were primarily concerned about the aesthetic, environmental and health quality of their neighbourhood. To what extent these responses were affected by comments from the then Victorian Premier, deriding powerline opponents as 'a bunch of yuppies concerned about their property values', can only be guessed at, but property values were certainly no longer a legitimate item on the agenda after this state-ment. Housing tenure is not, therefore, the only explanatory variable, merely one aspect of a very complex causal process. The fact that it **is** an aspect, rather than not, is, however, significant. Significant to the extent that concern over property values was for some a factor directly related to their activism, whilst for others it played a lesser role as a background factor perhaps provoking a heightened concern about the aesthetic, environmental and health threat from the powerline.

The significance of home ownership in the powerline opposition was acknowledged by many of the renters interviewed. These renters recognised the fact that the home owners of the neighbour-

hood had additional concerns in terms of property values and also
stated that if they were the owners of the houses they lived in, then,
they would not only be concerned about property values but
actively involved in the opposition as well.

A.   Well, speaking for myself, I'm sure if I was a home owner I'd
     be much more involved. Renters on the whole are a transient
     population. Whether the actual reasons for being involved are
     different I wouldn't know but I think they (home owners) are
     more likely to think of property value than a transient person.
     They'd be more concerned on a long-term basis.

     (renter/inactive/female/couple with children)

Interestingly, though, property value concerns in relation to the
powerline are not uniform over time for any one household. The
data show that tenure-based economic meanings such as these
vary over time in accordance with the specific circumstances of the
household. The quote below amply demonstrates how this process
occurs and how it can occur over a very short space of time.

Q.   Are those sorts of concerns (property values) any part of your
     opposition to the powerline?

A.   Only in a roundabout sense. Before, you asked me if we'd sell
     up and move if the powerline was built and my answer to that
     was 'no'. So in that sense the particular value that my house
     has is really an irrelevant question because it doesn't have any
     value as it is not for sale. If, however, we did decide we
     couldn't live with it and had to move, then obviously it would
     become a big issue.

     (owner/active/male/couple with children)

Moreover, inter household variation with regard to property
value concerns was also apparent. Owner households active in the
opposition, who intended residing in the neighbourhood for a very
long period of time and who were married with children tended to
be less concerned about property values. As the house had been
bought as the 'family home' where children would be brought up
and the family intended to stay, the fact of whether or not their
property value was rising was less relevant.

A.   ...getting back to the original intentions I didn't intend to
     make capital gains out of it, so I don't consider the money
     aspect that important. I hope to stay there for a long time.

     (owner/active/male/couple with children)

On the other hand owners who stressed the importance of
whether or not their property value was rising, were characterised
by households who intended staying in the neighbourhood in the
medium term and were single with no children. These households
saw themselves moving sometime in the future, most probably on
marriage or when having children and hence the transaction value
of their property was of greater concern.

Q.   Do you think there are any other issues at stake in the
     campaign?

A.   Yes I do. A lot of it is that it's going to devalue people's homes
     and of course if you are buying in the area then that is the key
     issue, that is something that hasn't been spoken about much
     but I'm sure that it is in everyone's mind.

     (owner/inactive/female/couple)

These distinctions highlight the need for a sophisticated understanding of home ownership, to indicate how different meanings
can be more or less important across household types within
tenures and how even within a household different meanings come
into play at different times.

Active home owners also related their activism in the powerline
issue to the political meaning 'security'. The notion of security
resulting in individual and familial well being, rather than physical
security related to fear of crime, is the meaning important to the
relationship between home ownership and collective action in the
powerline issue. Home owners active in the powerline opposition,
expressing a high degree of home-based legal and hence personal
security, interpreted the powerline as a threat to that security:

A.   It (the powerline) would threaten my security in that it would
     become a less pleasant place to live. It would threaten my
     feeling of comfort or happiness.

(owner/active/male/couple with children)

Yet renters did not see the powerline as a threat to their security, a fact directly related to their legal insecurity and their concomitant 'mobility'.

Q. Do you see the powerline issue as a threat in any way to those feelings of security?

A. No not here, not for me. If they do come through it will just make me move quicker than I would have.

(renter/active/male/couple)

This comment by an active renter demonstrates that this aspect of tenure was not a part of their participation as it was for the active home owners.

The legal insecurity of renting as a cause of the lack of participation by renters was frequently referred to by both inactive renters and active owners.

Q. What type of person do you think has not become involved in the campaign?

A. I'd probably say renting type people, those who don't own, those who are perhaps part-time residents and are only here for a short time.

(owner/active/female/single)

Q. What sorts of people do you think have not become involved in the campaign?

A. ...I know a couple of people living in the flats and they weren't involved and I had no hope at all of talking them into coming along to anything or doing anything but they're renting, they don't see themselves as staying here terribly long.

(owner/active/female/couple with children)

Though for some it was something simply about the fact of renting.

Q. Is there any particular reason why you have not become actively involved in the campaign?

A. Yes, a few reasons. One is that I'm renting, that I'm not
    living—I'm not purchasing a property so—I suppose that's not
    a very good excuse, if you like, but that's one of the reasons.

    (inactive/renter/female/single)

Though renters often commented on their legally insecure
position in terms of a 'forced mobility', it should be noted that it
was this very mobility that would allow them to evade the powerline were it to be built. Owners, on the other hand, faced a contra-
dictory situation in that whilst enjoying security of tenure and all
the associated benefits, they also bore the burden of relative
immobility.

Active home owners, who expressed high degrees of control
over their home environment also interpreted their activism in the
powerline issue in relation to the political meaning 'control'.

Q. Do you see the powerline issue as a threat to this control?

A. It is a threat to my control, to my environment and my
    extended environment outside my door.

    (owner/active/female/single)

A. Yes it gets back to the effects of the EMR [electromagnetic
    radiation]. The concern that the radiation will enter onto your
    property ... Not so much that it's on our land but that it will
    affect us in our daily lives.

    (owner/active/male/couple with children)

For renters, however, the threat to home control was just not an
issue as they felt they already had no control. Renters were,
however, quick to recognise that if they were owners then they
would feel that the powerline posed a threat to their home control.

A. I have all the control I want but if I owned it I wouldn't be
    able to control some great powerline they are proposing to
    build over the road, I wouldn't be able to stop that.

    (renter/inactive/female/single)

All owners felt they had sufficient home control and all but the
single renters with no children felt a distinct lack of home control.

For the single renters with no children this was not so much an issue, as they saw themselves as readily mobile, with no ties or responsibilities and at their stage of life, not wanting them.

Q.   Do you see the powerline as a threat in any way to those feelings of control?

A.   ...personally no, it isn't really because I can shift if I want to.

(renter/inactive/female/single)

Whilst it is clear from the data that there are distinct differences between the political meanings of home ownership and renting and that these differences impacted upon participation, there are also differences between the rights owners enjoy on their property and the extension of these rights into the neighbourhood. Neighbourhood control, as a ratepayer, was generally seen by home owners to be far weaker than the rights of control enjoyed on the property.

Q.   Do you feel you have sufficient control over what happens in and around your home?

A.   In the immediate area on my block I'll say yes, but in the less immediate area like the park across the road, my neighbours and us, we've got a little park out the back, no.

(owner/active/male/couple with children)

However, the fact of being a ratepayer seemed to be important in contributing to a notion of having any rights within the neighbourhood at all as owners expressed far greater feelings of control at the neighbourhood level than renters.

Q.   Do you think being a ratepayer affects how you view your neighbourhood?

A.   Yes, I think so because you are paying for things like the garbage and the streets. I mean O'Grady Street, that street is a disaster ...if we'd rented we'd still be annoyed but you have no comeback since you are only renting...

(active/owner/female/couple with children)

Significantly, only half the renters actually considered them-selves to be proxy ratepayers through their paying of rent; amongst those who did recognise this fact, some felt that they were not entitled to the same rights as home owners and unlike owners, none of them recognised this control as being at stake in the powerline issue.

A.   No, I don't have the right for absolute control ... I equate a lot of those rights with owning the property and I don't think I deserve some specific rights as I have no commitment to the area.

(renter/inactive/female/single)

One consequence of the home being a financial investment within which individual well being is fostered and through which self-expression is realised, is a strong 'home attachment'. Owners' expressions of this cultural meaning were accordingly far stronger than renters'.

Q.   What does that word 'home' mean to you?

A.   It's a concept of a base that you identify with and work from. It's more than somewhere you go and sleep. It's the place you feel comfortable in, it's part of you, in a sense, it partly expresses your personality, in some respects.

(owner/active/male/couple with children)

Renters' home attachment was weakened by limited feelings of security, by frustrated attempts at self expression within the home (there was either no point economically or it was simply not allowed by the terms of the lease) and by the knowledge that they were inevitably short term residents.

Q.   Do you call here home?

A.   Yes.

Q.   What does that word 'home' mean to you?

A.   Just somewhere to sleep, just the place where I'm living at the moment. No great attachment.

Q.   Really?

A. Yes, basically with renting I don't have much interest in this place or the community because I am not going to be here for long but if I own something it would be more permanent and I'd be inclined to put something into it.

(renter/inactive/female/couple no children)

This is an important part of explaining why home owners were far more actively involved in opposing the powerline than renters and is one of the key cultural meanings associated with home ownership.

Attachment to the home and attachment to the neighbourhood refer to the affective significance of place. At the neighbourhood level this often includes some notion of community feeling. Active owners were, thus, also likely to interpret the powerline as a threat to neighbourhood status, one further component of the causal process underlying the heightened activism on the part of home owners.

Q. Do you think the powerline is a threat to the standing or status of this neighbourhood?

A. ...this neighbourhood has spent a lot of its personal effort and a lot of feeling in trying to improve itself and I think that it would affect a lot of people to have the enormous slap in the face of slamming what is considered to be a monstrosity in an area that has been worked for so hard for so long...

(owner/active/male/couple with children)

A. I like to think of Clifton Hill being a reasonably desirable inner suburban neighbourhood, ...the powerline will dramatically affect that.

(owner/active/male/couple with children)

Owners' greater status concerns are part of an overall stronger neighbourhood-based identification. As with the cultural meaning 'home attachment', owners exhibited a higher degree of 'neighbourhood attachment' than did renters.

Q. How would you describe your attachment to this neighbourhood?

A. Fairly strong. Stronger than I would have thought actually.

Q. Why stronger than you might have thought?

A. Well we rented, have rented in the past for four of five years or so and we've been in various places and we've never really felt attached to any particular area, we've moved around where it suited. But when we moved here, I don't know, we just seemed to like it and when we thought of moving because the house isn't big enough, really big enough, it's not in good condition, we thought we'd sort of sell and move but we don't want to leave here, we've got too much here we like. So I don't know what it is but we just like it here and don't really want to move. Whether that is because it is our own place or not I don't know…

(owner/active/female/couple with children)

A. I think home owners on the whole feel more part of a neighbourhood because they own the home, they are a rate payer, they feel like a permanent resident and for that reason they tend, perhaps, to be more active in local issues.

(renter/inactive/female/couple with children)

Due to this attachment any threat to home or neighbourhood is far more likely to result in active opposition on the part of home owners.

As the range of quotes (above) across economic, political and cultural meanings illustrates, the tenure-based concerns home owners were experiencing in relation to the powerline, were for many an important factor in their political activism. For renters most of these meanings were either irrelevant, or if they were experienced, were so to a considerably lesser extent, thus weakening any motivation to become politically active in opposition to the powerline.

WAS THE PARTICIPATION OF HOME OWNERS ESSENTIAL TO THE NEIGHBOURHOOD ACTIVISM?

Posing this question enables us to reveal the nature of the causal role of home ownership. To phrase the question in another way, would the political activism have remained the same (i.e. the same in essential points), if the factor of home ownership had not been present? If the street had consisted only of renters would the activism have remained essentially the same? It appears not, primarily because the political activism would have been on a significantly smaller scale and if this had been the case it is doubtful whether the activists would have enjoyed the same success. This conclusion is based on two points.

First, inactive renters often stated that if they were home owners they would be actively involved. Second, fourteen sampling interviews with public tenants residing in a small block of flats that backed straight onto the proposed powerline route, revealed limited knowledge of the powerline issue (only two households were even aware of the issue) and not surprisingly no active opposition. This apparent apathy stood in marked contrast to the political activism of the owners, whose position was neatly summarised by one home owner as, 'Nobody who is an owner-resident would be ignorant of the position'. In sum, having specified a relationship at the level of typical probability between home ownership and activism and now established causality at the level of meaning, home ownership does seem to have been a causally adequate factor in this instance of political activism. To argue for causal adequacy is not to argue that home ownership was the only causal factor, nor that it is of a necessary nature (Saunders and Williams, 1988, p. 87; Savage, 1987) but that without the factor of home ownership this instance of political activism would have been essentially different, both in terms of the numbers involved and the tactics employed.

Having established the causal role of housing tenure in this social action, home owners' participation and renters' non-participation can be identified as tenure-based class, political force and status group action, to the extent that the range of economic, political and cultural meanings of housing tenures were drawn upon. This, however, says nothing about the nature of the social action engaged in.

THEORISING THE SIGNIFICANCE OF HOME OWNERS PARTICIPATION IN THE POWERLINE DISPUTE

The tactics that characterised the social action of powerline opponents varied from forms of direct protest action to letter writing and donations. All of these forms of social action were of a *zweck-rational* type (calculated means, rational ends). Opponents of the powerline had a specific objective in mind—to underground the powerline away from residential and environmentally sensitive areas. All of their actions (means) were calculated to achieve this objective (end).

The rational nature of this action is indicative of 'social group' action, the monopolisation of market interests in Weberian terms. Whilst this may accurately conceptualise aspects of opposition to the powerline it denies the public-minded or altruistic aspects of the political activism. Whatever their immediate gains from preventing construction of the powerline, opponents were also (perhaps unintentionally) making gains for the wider populous, for example, those people who use the parkland for recreation and raising community awareness of the health risks associated with electromagnetic radiation. If it were the case that the opponents were attempting to move the powerline from private land to public land then this would not be the case. Thus, the distinction between private and public centred social action, as was the case in Chapter 6, again appears to be an important aspect of the analysis. Tenure-based meanings are of a significance such that the social action of home owners and renters is affected in both the public and private spheres.

The collective nature of the social action of powerline opponents appears to have been characterised by both associative and communal social relations. Whilst the decision to engage in forms of direct protest action was calculated as the most appropriate means of preventing construction of the powerline (associative relations), the nature of the social relations that resulted in large turnouts to work-site protests were more of a communal nature. A strong sense of 'belonging together' and of being on 'one side' prevailed. A feeling that was no doubt reinforced through participating in the protest action. It was well known that a low turnout to a demonstration would weigh heavily on the momentum that the campaign had generated.

Having identified the nature of the social action engaged in and the social relations that characterised it, we are now in a position to comment on the (re)construction of social group consciousness in this instance of community activism and the role of housing tenure in it.

Though the actions of home owning powerline opponents contained elements of self interest, there are many aspects to their opposition that can be seen as progressive if not radical. First, powerline opponents, the bulk of whom were home owners, used non-violent direct protest action in the form of work-site occupations to disrupt work progress. These actions and their culmination in a number of arrests for trespass, can be seen as a somewhat ironic rejection of the property rights of the SECV. Second, opposition to the powerline amounted to a rejection of the commodification of Melbourne's parks and waterways and a replacement of notions of value and cost with non-monetary concepts such as aesthetic and environmental value, quality of life and attachment to home and neighbourhood. Third, a central part of the conservatism of home owners is argued to be their defence of the status quo. Opponents of the powerline were not attempting to maintain the status quo. They accepted the need for the powerline. In terms of how that powerline should be constructed, however, they argued for radically progressive health, environmental and aesthetic standards.

As Rose (1980) has argued, home ownership cannot be conceptualised as simply an ideologically functional tool for capital; on the contrary home ownership may, in some circumstances, provide a basis for active struggle against the status quo. Of particular significance, then, is the manner in which the meanings associated with housing tenure may lead to collective action in the public realm that is of a radical nature.

CONCLUSION

This chapter has attempted to answer three questions. First, is there a relationship between home ownership and collective action? Second, if there is a relationship, is it a causal one? Third, if it is causal then how is this revealed in particular empirical circumstances? These questions are raised in relation to our point in Chapter 3, that the causality of the relationship between housing tenure and social action has not been specified previously.

Whilst the findings of this case study go beyond the existing literature, in that they detail the nature of the causal relationship between housing tenure and political activism, it is worth noting that these conclusions point to areas of both agreement and disagreement with the existing literature. One point of agreement is that home owners are more likely to be active than renters in local political activism due to their private property interests. Importantly, however, as a point of disagreement, concerns regarding property values were not found to be the key factor.

The findings of this case study confirm Agnew's (1981) wider definition of private property interests associated with home ownership, as the facilitation of personal autonomy, the realisation of social esteem and the maintenance/enhancement of exchange value. All of these combine to require a heightened community consciousness on the part of home owners. Little support, however, is given to the findings of Cox (1982) and Cox and McCarthy (1982), in that none of the home owners opposing the powerline were active because it was 'cheaper to stay and fight' This again indicates that attention has been too focused on the economic aspects of home ownership and insufficiently focused upon the political and cultural aspects.

In response to the aim of specifying the causal nature of the relationship between housing tenure and political activism we have seen that there is a relationship between home ownership and collective action, that this relationship is of a causally adequate nature and that the empirical detail of this causal process is embedded in the economic, political and cultural meanings of housing tenures. This is not to argue for a deterministic relationship between home ownership and collective action, as obviously not all home owners were politically active whilst some renters were. Though other factors must also have been causally adequate in this instance of community activism, they have not been detailed here as our focus is upon housing tenure and its role in collective action, rather than on the causes of collective action per se. We have seen that the causal relationship between home ownership and collective action is multi-faceted with regard to the wide range of economic, political and cultural meanings drawn on by home owners and renters and that different households will draw upon the range of meanings in different ways at different times as circumstances change. To the extent that home owners and renters do draw upon tenure-based economic, political and cultural meanings in their social action then, such action can be analysed as tenure-based class, political force and status group action.

The *zweckrational* nature of the social action that powerline opponents engaged in was ambiguous. On the one hand it can be interpreted as a rational attempt to monopolise market interests. However, as the protest action centred on the use of public land (through which the SECV had an easement), there were inevitable gains for the wider public who enjoy the parklands in their current state. The collective nature of the protest action, characterised, in part, by communal social relations and located in the public sphere, created an environment in which social group consciousness could be 'radicalised'. The wider collective agenda and direct engagement in conflict took many individuals beyond their original concerns or allowed them to view those concerns in a different light. The actions of powerline opponents, grounded partly in housing tenure resulted in social change. This social change was wrought by home owners taking action of a radical nature.

This chapter has added further to understanding the social significance of housing tenure and the processes that underlie local political activism. The manner in which the meanings associated with the experience of housing tenure extend into the neighbourhood to affect social action has been made clear. What is more social action in the neighbourhood locale, being of a collective, public nature, offers significant opportunities for the (re)construction of social group consciousness in ways that otherwise might never have arisen. This then builds upon the conclusions of Chapter 6 in which the relationship between the meanings of housing tenures and home-centred social action is detailed. The manner in which such meanings may affect social action at the place of employment is the subject of Chapter 8.

Chapter 8

SOCIAL ACTION AT THE PLACE OF EMPLOYMENT

The case study of the Victorian nurses strike of 1986 examines the social action of striking and non-striking nurses. It does this to discover the role of housing tenure, especially housing costs, in relation to the decision about whether or not to strike. The case study thus explores the causal role of housing tenure in collective action at the place of employment. More specifically, the case study enables analysis of the interaction between housing/consumption based decisions, in terms of maintaining housing payments, *vis-à-vis* labour/production based decisions, with regard to issues of working conditions, staffing levels, professionalism, career structure and wages. Also, we are able to examine whether the interaction of consumption and production processes lead to varying courses of social action and hence the construction of a different social group consciousness. This then provides a further platform from which to view the formation of tenure-based classes, political forces and status groups.

The nurses strike was selected as a case study on the basis of an extensive newspaper search. The strike obviously had the necessary element of collective action and the strike's long duration (seven weeks) was thought to be sufficient to illustrate the conflict between being on strike and maintaining housing payments.

The following sections provide a brief history of the 1986 Victorian nurses strike, details of the selection of a particular hospital upon which to focus the case study and explain how the sample of nurses from this hospital was constructed, followed by the data analysis.

EVENTS LEADING TO THE VICTORIAN NURSES' STRIKE, 1986

The Victorian nurses strike of 1986 was the culmination of two years of industrial struggle and many years of exploitation of the Nightingale mystique of bed-side care. The devotion of nurses to their patients, as modelled by Nightingale, has been used to keep nurses on the wards whatever the circumstances. As a result of deteriorating work conditions, between June 1980 and June 1982 the number of registered nurses (RNs) employed full time declined by 20 per cent, whilst the number of public hospital patients increased by 3.8 per cent (Gardner and McCoppin, 1986, p. 29). In 1985 the Victorian Health Department estimated that there were 900 vacancies for RNs in Victoria and the Royal Australian Nurses Federation (RANF) Federal Secretary reported that 56 per cent of RNs were not working in nursing. By 1986 Victoria's public and private hospitals had 1400 vacancies for RNs that could not be filled, despite the fact that there were 10,000 people holding practising certificates (Kyle, 1987, p. 5). This chronic staff shortage, a result of poor wages and conditions combined with high stress and little opportunity for advancement, resulted in a log of claims being pursued on these issues between 1984 and 1986. Table 8.1 portrays the series of events that took place in the lead-up to the strike and during the strike. It was this long lead time and the conflict between nurses and management throughout that contributed to the intransigence of the two sides involved in the dispute with the resulting stalemate adding considerably to the length of the strike.

Table 8.1   Chronology of events: Victorian nurses strike 1986[a]

Year/Date	Events
1970	RANF affiliation with Australian Council of Salaried and Professional Associations (ACSPA).
1975	Selective bans on non-nursing duties for 12 per cent wage rise.
1977	Freeze on staffing levels in public hospitals by Liberal state government.
1979	RANF affiliation with ACTU.
1981	RANF warns state government of the 'exodus of nurses' from public hospitals because of working conditions.
1982	Work bans at St. Vincent's Hospital leading to temporary bed closures; work bans at Western General win a 1:5 nurse–patient ratio and ward closures if no staff.
1983	State Labor government budget cut: 1.5 per cent cut in hospital budgets leading to reduction of ancillary staff and indirectly increasing nurses' workloads. RANF (Vic. Branch) threatens strike action in December (i.e. before deletion of 'no-strike clause').
1984	Deletion of 'no-strike' clause from RANF rules in February after a national poll with 65.3 per cent in favour. Tertiary education for nurses by 1993.
June	Rally of over 2000 at Dallas Brooks Hall. Issues: nurse–patient ratios, admission–discharge policies, supervision of student nurses, decision making, nursing education. 28 resolutions passed! No.1 from June 1 all nurses in Victorian public hospitals no longer undertake non-nursing duties.
July 23	Government offers insult nurses and lead to escalation of bans. RANF and Government agreement on non-nursing duties.
August 16	Dispute flares again. Agreement on 22 non-nursing duties; commitment to develop career structure and admission/ discharge policies.
December	38 hour week for nurses.
1985	Victorian Health Dept. estimates 900 vacancies for RNs. RANF Federal Secretary says 56 per cent RNs not working.
September	Mass meeting leads to work bans.

Table 8.1 (Continued)   Chronology of events: Victorian nurses strike 1986[a]

Year/Date	Events
October 11	Mass meeting of 5,500 nurses. Nurses commence strike action.
October 21	Settlement of strike.
1986	Industrial Relations Commission of Victoria decision providing Victorian nurses with the first full scale review of their Award for 50 years; the first nursing career structure in Australia and an offer of a $42 million pay rise package to be implemented by Oct. 31. Dissatisfaction by nurses with the interpretation of the Industrial Relations Commission decision and the implementation of the new Award leads to bans on elective surgery admissions and to resignations by nurses in some public and private hospitals.
August	Government imposes stand downs.
October 30	Mass meeting leads to decision to strike indefinitely from Oct. 31 regarding 20 outstanding claims related to the new Award and its implementation. After 4 weeks 46 public and private hospitals on strike.
December 20	7 weeks later, return to work.

a. Adapted from Gardner and McCoppin, 1986.

The strike lasted 50 days, from October 31 until December 20 1986 and was prolonged (some nurses say unnecessarily) by a stalemate between the Industrial Relations Commission (IRC), which would not hear the nurses' case until they returned to work, and the Royal Australian Nurses Federation, which would not issue a call to return to work until their case was heard. The breach was finally filled by the Australian Council of Trade Unions who acted as a go-between for the two parties and finally negotiated a return to work. The hearing of the nurses' case resumed in January 1987.

THE CASE STUDY HOSPITAL

The case study focused on one large inner-urban public hospital, St Vincent's. St Vincent's was chosen as its large staff enabled sampling of a range of housing tenure types and because a friendly union representative was prepared to assist in finding participants. This latter point was particularly important as the sensitivity of the issue, even two years after the strike when the case study was conducted, made access to nursing staff through the hospital management impossible.

A public hospital, rather than a private hospital, was selected for the case study as working in the public sector was a strong indicator of participation in the strike. This variable was thus held constant to allow for a clearer focus upon housing tenure and strike participation. Strike activity in the public hospitals was greater as the RANF concentrated its energy on the larger public hospitals where their membership was higher. Management in the private sector at the time of the strike were apparently quick to point out the equation 'no patients, no money, no jobs' and nurses genuinely feared this threat resulting in low levels of strike participation in the private sector.

The inner-urban location of St Vincent's is typical of most of Melbourne's large public hospitals. The residential locations of the work-force can be typified as renters in inner-suburbs and owners in medium-priced, middle and outer-ring suburbs, in line with the nature of the housing stock in Melbourne.

By the time the strike call at St Vincent's came the division between the nursing staff and the hospital management was particularly acute. In the lead up to the strike this division had been hardened by a mass resignation of over 200 nurses filed in support of five fellow workers, who were stood down for adhering to a union ban on elective surgery admissions. The strike action at St Vincent's had a high public profile due to the hospital's location on a major commuter road and public transport route into and out of the city. In their tent village on the median strip of this wide boulevard, the pickets maintained a day and night vigil receiving both 'toots' of support and verbal abuse from passing motorists.

CONSTRUCTING THE INTERVIEW SAMPLE

Interviewees were selected using a sampling technique known as 'snowballing'. The 'snowball' for this case study began with the Royal Australian Nurses Federation, the union leading the strike. Union officials contacted job representatives at St Vincent's Hospital who in turn provided contact names of both strikers and non-strikers. At the end of each interview, the interviewee was asked to provide two or three other names of people who might be willing to be interviewed. Interviewees were then selected from the compiled list depending upon their social characteristics which were ascertained by phone (see Appendix 1 for copy of sampling interview schedule).

Twenty five in-depth interviews were carried out with nurses, both striking and non-striking, across three housing tenure positions including private renters, recent purchaser owners (less than five years) and established purchaser owners (over five years). The aim was to examine how the interaction between housing tenure and strike participation took place to affect the social action of nurses.

Before the interviews commenced six pilot interviews were conducted in three different rounds. After each round substantial modifications were made to the interview schedule (see Appendix 1 for copy of interview schedule). The pilot interviews were also used to gauge the social dimensions of the final interview sample other than those of housing tenure and participation.

On this basis it was decided that (with one exception) only women would be interviewed as the vast majority of nurses are women and the male experience of nursing is not 'typical'. Male nurses apparently enjoy an easier path through the career structure. One male nurse was interviewed as he was a job representative and thus a key actor in the strike. As the strike call was made by the RANF and membership of the union is probably a causal factor in willingness to strike, it was decided to only interview RANF members. Insufficient numbers of non-striking RANF members could be 'snowballed', however, thus non-striking non-RANF members had to be interviewed.

Primary and secondary income earners in the household were sought, as it was envisaged that if the primary income was lost the financial pressure to not strike would be greater. As the presence of children in a household adds further to financial pressures (school fees, clothing costs, etc.) single and couple households with and without children were included in the sample. The full characteristics of the interview sample are detailed in Table 8.2, below.

Table 8.2 shows that most of the sample were aged under 40. All of the renters were single, with no children, and they typically had one household income of $15–20,000 and were State Registered Nurses (SRNs). The owners, on the other hand, were of all household types but primarily couples with children. They were frequently in two income households being in either the upper income brackets if they worked full-time or the lower income brackets if part-time. Owners were also more likely to occupy a senior position in the hospital such as Charge Nurse.

The results of the qualitative analysis of these interview data are presented below. The detail of the interaction between housing market and job market is examined through a comparison of the causal significance of housing tenure upon the social action of strikers and non-strikers, bearing in mind that inaction is also a form of social action. Having compared these groups, we then examine each group separately to see if 'striking' home owners and 'striking' renters participated in the strike action in different ways, because of their tenure; similarly with non-strikers and their non-participation in the strike.

In order to examine the causal significance of housing tenure in the social action of nurses during the strike and the (re)construction of their social group consciousness, discussion of the case study data is organised around three main questions. Does housing tenure differentiate the social action of, first, strikers compared with non-strikers, second, amongst strikers themselves and third, amongst non-strikers?

It will be argued that, amongst the nurses out on strike during the seven week dispute, purchaser owners and private renters experienced very different consequences of the loss of their

Table 8.2 Characteristics of the interview sample.

	owners	renters	no tenure[a]	total
20–30	3	5	2	10
31–40	8	1	0	9
41–50	1	0	1	2
51–60	1	0	0	1
total	13	6	3	23
single no kids	3	8	2	13
single with kids	1	0	0	1
couple no kids	3	0	0	3
couple with kids	8	0	0	8
total	15	8	2	25
ranf member	11	7	1	19
non-ranf member	4	1	1	6
total	15	8	2	25
1 income	6	8	2	16
2 incomes	9	0	0	9
total	15	8	2	25
primary earner	9	8	2	19
secondary earner	6	0	0	6
total	15	8	2	25
less than $10,000	3	0	0	3
$10–15,000	2	0	0	2
$15–20,000	0	6	1	7
$20–25,000	3	0	1	4
more than $25,000	5	2	0	7
total	13	8	2	23
SRN	9	7	1	17
clinical specialist	1	0	1	2
charge nurse	5	1	0	6
total	15	8	2	25
strikers	9	6	1	16
non-strikers	6	2	1	9
total	15	8	2	25

a. No tenure means that the interviewee was not responsible for housing costs in the household. In the cases documented this was because they were living in the parental home.

NB: this table is not a complete data set as some interviewees were unwilling to reveal their age, RANF membership and income. Where totals equal less than 25, this information was not provided by some members of the sample.

income. The social action of nurses on strike was differentiated by their housing tenure position to the extent that different courses of social action were engaged in by striking owners and striking renters. The result of this is that a different social group conscious-ness was being constructed for owners and renters. This is an example of the manner in which housing tenure can affect collec-tive social action beyond the residential environment and of inter-action between consumption and production in the (re)construction of social group consciousness.

Furthermore, spatial separation between home and place of employment (the spatiality of the consumption–production relation) was instrumental in shaping the social action and hence social group consciousness of part-time nurses who did not engage in strike action. This is further evidence of the manner in which housing market and job market processes interact to affect courses of social action.

STRIKERS AND NON-STRIKERS

After Pratt (1986a, p. 391), who concludes that home owners are 'less willing to chance the economic hardship associated with a prolonged strike', we may hypothesise that home owning nurses would be less likely to participate in strike action than nurses who rent due to the higher housing costs home owners have to bear. In this case study, however, this did not occur. Home owners and renters appear to have applied the same reasoning in their decision to go out or not go out on strike and this reasoning was almost exclusively unrelated to housing tenure per se. An explanation of these conclusions can be arrived at by examining three different time phases of decision making—the decision to: go out on strike; stay out on strike; and go back to work.

To Go Out On Strike?

Pratt (1986a) suggests that economic factors associated with home ownership, such as mortgage debt, will have a direct impact upon support for strikes. However, this was not the case in the Victorian nurses strike for it was anticipated that the strike would last, at the most, only one or two days (in some cases people quoted 20 minutes as the expected duration of the strike). Housing based economic factors did not, therefore, play a major role in deciding whether or not to go out on strike.

Q. When making the decision to go out on strike did you have any financial worries?

A. No because I didn't think it would go on so long. I think a lot of people thought it would be over in a couple of days or a week, but not six or seven weeks, no one thought it would last that long, so financially that didn't come into it.

(striker/no tenure status/single/1 income)

(See Appendix 3 for explanation of abbreviations).

A. You also had the financial thing, no one ever dreamed that we'd be out for seven weeks, everyone thought we'd be out for two or three days and everyone could afford two or three days.

(striker/renter/single/1 income)

In fact it appears that job related ideological factors were far more prominent in people's decision to go out or not go out on strike than tenure-based economic ones.

A. With some people, you wonder if it was financial, but then it's just that they didn't want to lose money, but then they wouldn't have known how long it would go on for anyway, so—I think it was mainly that they didn't think it was right to strike.

(striker/no tenure status/single/1 income)

The analysis of non-strikers reasons for not going out on strike indeed bear out the above observation. Job related ideological factors seem to have dominated their decision making and we can specify two main factors that appear to have affected the decision not to strike: 'couldn't leave the patients' and 'don't believe in strikes'

'Couldn't leave the patients'

This was by far the most common reason given for not going out on strike, that to walk-out on one's patients was to go against everything nursing stood for. Despite the fact that most non-strikers supported the cause, they simply could not bring themselves to leave 'their' patients.

Q. Why did you decide not to go out on strike?

A. I decided to become a nurse at a very early age, about five years of age and I always put the patients first which at times, apart from the strike, has put me in a position where I've thought if only I didn't put the patient first, like sometimes with a change of jobs. I love my work too much and I'm willing to put up with a lot of rubbish just so I can look after patients because that's my real love, is just being there. So it was a combination of putting the patients first and my upbringing, my principles and seeing that I've never seen strike action in the past assisting the worker, so I didn't see it was going to help the nurse at this stage either.

(non-striker/no tenure status/single/1 income)

Q. You say you just couldn't leave the hospital, why?

A. Because there were people there who were sick. They were pouring out of ICU (Intensive Care Unit), because every time anyone came into 'cas' (casualty) they were often people who were so sick they had to go in twice a year and I just couldn't come out.

(non-striker/recent purchaser owner/single/1 income)

A. ...striking in the nursing profession is different from working in a factory where people aren't directly affected. A lot of people agreed entirely with the cause, as I did, but just couldn't leave the patients... I think the nursing profession is quite unique in that it's up to the person themselves emotionally to find out if they can handle leaving their patients or not.

(non-striker/renter/single/1 income)

'Don't believe in strikes'

For some the decision not to strike was part of a general political philosophy. This was that they just didn't believe striking was a fair or responsible tactic.

A.   I've never supported strike action.

    (non-striker/no tenure status/single/1 income)

However, when questioned further these people could rarely suggest alternative courses of action that the RANF could have taken.

As the reasons for not going out on strike were predominantly job related so, not surprisingly, were the reasons for going out on strike. The following comments are typical of the reasons why so many Victorian nurses went out on strike in 1986.

Q.   What would you say were the main aims of the strike?

A.   To improve our conditions definitely, and to improve our conditions meant that we had to improve our career structure and our wages, but I also think that there were other aims of politicising nurses. It was the first time ever that we had showed some unified stance. It was a real statement for women in general because nursing is a predominantly female profession. I think they were aims that weren't realised until the strike began, those other ones, but the major one, the reason why we went out, was for a better career structure.

    (striker/recent purchaser owner/couple/1 income)

To Stay Out On Strike?

The second time phase during which we may have anticipated, on the basis of Pratt's (1986a) conclusions, that economic factors associated with housing tenure would causally relate to social action in the nurses strike, is the decision to stay out on strike rather than return to work. This time phase appears to have lasted from approximately week three or four of the dispute until the official call to return to work came from the union leadership in week seven.

Again the results from this case study are contrary to those we may have anticipated from a reading of Pratt (1986a), as very few nurses at all appear to have returned to work whilst the strike continued. It is difficult to assess the exact scale of this, though, as those who did return are unlikely to have broadcast the fact and in the one or two incidents that emerged, it appears the persons concerned deliberately went on night duty to avoid being noticed by the large day-time picket.

To explain why so few nurses appear to have returned to work during the strike, despite desperate hardship in many cases, three points are germane: first, the long build up to the strike led to the divisions between the RANF and hospital management being hardened to a state of complete intransigence. Second, it was never clear to those who were out on strike that they would not be going back tomorrow. Each day, it appears, the nurses thought they would be returning to work.

Q.   After the first few days had passed did you think the strike was going to be over quickly or drawn out still further?

A.   No we still kept expecting it to finish. Every few days we'd expect it. We never thought now right I've got to sit it out, we always thought it was going to be finished.

(striker/renter/single/1 income)

Third, amongst some there was a fear of being ostracised if they did return to work.

A.   Like when I was out on strike did I ever think I would have to go back because of any of those hardships? No I didn't because there was always that pressure. I don't think anybody would have been abused if they'd gone back to work—I don't think anyone out on the picket line would ever say anything, but there was that sort of untold pressure on you, it was a quiet thing—you just couldn't do it.

(striker/recent purchaser owner/couple/2 incomes)

In the second time phase, then, deciding whether or not to return to work, it seems again that job-related ideological factors outweighed tenure-based economic concerns.

To Go Back To Work?

It is only when we reach the final decision phase, the decision to go back to work, that, fairly logically, we get some indication that tenure-based economic factors come to outweigh job related ideological factors with regard to strike-oriented social action. The evidence for this is limited, however, as the decision to go back to work was one not made individually but collectively at a union mass meeting. The only indication that tenure-based economic concerns were coming to exceed job-related ideological factors, at this time, are the comments of key union representatives which suggest that the union mooted the return to work as it feared a mass informal return anyway. Tenure-based economic concerns are, however, likely to be only one small part of the equation that was prompting the return to work, for with Christmas and the summer holidays approaching, households were facing a range of economic concerns broader than just their housing costs.

The reasoning behind the social action of strikers and non-strikers has been compared through three decision time phases, to examine whether or not housing tenure is a key discerning variable in their different courses of social action. It has to be concluded, on the basis of the above data, that in this particular instance of labour activism housing tenure appears to have played a minimal role in differentiating the social action of strikers and non-strikers. The reasons for this have been outlined above and on this basis we can conclude that non-strikers' reasons for not striking had nothing to do with anticipated problems with meeting housing costs. Furthermore, strikers do not appear to have been forced back to work on any significant scale due to economic concerns associated with their housing tenure.

Why these results should differ so markedly from Pratt's (1986a) is largely a matter of speculation. First, broad structural factors such as interest rates, percentage of household income dedicated to housing costs, the nature of the industrial relations system and wage rates may differentiate the two studies. Second, methodological differences between the studies may be important. Pratt's work was not a study of a strike but a study of people discussing that scenario. The case study reported here is one of individuals who were actually embroiled in a strike. This distinction may reflect upon the difference between what one would hope to do rationally and what one actually does emotionally. Finally, this case study may be of an atypical strike, though what is a typical strike? The Victorian nurses strike of 1986 was the very first time the nurses of Victoria had been on strike. They went on strike due to what they perceived as a crisis in their profession. For these reasons decision making at this time was permeated with emotion. May be in less dramatic circumstances the economic rationality that Pratt reported on would have prevailed.

HOME OWNERS AND RENTERS ON STRIKE

Whilst housing tenure does not differentiate the social action of strikers and non-strikers, it does appear more important when considering the comparative ability of owners and renters to cope with being on strike. Notably, the economic, cultural and political meanings of housing tenures that differentiate owning and renting had a significant causal impact upon the social action and hence social group consciousness of striking nurses. Though the economic factors associated with different housing tenures did not cause a return to work (as was pointed out above), they do appear to have affected the primary production based experiences of nurses during the strike. That is, owners and renters differed significantly in their ability to engage in social action that directly supported the strike (other than simply not being at work), the most obvious outcome being that renters (due to reasons outlined below) were unable to attend the picket line.

In this regard the results from the strike case study again contradict Pratt's hypotheses in that owners, who generally have higher housing costs than renters, should, on the basis of Pratt's evidence, have coped the least well with the loss of income in relation to their housing situation. The opposite is the case in the 1986 nurses' strike. The reasons for this apparent contradiction lie with understanding the manner in which the economic, cultural and political meanings of housing tenures affected the social action of striking nurses.

Particularly important with regard to the comparative ease owners had coping with the strike was the legal security that home ownership affords, plus the differing economic arrangements between the two groups in terms of the temporal structure of their housing payments. Renters' housing payments were due fortnightly or monthly, compared with quarterly for owners, with the effect that renters had to pay an extra two to four housing payments during the strike. Obviously, meeting such payments without any income would be difficult but what compounded this situation was the legal insecurity experienced by renters. They felt if they did not make these payments then eviction was a very real possibility. These two factors of legal insecurity and the temporal structure of housing payments appear in an interrelated fashion in the statement below.

Q.   Do you think it might have been easier to perhaps go/have been on strike if you were renting or owned your house outright instead of buying?

A.   No you can get evicted and its a lot easier to get evicted than for banks to kick you out. I think from a housing point of view renting would present more difficulties. Also bills for rent are almost always fortnightly and ours are quarterly, so you can pretend that it hasn't arrived which you couldn't do if landlords are hassling you. They (renters) would have had at least three rental payments during the period of the strike, we had one mortgage payment.

(striker/established purchaser owner/couple with children/1 income)

This point directs our attention away from an exclusive concern with the economic factors associated with tenure, to consider political factors such as differences in the security of tenure.

Further factors that worked against the renters were that they were usually a single income household (but with few family commitments), thus their only source of household income was lost, whereas many of the owner households had two incomes (but usually more family commitments). Second, landlords with one or two properties may not be as able or willing to forego rental payments for a couple of months as are large financial institutions such as banks or building societies and therefore, may have placed, or renters may have felt, more pressure to keep up to date with their payments. No doubt their feelings of legal insecurity would have played a substantial role in this.

Q. Do you think it might have been easier to perhaps go/have been on strike if you were purchasing or owned a house outright?

A. Yes you probably would have got more concessions than when you're renting. Concessions from the banks, 'don't worry about the payments this week we'll get it when you go back to work', whereas I don't think the landlords would like that too much.

(striker/renter/single/1 income)

Many nurses who rent houses form group households and those households that consisted entirely of nurses suffered acutely. Those who shared with others, either not in nursing or in nursing but not on strike, were often financially aided by other household members (e.g. rent, kitty, bills) in much the same way as many of the two income owner households.

Q. Was there anything about your personal situation that made it less difficult to go on strike for this length of time?

A. Yes I think probably because I was renting with a couple of other people, they were pretty understanding and I think financially that wasn't quite as bad...

(striker/renter/single/1 income)

The tenure-based differences outlined above had a significant impact upon the coping strategies of owners and renters during the strike. The extent of this was that owners and renters pursued different courses of social action during the strike thus affecting the construction of social group consciousness. Renters, unable to meet housing costs, were often forced to return home to live with their parents, typically in country Victoria. Being away from

Melbourne prevented them from participating fully in the labour
activism by joining the picket line, blockading linen deliveries, etc.
Others tried to find alternative sources of income ranging from
car-washing to baby-sitting to strawberry picking, and again this
prevented many renters joining the picket line, a problem which
owners did not have to confront. In this manner it is possible to
argue that housing tenure was causally adequate in the construction of social group consciousness along the lines of tenure, for it
was the combination of factors outlined above that caused the
divided courses of social action of owners and renters during the
strike.

The major reason why owners found it comparatively easy to
cope with the strike, and thus didn't have to engage in courses of
social action that took them away from the picket line, is that the
banks and building societies were prepared to postpone their
housing repayments.

Q.   Have you ever had to postpone or rethink any particular deci-
     sions due to the level of your housing costs?

A.   Well just that once (during the strike) when I had to ask the
     bank for the monthly repayment... The only thing the bank
     said to me that day when I asked to postpone, was if it (the
     strike) goes on you might consider a 25 year term...

     (striker/recent purchaser owner/single/1 income)

Q.   Did your concern over house payments in any way affect your
     participation in the strike?

A.   Well it did, I even went up to the bank to ask them if I could
     have it extended for another quarter and they said I'd be able
     to.

     *(striker/established purchaser owner/couple with children/2
     incomes)*

Some of the reasons for the banks' apparent leniency are as
follows. First, the costs to a bank or building society of foreclosing
a mortgage are substantial, far more than it costs a landlord to
evict a tenant. Hence, the banks were very unlikely to act for the
sake of one or two payments which they knew would be paid once

the strike had ended. Second, as pointed out above the banks could weather a storm such as the nurses strike with relative ease, a number of nurses postponing their repayments was unlikely to cause the banks any serious financial problems since their mortgage loan portfolios are widely dispersed throughout the community. Third, re-possessing nurses' homes whilst they were out on strike would no doubt have caused an avalanche of bad publicity, something the image conscious banks would be keen to avoid. Lastly, being on quarterly repayment terms, a large number of owner households had paid their last instalment in September, the month before the strike began and were not due to pay another instalment until December or January by which time the strike was over.

Q. Do you think it might have been easier to perhaps go/have been out on strike if you were renting or owned your house outright instead of buying?

A. I don't know, I think with rent costs these days there would be much—you still had to put out your rent money. We were fortunate in that our payments were quarterly as well, because we'd only just made a payment before we went out. We were able to postpone payments, free credit from banks.

(striker/established purchaser owner/couple with children/2 incomes)

Q. Did your loss of income during the strike mean that you could not meet your loan repayments?

A. Well yes I had to put it on overdraw.

(striker/established purchaser owner/couple with children/2 incomes)

This section has argued that housing tenure is an important cause of variation in the social action of strikers during the Victorian nurses strike. Housing tenure structured different types of coping strategies which led to renters playing a significantly reduced part in the labour activism. This reduced part resulted in the (re)construction of a different social group consciousness along the lines of tenure.

HOME OWNERS AND RENTERS NOT ON STRIKE

Amongst non-strikers the reasons for not going out on strike differ between full and part-time staff. Full-time non-strikers' reasons for not striking relate primarily to 'the job' and fall into the 'couldn't leave the patients', 'don't believe in strikes' brackets stated above. However, part-timers' reasons for not striking are more closely related to home oriented factors rather than employment. This seems largely due to different experiences of the way in which home and place of employment interact; a different dual role for these women which is fundamentally shaped by the spatiality of the home-employment split.

At employment part-timers are not fully integrated into existing social networks. This is partly due to them only working one or two days a week. Also, many part timers work 'bank' (emergency replacement of absentees), which prevents them forging strong links in the hospital because they are always working in different parts of it and don't know where they will be working until they arrive on shift. A reflection of their lack of identification with their job is that part-timers, it seems, are less likely to be members of the RANF.

A.   I think you'd find that a lot of people with children aren't working full time, it's only a minority that are working full time. I just think if you're working part time and you've got a family why put money into a union when it's not compulsory. I think a lot of people would say well I can do better with the money, much to the disgust of the RANF.

(non-striker/established purchaser owner/couple with children/2 incomes/part-time)

Due to their weak social ties to the place of employment and their lack of identification with their jobs and the hospital, part-timers were more likely than full-timers to interpret the strike as not their struggle.

Q   Why did you personally not want to go out on strike?

A. Well I wasn't a union member for a start and I just didn't—I
    could not afford to lose the money, there was no way I could
    drop the money, so I wouldn't even consider it. But working
    only one day a week, I didn't sort of feel it was my fight either.

    *(non-striker/established purchaser owner/couple with children/ 2
    incomes/part-time)*

For many part-timers, who can be characterised as having
school age children and a mortgage, their reasons for working were
that they needed the money (see quote above), nursing was a job
not the career that it was for many of the full-timers. For this sub-
group the economic dimension of home ownership is obviously
more important.

A. I couldn't have dropped that money and I didn't feel that
    committed anyway. We would have just gone further down the
    tube.

    *(non-striker/established purchaser owner/couple with children/2
    incomes/part-time)*

Indeed, the new career structure that the RANF was pushing
for would put pressure on part-timers to upgrade their qualifica-
tions if they wanted to increase their pay, which many had neither
the time, money nor inclination to do.

The position of these women in the job market as part-timers is
closely related to a series of factors such as caring for children and
managing the home, balanced against the need for money to pay
for the mortgage, school fees, clothes, etc. It is the interaction
between consumption and production forces that not only defines
the employment of these women as part-time but also affects their
self-definition. These women tend to identify more with home
rather than employment related pressures. To this extent the part-
timers would have been one of the least supportive groups of the
strike.

CONCLUSION

This chapter has shown that, in the case study of the Victorian nurses strike of 1986, home owners appeared to be just as willing as renters to enter into labour activism (if not more able) and that throughout the course of the strike housing tenure was not a significant factor in differentiating the two groups, strikers and non-strikers. If, however, we scrutinise each of these groups separately, then amongst strikers it is possible to identify different courses of social action along the lines of housing tenure divisions. With non-strikers, consumption processes more generally, rather than housing tenure, were important in explaining the different courses of social action followed by full and part-time nurses.

Contrary to expectations stemming from the literature (Pratt, 1986a) housing tenure did not differentiate the actions of strikers and non-strikers. Home owners were going out on strike in the same way and for the same reasons as renters despite the fact that they were responsible for mortgage repayments. These actions cannot be interpreted as tenure-based class, political force and/or status group actions. However, amongst the group 'strikers', social action was differentiated by tenure. The different courses of social action that striking home owners and renters undertook can be interpreted as tenure-based class, political force and status group action to the varying extent that the economic, political and cultural meanings of housing tenures were drawn upon. Particularly significant were the legal security and temporal structure of housing payments that differentiate the tenure groups. The combined result was that renters were compelled to find alternative work so that they could make their rental payments, or to return to the parental home, often outside Melbourne. Both of these courses of social action took renters away from the picket line and other strike related activities, but left home owners engaging in a daily struggle with their employers on the picket lines.

In further reference to the literature, the results of this case study concur with the findings of Pratt (1987) whereby she suggests that the political values of white collar workers will be differentiated by housing tenure. Recognising the professional 'white collar' status of nurses, this case study has shown how the courses of social action engaged in by home owners and renters differed according to housing tenure. The result of engaging in different courses of social action, one collective, conflictual and radical, the other individual, away from the conflict and basically a coping strategy, would be the (re)construction of different political attitudes along the lines of tenure. In other words, one may expect the experience of the strike to have been a more politicising experience for those (home owners) who stood on the picket line day in day out, than those (renters) who returned to the parental home or picked strawberries.

Reflecting on the results of this case study in relation to the theoretical framework detailed earlier, it is suggested in Chapter 4 that economic action, '...a peaceful use of the actor's control over resources, which is primarily economically oriented' (Weber, 1947, p. 158), may typify the social action of this case study. Whilst the conflictual nature of the strike situation does not sit comfortably with this ideal type of *wirtschaften* or economic action, an example of this type of action includes the way in which home owners were able to draw upon their housing tenure as an economic resource that enabled them to pursue particular courses of social action during the strike. In contrast renters were unable to draw upon their tenure as an economic resource, which also affected the course of their social action. In many ways, however, it was the political meanings of housing tenures that governed the way in which these economic resources could be drawn upon. The legal security that owners enjoy and the legal insecurity that renters endure, had a significant impact on owners' and renters' anticipation of the consequences of non-payment of mortgage or rent.

Whilst the tenure-related elements of the nurses strike show elements of *wirtschaften* (economic action), the strike action in general was *zweckrational* in nature, calculated as it was to achieve certain demands (ends). *Wirtschaften* and *zweckrational* are those ideal types of social action at the 'rational' end of the spectrum. This gives some indication of the degree to which the strike action was oriented towards the monopolisation of market interests (rational social action in our framework) and therefore, the extent to which it is definable as 'social group' action. The monopolisation of market position being a key aspect of social group formation.

As with the powerline case study the social relations that characterised this rational action, were both associative and communal in nature. They were associative in as much as the decision to join the strike was a calculated response aimed at achieving a particular outcome and communal in that the collective endeavour engendered strong feelings of unity. If the nature of the social relations was both associative and communal, the type of social action both *wirtschaften* and *zweckrational*, what of the nature of the social group consciousness constructed through the tenure differentiated courses of social action of home owners and renters?

To the extent that strike action challenges the balance of power in the labour relation, a cornerstone of capitalist formations, engagement in such action is obviously radical in that it challenges the status quo. The demand for professional recognition by largely female nurses represented a challenge to the domination and power of the established medical profession, the predominantly male doctors and hence a challenge to the existing social order. The nurses strike, however, was also an attempt to gain recognition by the social order, to gain professional status. This aim can perhaps be seen as self-serving, oriented towards the monopolisation through professionalisation of one's market niche. Whilst the activity of the strike challenged the status quo, the outcome of it may well be simply the establishing of a slightly different social order.

To the extent that home owners, because of their tenure-based experiences during the strike, were more able to participate fully in the strike action they had greater exposure to radical action. To the extent that renters, because of their tenure-based experiences during the strike, were less able to fully participate in the strike action they had less exposure to oppositional action. It is this exposure to oppositional action that is seen as the key to the (re)construction of a radical social group consciousness, an outcome far more likely for home owners than renters in this instance. This conclusion, as did that of Chapter 7 again questions the incorporation thesis (Pratt, 1989). If home owners are being exposed to radical social action to a greater extent than renters, they may not be the 'pillars of social responsibility' that is generally expected. Or if they are, then this conservative social group consciousness has its roots in another part of the social order, not just home ownership.

Chapter 9

CONCLUSION
The Radical Home Owner?

No longer can we assume that home ownership will provide a 'bulwark against Bolshevism' and maintain the status quo, for the suburbs and lands of the new gentry may be the seed-beds of radical opposition in the 1990s. We have seen how the interests and meanings of home ownership can cause social action that both supports and challenges dominant social relations. As home owners comprise 60–70 per cent of all households in Britain, the U.S., Canada, Australia and New Zealand, and are on the rise throughout western Europe, it is important we consider the potential sociological impact of these tenure-based classes, political forces and status groups.

First, is this something new that we are revealing or have housing tenure relations always entailed such contradictions and social science simply failed to recognise them? Or, are we witnessing a re-definition of housing tenure relations? It would seem unlikely that the private property relations at the core of home ownership have altered over time, for the rights of use, control and disposal are essential to the very notion of home ownership—they are a part of its definition. That social science has failed to recognise the oppositional potential of home ownership is quite possible and the inadequacies of both the collectivist and anti-collectivist approaches to the theorising of housing tenure have been discussed in Chapter 2. A re-interpretation and re-conceptualisation of past urban struggles through the framework developed above, then, may well prove fruitful. The limit to such an historical re-interpretation, however, is that the association of home ownership with conservatism goes beyond the realm of social scientific explanation and has been a common-place under-standing for much of this century. Whilst such a popular under-standing should rightly be treated with caution, it does lend weight to the idea that home ownership has not always housed the possi-bilities of opposition we have revealed. The conclusion we are drawn towards, then, is that more recently the socio-spatial nexus, of which home ownership is a part, has changed to such an extent that the social relations of housing tenure have been redefined.

The key forces that may have brought about such a re-definition are those of global economic restructuring that have commanded new spatial patterns of production and consumption. Office suburbanisation, the manufacturing shift to small rural towns and the shoring-up of CBD investment through new infrastructure and the creation of 'spectacle' have all impinged upon home owner interests in ways that the modernist separation of functions attempted to avoid. This re-shaping of land-use through the re-assertion of the rights of capital in harness with the state, has threatened the interests of home ownership in ways perhaps not previously encountered. In particular, a rising entrepreneurialism on the part of the state (Harvey, 1989a) has led states to attempt the capture of investment and development funds, with the aim of attaining urban and economic regeneration. This response by the state to changing structural conditions, manifests itself in the hindrance of public participation and a weakening of democratic accountability as we witness the privatisation of land assets, the liberalisation of land-use regulations, subsidisation of private sector developments and commercialisation of government department operations (Winter and Brooke, 1993; Winter, 1993). It is these changing forms of land-use and land-use regulation that are bringing new pressures to bear on the interests of home owner-ship.

Furthermore, mass unemployment, the growth of female labour force participation rates, particularly part-time, increasing numbers of working poor, falling union membership rates, and the collapse of union power via the efforts of new right governments and/or through shifts to enterprise bargaining and the consequent demise of collective bargaining (Lash and Urry, 1987)—suggest a re-definition of the home-employment nexus and that the place of employment is less and less likely to be an effective site of opposi-tional strategies. As employment relations become less secure, the home and the relations of housing tenure may become increas-ingly important bases around which opposition is centred. This will not be the opposition centred around collective consumption of Castells' urban social movements and will not be simply an opposition focused upon consumption as some of the defensive 'Not In My Back Yard' (NIMBY) protests are. Here we are talking of opposition that is focused by the sphere of private consumption to span both production and consumption.

If the essence of the analysis advanced here is correct, that home ownership can become increasingly a focus for oppositional strat-egies, then, perhaps states will also be less enthusiastic in their support of home ownership. The temporariness and alienation that characterises private renting might be preferred to an involved, active and sometimes oppositional citizenry founded upon home ownership. A recent review of housing policy in Australia, the National Housing Strategy (NHS) advocates a policy of 'tenure neutrality' to redress the imbalance between home ownership and private renting. However, by advocating income support for private renters and taxation of capital gains reaped by home owners, the NHS proposals are as limited as the early housing classes debate in that they are one-dimensional, solely being concerned with the economic inequalities that exist between the tenure forms. Whilst in itself this is important, it disregards the poignant political and cultural inequalities that persist between home ownership and private renting. If the NHS position of tenure neutrality is implemented this will make it easier to access and remain in private renting whilst doing nothing about the alienating aspects of insecurity and temporariness.

As home ownership becomes the dominant tenure form in more and more countries it is argued that the differences between home owners and private or public renters will become less marked than the differences amongst home owners themselves (Murie, 1991; Forrest, Murie and Williams, 1990). This process, it is argued, will reduce the relevance of the category housing tenure for sociological analysis. However, whilst social differentiation will inevitably occur amongst the incumbents of a housing tenure as it grows to 70 or 80 per cent of all households, we have demonstrated through the course of this book that in countries where home owners constitute 60 to 70 per cent of all households (Australia, New Zealand, U.S., Canada and Britain) there remains a common set of meanings which underlie the experience of living in a particular form of housing tenure. We have then shown how such meanings causally relate to courses of social action. Despite a social differentiation amongst home owning households, housing tenure remains an important focus for sociological analysis.

These somewhat speculative conclusions rest upon primary data from the three Australian case studies and secondary data from a range of other countries that has assessed the causal significance of housing tenure relations for social life. Drawing upon the housing classes debate the parameters which might guide a Weberian informed analysis of housing tenure have been established and the key concepts appropriate to such an investigation detailed. Data from Australia, New Zealand, Canada, the U.S. and Britain established that objective inequalities and different subjective meanings of an economic, political and cultural nature causally relate to the experience of differing private property rights. The three Australian case studies then examined the causal significance of these economic, political and cultural inequalities and meanings in relation to social action in the home, neighbourhood and place of employment. What remains is for us to summarise the key points of the analysis and to establish its limits.

The key points of the analysis are that:

1. The attribution of meaning to housing tenure occurs across each of the economic, political and cultural dimensions of inequality.
2. There is a causally adequate relationship between housing tenure-based meanings and certain forms of social action.
3. Through such social action social groups are formed.
4. Tenure-based social groups engage in oppositional strategies that result in social change through challenging dominant social relations. Social action in the public domain that draws on each of the three dimensions of power, economic, political and cultural is more likely to affect social change than social action that draws on any one of these dimensions alone. These points are examined in greater detail below.

THE ATTRIBUTION OF MEANING TO HOUSING TENURE OCCURS ACROSS EACH OF THE ECONOMIC, POLITICAL AND CULTURAL DIMENSIONS OF INEQUALITY

By examining the subjective dimension of householders' experiences it becomes clear that the nature of inequality constructed through housing tenure is wide ranging. Other authors have tended to treat housing tenure as simply an economic or political phenomenon, however, it is clear that each of three aspects of inequality, economic, political and cultural, is constructed through housing tenure relations. Such inequalities are apparent in the individual's interpretation of the experience of private property rights.

For home owners, meanings of an economic nature include investment, making money, saving money, financial security and inheritance, i.e. 'leaving something for the kids'. These meanings fall into two broad categories, those dependent upon generally rising property values and those independent of generally rising property values. For renters, economic meanings include financial insecurity, rent as 'dead' money, the inability to save whilst paying rent and limited control at a price (bond money being sacrificed to make desired but unauthorised changes to the dwelling). More positively, but paradoxically with regard to 'dead money', renting is also said to be cheaper than owning.

The political meanings of housing tenures refer to notions such as control and security. These meanings are held in a positive sense by home owners and a negative sense by renters. Control refers to the autonomy that home owners enjoy in their homes; they can do whatever they want to (within the law). Renters, however, speak of a lack of control. This is because the private property rights associated with renting place control not with the tenant but with the landlord or property agent, reinforced by the authoritative and routine force of the state.

The security that home owners enjoy and the insecurity that renters endure is also grounded in differing experiences of private property rights. The main distinction here is one of legal security. Outright owners can only be ousted involuntarily from their property via compulsory acquisition by the state. Purchaser owners, as long as they maintain their mortgage repayments, enjoy similar security. A tenant in Melbourne, however, even if s/he 'plays everything by the rules' can be asked, legally, to vacate a property with just two months notice. If a rental payment is missed or the lease broken in any way the landlord has the right to evict within one month.

The cultural meanings of housing tenure refer to notions such as status and attachment. For home owners, status and attachment are positive meanings whilst for renters they are negative. Being a home owner conveys social (self) respect and such respect can be enhanced through the considered presentation of house and garden. For renters, on the other hand, stigma, rather than status, is associated with their tenure form. Renters have not 'made the mark' and a lack of control over the dwelling leaves few opportunities for the positive reinforcement of status through the display of house and garden. With regard to attachment, again this is a positive meaning for home owners and a negative one for renters. Home owners develop a strong attachment to their homes and neighbourhoods, a feeling that is rarely present for renters, due to the politically guaranteed advantages of the former group's private property rights.

This range of meanings, as elicited by the primary data and reinforced by the secondary data, is important in two ways. First, that each dimension of inequality is reproduced through housing tenure and second, that these meanings are the interpretative means through which social action occurs.

The attribution of meaning by home owners and renters to the experience of housing tenure is not a contingent process. Causal adequacy in the relationship between housing tenure and particular meanings has been demonstrated in each of the case studies. This moves debate beyond notions of mere 'association' (Williams, 1989) or 'link' (Pratt, 1986d) to the proposition that the experience of private property rights causes certain understandings and interpretations of housing relations rather than others. For example, the experience of home ownership is essential to the positive meanings of control and security that home owners spoke of. Renting does not provide the appropriate experience for these meanings to evolve.

Whilst 'housing class debaters' have generally been content to search for the objective inequalities between tenure forms, this book has revealed how the subjective understanding of objective inequalities is equally important. For it is an individual's subjective interpretation of material inequalities that will finally determine what course of social action occurs.

THERE IS A CAUSALLY ADEQUATE RELATIONSHIP BETWEEN HOUSING TENURE-BASED MEANINGS AND FORMS OF SOCIAL ACTION

In each of the three case studies a causally adequate relationship is apparent between the meanings of housing tenure and social action. The emphasis of the data lay with establishing causality at the level of meaning, yet, causality at the level of typical probability has also been demonstrated with the combined data sets indicating causal adequacy overall.

For example, in the Neighbourhood Watch case study home owners were more active than renters. In the particular NW Area studied this heightened activism took the form of physically securing the dwelling and marking possessions. The causally adequate relationship between these forms of social action and housing tenure stems from the political advantages of control and security that home owners enjoy over renters. The control that home owners experience, because of their property rights, freely enables them to install dead locks, window locks, security doors, etc. Whilst renters may be 'allowed' to do this, with the permission of their landlord, the legal insecurity they endure through their limited property rights and consequent forced mobility means that such an investment is hardly worthwhile. The legal insecurity of renting also relates to the second identified aspect of participation in NW, the marking of valuables. The forced mobility of renters works against the accumulation of goods of value, precluding the need to mark anything, thus closing off this avenue of activity. The reduced accumulation of goods of value by renters is reinforced by the previous point that renters' homes are less likely to be secured against burglary due to the lack of control they have over their dwelling.

In the Brunswick–Richmond powerline dispute home owners were again more active than renters. The activism of home owners drew, amongst other things, upon the economic, cultural and political meanings of home ownership. Active home owners related their activism to home ownership in that the powerline was perceived by them as a threat to the economic value of their homes, to control over their homes, to the security they enjoyed in those homes and the attachment they felt to those homes. Renters did not identify with any of these concerns though they recognised the legitimacy of them for home owners and were, consequently, less politically active.

In the nurses strike case study the impact of the experience of private property rights upon social action again emerged. Contrary to expectations, derived from Pratt (1986a), home owners were as willing and able to enter labour activism as renters, if not more so. Housing tenure was not, therefore, a key factor differentiating the social action of strikers *vis-à-vis* non-strikers. However, housing tenure did differentiate internally the social action of the groups 'strikers' and 'non-strikers'. Amongst the group 'strikers', renters had more housing tenure-related difficulties coping with the prolonged loss of income associated with the strike than home owners. The result of this was that renters were compelled to engage in courses of social action that took them away from direct participation in labour activism, notably the picket line. Home owners, however, were able to commit themselves to full participation in the strike as banks and building societies were willing to postpone housing repayments.

Amongst the group 'non-strikers', the reasons for not joining the strike differed according to whether or not the individual worked full or part-time. Full-time nurses' reasons for not joining the strike related solely to job related ideological factors. Part-time nurses' reasons for not joining the strike emphasised the influence of the domestic sphere. The difference between the two groups lay with the difficulties part-time nurses had establishing significant ties within and to the workplace. The reasons why many such nurses work part-time, though, are related to factors such as family life cycle and housing tenure. In this unexpected manner, housing tenure was again affecting social action.

So, the relationship between home ownership and social action is multi-faceted and non-deterministic. A causally adequate relationship exists between home ownership, specific sets of interests and certain meanings. The interests and meanings of home ownership, when threatened, do relate in a causally adequate fashion to a heightened degree of participation but it is contingent or in Weber's terms 'accidental' whether or not such interests are ever threatened.

HOUSING TENURE IS A CAUSAL FACTOR IN THE FORMATION OF SOCIAL GROUPS

In each of the three case studies the interpretation and understanding of the experience of private property rights is a significant dimension of people's lives. Its significance lies with the fact that owning or renting a home means something in particular rather than nothing in general. As these meanings causally relate to the social action of home owners and renters so are tenure-based classes, political forces and status groups formed.

The criteria for the formation of classes, political forces and status groups are of a similar nature. The common criteria are, the specification of particular objective inequalities, the attribution of meanings in relation to such inequalities and the pursuit of social action on the basis of such meanings; each being of an economic, political and cultural nature respectively.

The analysis has shown that it is possible to identify home owners and renters as distinct tenure-based classes, political forces and status groups. These social groups form, re-form and overlap depending upon; (i) whether economic, political or cultural tenure-based interests are being threatened, (ii) how these interests and threats are being interpreted and (iii) the consequent social action unleashed. The empirical intertwining of such tenure-based social groups is not problematic, rather, inevitable. Status group formation, on the basis of housing tenure, does not exclude the possibility of class or political force formation and vice versa. As each of the axes of power, economic, political and cultural, co-exist and overlap ontologically, so will the social groups that form around these dimensions of inequality.

Data from each of the case studies support the above conclusion as in each case study the significance of tenure in terms of meanings is clear. The manner in which these meanings affect social action is also clear. In the NW case study home owners were more active largely due to the meanings of control and security. In the powerline case study, home owners were again more active, this time due to a wide range of tenure-based economic, political and cultural meanings. In the strike case study home owners were not more active than renters but the former group's ability to participate successfully in the strike action was related to the meaning of legal security and the organisation of housing payments.

We can, therefore, identify ideal types of class, political force and status group in relation to housing tenure. For example, home owners who acted collectively on the basis of tenure-related economic meanings, as some opponents of the powerline did, acted as a housing tenure class. These home owners were well aware of the economic interests associated with their home owning and were engaged in collective social action to defend these interests. This was not the only motivation for opposition to the powerline, as has been pointed out previously, but the fact that it is a part of the activism is significant and important to explaining that activism. This example of tenure-based class action can be compared with the action of home owners deciding whether or not to join the nurses' strike.

Whilst it was hypothesised that home owning nurses would be reluctant to join the strike due to the economic pressure of maintaining mortgage repayments, this was not the case. The economic interests of home owning played no part in the decision of whether or not to go on strike. This action could not, then, be interpreted as housing tenure class action. Similarly, the fact that neither the cultural nor political meanings of housing tenure were drawn upon, means that there was no tenure-based status group action, nor tenure-based political force action in this instance of social action, i.e. deciding whether or not to go out on strike. However, the extent to which home owners and renters were able to engage fully in the strike action, having made the decision to go out on strike, was related to their tenure-based experiences. In differentiating the experiences of home owners and renters both economic (organisation of housing payments) and political (legal security) tenure-based meanings appear to be important. To this extent then, it is possible to describe the social action of striking home owners and renters as that of a tenure-based class and a tenure-based political force.

In the Brunswick–Richmond powerline case study, home owners readily made links between the cultural meanings of their home and neighbourhood, such as status and attachment, and their opposition to the powerline. Action carried out on the basis of these cultural meanings can be interpreted as tenure-based status group action. The political meanings of control and security were also linked by home owners to their actions against the powerline. Home owners, therefore, were not only acting as a tenure-based status group but as a tenure-based political force as well. The inaction of renters in the powerline dispute can also be identified as tenure-based political force (non-)action. One of the major reasons why renters were inactive was because of the political meanings of renting, such as legal insecurity. This meaning contributed to an attitude amongst renters that, as they had no long-term future in the area, it was not worth fighting the SECV. In the NW case study home owners were active partly because of the political meanings of control and security and, thus, can also be seen to be acting as a tenure-based political force.

HOME OWNERSHIP CAN BE A SITE FOR OPPOSITIONAL STRATEGIES THAT RESULT IN SOCIAL CHANGE

It is clear then that housing tenure causally relates to social action at both the level of meaning and typical probability. To have established this is important for previously 'links' and 'associations' were the language of housing tenure studies. In as much as the causal significance of housing tenure has had an assumed status in earlier work, so has the stable citizen been associated with home ownership. The socio-political impact of home ownership has always been thought to be one of shoring-up capitalist relations through an extension of private property relations and a 'chain of debt'. The analysis presented here, however, identifies home ownership as a site of potentially oppositional strategies, strategies that may result in social change.

In the Brunswick–Richmond powerline case study home owners were engaged in action that challenged the dominance of existing social relations. Powerline opponents, the bulk of whom were home owners, used non-violent direct action in the form of work-site occupations to disrupt work progress. These actions and their culmination in a number of arrests for trespass can be seen as a somewhat ironic rejection of the property rights of the State Electricity Commission of Victoria (SECV). Opposition to the powerline also amounted to a rejection of the commodification of Melbourne's parks and waterways and a replacement of notions of value and cost with non-monetary concepts such as aesthetic and environmental value, quality of life and attachment to home and neighbourhood. More broadly this action opposed the socio-spatial logic of global economic restructuring for the new power-line was to secure the electricity supply to the CBD of Melbourne. This had become all the more important as development pressures wrought by global economic restructuring mounted on the CBD. For example, transnational corporations desired bases for Australian and southeast Asian development, foreign banks arrived with the deregulation of the Australian finance and banking system (Berry, 1986, p.39) and the per capita consumption of office floor space increased from fifteen to twenty-three metres per person between 1982 and 1989 due to the increasing use of 'high-technology' office equipment (Low and Moser, 1991, pp.12–13), a technology which of course is entirely dependent upon electricity. These CBD development pressures arguably brought about the need for new infrastructure, thus bringing the SECV into conflict with residents who saw the Yarra River valley as more than a conduit for infrastructure provision.

In the case study of the nurses' strike home owners were as radically active as renters, if not more so, through their challenge to the labour relation. The 'chains of debt' that are supposed to 'tie home owners into the property relations of advanced capitalism' did not prevent any of the interviewed home owners from joining the strike. In fact, home ownership may have enabled home owners to participate more fully in this action than renters. Their security of tenure and credit worthiness enabled them to cope more readily with the protracted but temporary loss of income. The strike can also be interpreted as resistance to the socio-spatial logic of global economic restructuring. The rise of nursing as a profession cannot be separated from an increasing use of medical technology, growth in the size and status of service industry jobs and greater female labour force participation rates. Each of these trends has been associated with the emergence of a new regime of accumulation (Harvey, 1989). The causal role of housing tenure in enabling greater participation in such strike action, thus, identifies home ownership as a potential locus of opposition to the contemporary restructuring of capitalist economies.

Home ownership, however, can also lead to strategies that reinforce dominant social relations. For example, those active in the NW case study engaged in two forms of activity, physically securing the dwelling and marking possessions. These actions represent little more than a maintenance of the status quo; those who have defending what they have.

The interests of home ownership, as Pratt (1989) suggests, can lead to both incorporation into and resistance to the status quo. Though the defence of domestic property interests may often be a conservative reaction, this defence can lead to both intended and unintended oppositional strategies. Through the experience of such oppositional strategies the construction of a 'radical' social group consciousness, grounded in housing tenure relations can form. Whether or not a radical form of social group consciousness arises appears dependant upon two things: first, the locale of the social action and second, the extent to which the social action encompasses the economic, political and cultural, that is all three dimensions of power, rather than any one or two.

On the significance of locale, the case studies reveal the impact of tenure-based interests upon social action within the home (NW case study), within the neighbourhood (powerline case study) and at the place of employment (nurses' strike case study). The wide ranging nature of social action causally related to tenure-based interests highlights the complexity of interwoven forces acting upon any one individual. The interaction of the housing and labour markets is particularly noticeable in the nurses' strike case study. Comparing the case studies, home-oriented social action appears less important in the construction of a radical social group consciousness and thus in bringing about social change, when compared with collective action in the public realm. For example, Chapter 6 suggests that to the extent that social action is home-centred, it appears more likely to be either rational and thus oriented towards a monopolisation of market position, or based on absolute ends to suit the private realm that are inherently conservative. On the other hand, Chapter 7 suggests that engaging in collective action in the public realm, in this case, to prevent the construction of intrusive powerlines, can result in a challenging of dominant social relations and thus social change.

The impact of housing tenure is not restricted to the private sphere; we are not concerned simply with the sociology of consumption if this is defined as the sociology of everything that takes place in the home. First, the way in which social relations such as housing tenure affect social action in the home, neighbourhood and place of employment, the spatiality of social relations, should be borne in mind. Second, with regard to an analytical separation of consumption from production, the interaction between structures such as the housing market and job market deny the usefulness of such a conceptual separation.

The second key factor that affects the construction of a tenure-based social group consciousness is the extent to which all three axes of power are drawn upon in the social action. Social change, it appears, is more likely when social action encompasses all three dimensions of power, rather than simply any one or two. This is supported through the analysis of the case studies and is implicit in the ontology of the adopted theoretical framework. The social is defined as comprising economic, political and cultural relations. With action and change taking place in each of the parts, significant change of the whole is also more likely.

In the NW case study home owners were only drawing upon the political meanings of housing tenure to inform their social action and such action was of a conservative nature. In the nurses strike case study the economic and political meanings of housing tenure were important and whilst dominant social relations were being challenged, nurses were perhaps challenging them in order to gain acceptance by them, rather than fundamentally replacing or re-aligning such social relations. Nurses were essentially striking for professional recognition, rather than articulating a de-profession-alisation of medicine that placed the patient in an equal relation-ship, for instance. In the Brunswick–Richmond powerline case study, active home owners drew upon economic, political and cultural meanings to inform their social action. The social action engaged in was ultimately confrontational with work-site occupa-tions that trespassed the private property of the SECV. The commodification of the valley was challenged with notions of use value and the legitimate authority of the state was challenged through communal relations and collective action. The overhead powerline proposal was defeated with the powerline eventually being undergrounded away from environmentally sensitive areas and with the SECV now in a position of being unable to place any new high transmission cables overhead.

Finally, we need to examine the limitations of this analysis. First, this book has simply examined whether or not housing tenure is causally related to courses of social action and the forma-tion of social groups. Some differentiation in the experience of housing tenure was noted. Further work is necessary to uncover how housing tenure interacts with other social characteristics, such as gender, ethnicity and occupation. These questions are not only about how such interaction takes place to affect the formation of social groups but in what social contexts and locales does housing tenure become more or less important?

Second, this book examines the attribution of meaning to housing tenure from the point of view of the individual user. How this process of attribution is mediated through and by private sector marketing strategies and state policies has not been examined. If we are to understand the significance of housing tenure still further it will be necessary to examine the ways in which capital, the state and civil society have combined in the past and do so today to forge the significance of contemporary housing tenure relations.

Third, more work needs to be done that examines the process of the (re)construction of social group consciousness. What forms of social action in what sorts of social contexts and locales lead to the continuing reformulation of social group consciousness? What does a radicalising or conservatising experience consist of? If an individual's social group consciousness is reshaped through social action, how does this then affect the way in which people give meaning to their lives?

Finally, how are the social groups of class, political force and status group formed through other spheres of life such as employment and how does this social group formation interact with that of spheres such as housing tenure?

These are all issues that we have not attempted to grapple with. They represent distinct and comprehensive areas of research in their own right. Hopefully this book will generate interest in finding the answers to such questions.

Appendix 1

THE INTERVIEW SCHEDULES

A. NEIGHBOURHOOD WATCH SAMPLING INTERVIEW SCHEDULE

DATE:

TIME:

NAME:

ADDRESS:

AGE:

SEX:

1. Would you describe yourself as active or inactive within Neighbourhood Watch?   ACTIVE / INACTIVE
2. Have you ever been burgled?   YES / NO
3. In which country were you born?
4. Do you speak English as your first language at home? YES / NO

5. Are you PURCHASING YOUR HOUSE WITH A MORTGAGE / Are you RENTING / Do you OWN IT OUTRIGHT / OTHER?

6. Are you married or living in a de facto relationship?
YES / NO

7. Are there any children in your household?   YES / NO

8. Are there any elderly people in your household?   YES / NO

9. How long have you lived in this neighbourhood?

10. What level of education did you complete?
NONE / PRIMARY / SECONDARY / TERTIARY

11. What is your occupation?

12. What is the nature of your work?

13. Are you a: MEMBER OF A TRADES UNION / MEMBER OF AN ASSOCIATION?

14. What are/were your parents occupations?
FATHER:
MOTHER:

15. What level of education did they complete?
NONE / PRIMARY / SECONDARY / TERTIARY

16. Are you willing to be interviewed?   YES / NO
TELEPHONE NUMBER:

B. NEIGHBOURHOOD WATCH IN-DEPTH INTERVIEW SCHEDULE

I. How the individual perceives NW, crime and the police

1. When did you first hear of NW?

2. How did you first find out about NW?

3. What would you describe the aims of NW as being?

4. Which of these aims do you think NW has successfully achieved?

5. How involved would you say you have become in NW?

6. [*Active only*] Why do you feel it's important to do those things?

7. [*Inactive only*] Why have you decided not to become actively involved in NW?

8. Would you describe yourself as a supporter of NW?
   Any particular reason why or why not?

9. Have you carried out any particular activities that you think are an indication of the fact that you support NW?

10. Do you think any particular type of person has become involved in, or tends to support NW?

11. Do you think any particular type of person has NOT become involved in or tends NOT to support NW?

12. Have you generally speaking been concerned about local issues in the past?

I am now going to read out a series of statements, after each of which I'd like you to state whether you AGREE or DISAGREE with the statement.

13. Women support NW for different reasons than men.

14. Single or elderly people support NW for different reasons than either families or group households.

15. People from differing ethnic backgrounds support NW for different reasons.

16. People in differing occupations support NW for different reasons.

17. Home owners support NW for different reasons than renters.

    Ask why they agreed to the statements they did, if any.

18. Do you think any of the factors that we have just discussed are important in why you do or do not support NW?

19. What do you think the benefits of living in a NW zone are?

20. Do you think there are any crime rate related benefits?

21. Do you think there are any benefits related to how you get on with your neighbours? Explain.

22. Do you think there are any economic related benefits, for instance with regard to house values or insurance premiums? Explain.

23. Do you think having NW in the neighbourhood offers some means of keeping tabs on the perhaps less desirable elements of the community? Explain.

24. Do you think that having a NW programme in the neighbourhood helps to keep intruders out of your home?

25. Do you think there are any disadvantages of living in a NW zone?

26. Are there any changes you would like to see made to the NW programme?

27. If you were moving house how important would it be to you to move somewhere where there was a NW zone?

28. What particular type of crime in the neighbourhood do you fear, or concerns you the most?

29. Generally speaking, how important a part of your life are these fears or concerns?

30. What do you fear most about being burgled? LOSS OF POSSESSIONS / INVASION OF PRIVACY AND LOSS OF CONTROL OVER HOME ENVIRONMENT / PERSONAL SAFETY.

31. Does NW offer some means of allaying these fears?

32. Is there anything particular about your own situation that influences your: FEAR OF / LACK OF FEAR OF / CONCERN OVER / ATTITUDE TOWARD THE ISSUE OF/ crime?

33. How do you feel about the police being involved in the neighbourhood through NW?

34. Do you think NW helps the police control the neighbourhood?

35. How important do you think the following personal characteristics are in shaping your attitudes towards crime in the neighbourhood?

II. How the individual regards the neighbourhood

36. How would you describe your attachment to this neighbourhood?

37. Why did you choose to move to this neighbourhood? Due to choice of school?

38. How long have you lived here?

39. How long do you intend living here?

40. Would you consider leaving the neighbourhood because of the crime rate?

41. How would you describe your ability to influence events in the neighbourhood? Why do you feel like that?

42. Do you feel that crime in the neighbourhood threatens your, or the community's ability, to maintain control over events in your neighbourhood?

43. [*If yes*] Is that an important part of your participation in/ support of NW?

44. [*Home owners only*] Do you think that being a ratepayer affects how you view your neighbourhood?

45. [*Renters only*] Do you consider yourself a ratepayer of this neighbourhood? [*If yes, ask previous question*]

46. What for you would be the most important factors in creating your ideal neighbourhood?

47. What is it do you think that contributes to the standing or status of this neighbourhood?

48. Other people have suggested that they thought the following factors important. How important do you think they are?

49. If the Ministry of Housing announced plans to build some housing in your street how would you feel about the proposal?

50. How do you think this neighbourhood ranks in terms of its status compared with Richmond, Hawthorn, Toorak?

51. Do you think the level of crime in this neighbourhood threatens the standing or status of the neighbourhood?

52. [*If yes*] Do you think NW offers some means of protecting the standing of the neighbourhood?

53. What would you say are the predominant social groups in this neighbourhood?

54. Are there any sorts of people in the neighbourhood you don't identify with?

55. How would you describe your own social status?

C. POWERLINE SAMPLING INTERVIEW SCHEDULE

DATE:

TIME:

NAME:

ADDRESS:

AGE:

SEX:

1. Are you aware of the community campaign against the SEC's proposed powerline?   YES / NO

2. Would you describe yourself as active or inactive within the powerline campaign?   ACTIVE / INACTIVE

3. Do you think you live close to the proposed powerline route? YES / NO

4. Are you or do you see yourself as becoming a long-term resident of this neighbourhood?   YES / NO

5. Do you OWN YOUR HOUSE OUTRIGHT / are you PURCHASING IT WITH A MORTGAGE / are you RENTING / OTHER?

6. Are there any children in your household?   YES / NO

7. Are there any elderly people in your household?   YES / NO

8. Are you of English speaking or non-English speaking ethnicity? ENGLISH SPEAKING / NON-ENGLISH SPEAKING

9. What level of education did you complete?
   NONE / PRIMARY / SECONDARY / TERTIARY

10. What is your occupation?

11. What is the nature of your work?

12. Is it a secure job?   YES / NO

13. Are you a: UNION MEMBER / MEMBER OF AN ASSOCIATION?

D. POWERLINE IN-DEPTH INTERVIEW SCHEDULE

I. How do participants articulate the reasons behind their activism?

1. When did you first find out about the powerline issue?

2. How did you find this out?

3. At that time what did you think the key issues about the powerline were?

4. Do you still see those as the key issues?

5. What other issues do you think are at stake in this campaign?

6. [*Active only*] How have you been participating?

7. [*Inactive only*] Is there any particular reason why you have not become actively involved in the campaign?

8. Could you please tell me if you are concerned about any of the following and how important they are to you?

9. Do you think you would be PARTICIPATING IN THE OPPOSITION or MORE / LESS CONCERNED if you HAD / DID NOT HAVE children?

10. Do you think you would be PARTICIPATING IN THE OPPOSITION or MORE / LESS CONCERNED if you lived WITHIN / OUTSIDE the directly affected area of the proposed powerline route?

11. [*Active only*] Which of the proposed alternative routes or any other alternative do you think would be the best solution?

12. Do you think you would be PARTICIPATING IN THE OPPOSITION or MORE / LESS CONCERNED if you WERE / WERE NOT going to be a long-term resident of this neighbourhood?

13. What type of person do you think has become involved in this campaign?

14. What type of person do you think has *not* become involved in this campaign?

15. Have you ever experienced any kind of political struggle at your workplace?

16. Do you think your work based experiences have affected your response to the issue in any way?

17. Have you had any previous experience of this type of campaign?

18. What about other health or environmental issues?

19. [*Active only*] What was it about this issue then, that has provoked this response in you? Because it was local?

20. Have you, generally speaking, been concerned about local issues in the past?

21. Is there anything particular about your own situation that has influenced your CONCERN / LACK OF CONCERN over this issue?

I am now going to read out a series of statements, after each of which I would like you to state whether you AGREE or DISAGREE.

22. The women involved in this campaign have different reasons for participating than the men involved.

23. The families with children involved in this campaign have different reasons for participating than either the single or elderly people involved.

24. People from different ethnic backgrounds have different reasons for being involved in this campaign.

25. People in different occupations have different reasons for being involved in this campaign.

26. Home owners involved in this campaign have different reasons for participating than the renters involved.

Then ask why they agreed to the statements they did, if any.

II. Do participants recognise tenure based economic, political and cultural interests?

Neighbourhood based concerns

27. How would you describe your attachment to this neighbourhood?

28. Why did you choose to move to this neighbourhood? Due to choice of school?

29. How long have you lived here?

30. How long do you intend living here?

31. Would you leave the neighbourhood if the powerline was built? If yes, what is your main reason for wanting to leave? If no, why not? Are moving costs any barrier?

32. How would you describe your ability to influence events or developments in the neighbourhood? Why do you feel like that?

33. Do you see the powerline issue as a threat to the extent of that ability or personal control?

34. [*Active only*] How important a part, is that, of your opposition to the powerline?

35. [*Home owners only*] Do you think that being a ratepayer affects how you view your neighbourhood?

36. Do you think that has affected your response to this issue in any way?

37. [*Renters only*] Do you consider yourself a ratepayer of this neighbourhood?
    [*If yes ask previous question*]

38. What for you would be the most important factors in creating your ideal neighbourhood?

39. What is it do you think that contributes to the standing or status of this neighbourhood?

40. Other people have suggested that they thought the following factors important. How important do you think they are?

41. If the Ministry of Housing announced plans to build some houses in your street how would you feel about the proposal?

42. How do you think this neighbourhood ranks in terms of its status compared with, Richmond, Hawthorn?

43. Do you think the powerline proposal is a threat to the standing or status of the neighbourhood?

44. What effect do you think the campaign has had upon the neighbourhood?

House based concerns

45. Given complete freedom of choice, what is your preferred housing option? OWNING / RENTING

    Why? MADE IT / STATUS / COSTS / SAVINGS / FLEXIBILITY / FREEDOM / CONTROL / SECURITY

46. Again with complete freedom of choice, which tenure would be the most likely in which you would establish a home? OWNING / RENTING

47. [*Home owners only*] Could you describe to me your feelings when you bought your first home?

48. Would you call where you now live home?

49. What does that word 'home' mean to you?

50. Do you feel sufficiently secure in your own home?

51. What does SECURITY / LACK OF SECURITY mean to you?

52. What is it about your own [housing] situation that contributes to those feelings of SECURITY / LACK OF SECURITY?

53. Do you see the powerline issue as a threat in any way to those feelings of security?

54. Do you feel you have sufficient control over what happens in and around your home?

55. What does that control mean to you?

56. What is it about your own [housing] situation that contributes to those feelings of CONTROL / LACK OF CONTROL?

57. Do you see the powerline issue as a threat, in any way, to those feelings of control?

58. Do you think owning a house as opposed to renting one is an important part of those notions of 'home', 'security', and 'control'?

59. [*Home owners only*] Do you think buying a house has been a good investment decision? – In what way? TO MAKE MONEY / TO PROTECT SAVINGS / TO SAVE MONEY

60. Is the appearance (external and internal) of your house of importance to you?

61. Is the appearance of your garden of importance to you?

62. Is it important to you that your house should be seen to blend with the rest of the neighbourhood?

63. [*If yes*] Why is this important to you?
STATUS / HOUSE VALUE / OTHER

64. If you were to think of your neighbours, what factors do you think would be important in influencing their attitudes towards their homes?

65. And their neighbourhood?

66. How important do you think the following personal characteristics are in influencing people's views about their home and neighbourhood? a. Gender; b. cultural background/ethnicity; c. age; d. occupation; e. being a parent.

67. You said that you thought... (any of a–e) important in shaping people's views about their home and neighbourhood. Do you also see those as important in influencing your views?

House based economic concerns for owner occupiers

68. Do you know what your house is currently worth?

69. What was its original price?

70. [*Only if no answer to above 2 questions*] Have house values been rising or falling in this neighbourhood recently?

71. When you bought your house did you expect it to rise in value?

72. How important a part of your home owning is that expectation?

73. Do you think the campaign about the powerline and its associated publicity has affected house values in the area?

74. If the powerline is actually built, do you think that will affect house values in the area?

75. Are those concerns any part of your opposition to the powerline?

76. If the political party you don't normally vote for were to propose the re-introduction of income tax relief on mortgage repayments (i.e. if the tax rate were say 30% you would only pay approximately two thirds of the interest you currently pay) would you be prepared to change your vote?

III. How the individual regards their house

77. Given complete freedom of choice, what is your preferred housing option? OWNING / RENTING

    Why? MADE IT / STATUS / COSTS / SAVINGS / FLEXIBILITY / FREEDOM / CONTROL / SECURITY

78. Again with complete freedom of choice, which tenure would be the most likely in which you would establish a home? OWNING / RENTING

79. Do you think people respect home owners more than those who don't own their own homes?

80. [*Home owners only*] Could you describe to me your feelings when you bought your first home?

81. Would you call where you now live home?

82. What does that word 'home' mean to you?

83. Do you feel sufficiently secure in your own home?

84. What does SECURITY / LACK OF SECURITY mean to you?

85. Is there anything particular about your own situation that contributes to those feelings of SECURITY / LACK OF SECURITY?

86. Do you see burglary as a threat to those feelings of security?

87. Does having NW in the neighbourhood make you feel more secure in your home?

88. Do you feel you have sufficient control over what happens in and around your home?

89. What does that control mean to you?

90. Is there anything particular about your own situation that contributes to those feelings of CONTROL / LACK OF CONTROL?

91. Do you see burglary as a threat to your ability to maintain control over your home environment?

92. Do you think having a NW scheme in the neighbourhood helps you or the community to feel in control of the neighbourhood?

93. Do you think ownership of a house as opposed to renting is an important part of those notions of 'home', 'security' and 'control'?

94. Do you think buying a house has been a good investment decision? In what way? TO MAKE MONEY / TO PROTECT SAVINGS / TO SAVE MONEY

95. Are the contents of the house insured? What value?

96. Have you spent any money on improving the security of this house? DOORS / WINDOWS / BOLTS / ALARMS / LIGHTS / DOG

97. Is the appearance (external and internal) of your house of importance to you?

98. Is the appearance of your garden of importance to you?

99. Is it important to you that your home should be seen to blend with the rest of the neighbourhood?

100. Why is this important to you? STATUS / HOUSE VALUE / OTHER

101. How important do you think the following personal characteristics are in shaping OTHER PEOPLE'S / YOUR views about THEIR / YOUR home and neighbourhood?

E. STRIKE SAMPLING INTERVIEW SCHEDULE

TIME:

NAME:

ADDRESS:

AGE:

SEX:

POSITION WITHIN HOSPITAL:

MARITAL STATUS:

DEPENDENTS:

1. Are you a member of the RANF? YES / NO

2. Did you go out on strike in November 1986? YES / NO

3. For how many days/weeks?

4. Are there one or two income earners in your household? ONE / TWO

5. Is your income the primary or secondary income of the household? PRIMARY / SECONDARY

6. Are you PURCHASING YOUR HOUSE WITH A MORTGAGE / RENTING / do you OWN IT OUTRIGHT / OTHER?

7. At the time of the strike: were you ABOUT TO BUY YOUR OWN HOUSE / had you RECENTLY BOUGHT YOUR OWN HOUSE (under 5 years) / had you BOUGHT YOUR HOUSE SOME TIME AGO (over 5 years) / did you OWN YOUR HOUSE OUTRIGHT?

8. At the time of the strike did you earn:
   - under $10,000
   - $10–15,000
   - $15–20,000
   - $20–25,000
   - above $25,000

F. STRIKE IN-DEPTH INTERVIEW SCHEDULE

I. Attitudes towards the strike

1. In your opinion what were the key issues in the strike?
2. What would you say were the main aims of the strike?
3. Which of these aims did you support?
4. Which of its aims do you think the strike achieved?
5. Did you think strike action was the best way of achieving those aims?
6. How easy or difficult was it to make the decision to STRIKE / NOT TO STRIKE?
7. Do you think that as you were working in a PRIVATE / PUBLIC hospital this made a difference to the numbers that went out on strike?
8. [*Strikers only*] What form did your support of the strike take? How long were you out?
9. Do you think there was a difference in attitude towards the strike between college and hospital trained nurses?
10. Do you think this affected strike participation in any way?

11. What factors outside of the workplace did you consider when deciding whether or not to go on strike?

12. Other people have suggested they had to consider some of the following factors, how important were these to you? a. Housing costs; b. schooling costs; c. welfare of your children; d. welfare of aged dependents; e. your position within the hospital; f. patient welfare; g. whether you could afford it; h. credit card debts; i. personal loans; j. an alternative source of income.

13. Had you, or other members of your household, ever previously been on strike either as a nurse or in another job?

14. Do you think there may be need in the near future for a strike to be called again?

15. If need be would you be prepared to go on strike again?

16. When the strike began, how long did you expect the strike to last?

17. After that period of time had passed, did you think the strike was going to be over quickly or drawn out still further?
For how long?

18. After the strike had been going for a month were you experiencing any problems because of the strike?

– If 'yes', what were the important factors in your situation?
– What form did these problems take?
– If 'no', was there anything about your personal situation that made it less difficult to go on strike for this length of time?

19. If the strike had lasted another 2 months how do you think you would have coped?

20. What do you think would have been your greatest difficulty if the strike had lasted another 2 months?

21. Did you at any time during the strike consider looking for other employment?

22. At what stage do you think you might have had to consider looking for other employment?

23. Did you at any time during the strike consider applying for a personal loan?

24. If the strike had gone on a further 2 months would you have been prepared to take out a loan to tide you over?

25. How did STRIKERS / NON-STRIKERS explain to you their reasons for GOING / NOT GOING on strike?

26. Do you think those people were in particular situations that made it EASIER / MORE DIFFICULT for them to GO / NOT TO GO on strike?

27. [*Strikers only*] Other people have suggested that some of the following factors caused them to review whether or not they could remain on strike. How important were these for you? a. Housing costs; b. schooling costs; c. welfare of your children; d. welfare of aged dependents; e. your position within hospital; f. patient welfare; g. whether you could afford it; h. credit card debts; i. personal loans.

Returners only

28. When did you decide to go back to work?

29. Why did you make that decision at that particular time?

30. Were there any particular factors that influenced your decision to go back to work at that time?

31. Other people have suggested that some of the following factors were important in their decision to return to work. How important were these for you? a. Housing costs; b. schooling costs; c. welfare of your children; d. welfare of aged dependents; e. your position within hospital; f. patient welfare; g. whether you could afford it; h. credit card debts; i. personal loans; j. maintaining unity of action with fellow strikers.

II. Attitudes towards union

32. How long have you been a member of the union?

33. Generally speaking, how well do you think the union represents nurses' interests?

III. Attitudes towards pay

34. At the time of the strike how fair did you think the level of your wage was in relation to the number of hours worked?

35. Did you have to do overtime, shiftwork or agency work to earn that wage? How much?

36. Did you experience any problems coping with a wage at that level?

37. I'd now like to talk to you about the sorts of decisions that the level of your pay may have affected. Did you ever have to postpone or rethink any of the following decisions due to the level of your wage and how important were they at the time? a. Whether to get married or not; b. to live on your own; c. to buy a house; d. to furnish a house; e. to extend or improve a house; f. to have children; g. to buy a car; h. to go on holiday.

IV. Attitudes towards the career structure

38. How did you feel about the career structure at the time of the strike? What is the concern? WAGES / STATUS / AUTHORITARIAN POWER

39. If nurses were mostly men do you think pay and conditions would be any different?

V. Social factors important in explaining activity / non-activity.

I am now going to read out a series of statements, after each of which I'd like you to state whether you AGREE or DISAGREE with the statement.

40. Male nurses involved in the strike had different reasons for participating than the female nurses involved.

41. Nurses with children and nurses with older families *not* involved in the strike had different reasons for *not* participating than single nurses.

42. Nurses from different ethnic backgrounds had differing reasons for going or not going out on strike.

43. Nurses in different positions within the hospital, had differing reasons for going or not going out on strike.

44. Nurses who owned their homes and were not involved in the strike had different reasons for not participating than the nurses who rented.

Ask why they agreed to the statements they did, if any.

VI. House

All home owners

45. Why did you decide to buy your own house?

46. What advantages did you see in home ownership when you bought your first house?

47. What do you think the advantages of owning your own house are now?

48. What disadvantages did you see in home ownership when you bought your first house?

49. What do you think the disadvantages of owning your own house are now?

50. What was the approximate value of your house at the time of the strike?

51. What was the approximate amount of your original deposit?

52. How did you obtain the money for your deposit?

53. [*If saved*] How long did it take to save it?

54. In what year did you buy your first house?

55. In what year did you buy this house?

56. How much money have you spent on renovating and redecorating?

57. How much are your council and MMBW rates per year?

58. What was the value of this house when you bought it?

59. How much of a burden were your removal costs, legal costs and government charges?

60. Did they affect your decision to buy in any way?

61. Would you support or oppose the Federal Government if it introduced a capital gains tax on houses valued at over $300,000?

Purchaser owners only

62. At the time of the strike, what was the full value of your mortgage, and at what interest rate was it issued?

63. At the time of the strike, how much were the repayments on this loan?

64. Roughly, what percentage of your *disposable* income (after tax and super) were these payments?

65. Do you think it might have been easier to perhaps go (or have been) on strike if you were renting or owned your house outright instead of buying?

Renters only

66. How long had you been renting this house at the time of the strike?

67. How long have you been a renter altogether?

68. How long do you intend to continue renting?

69. What do you think the advantages of renting are?

70. What do you think the disadvantages of renting are?

71. At the time of the strike how much was your weekly rent?

72. Roughly, what percentage was this of your disposable weekly income (after tax and superannuation)?

73. Had you spent any money on improvements to this house up to the time of the strike?

74. What would you estimate your removals cost to have been?

75. At the time of the strike, how long did your lease have to run?

76. Do you think it might have been easier to perhaps go (or have been) on strike if you were purchasing or owned a house outright?

About to buy

77. Why had you decided to buy your own house rather than continue renting?

78. What do you think the advantages of owning compared to renting are?

79. What do you think the disadvantages of owning compared to renting are?

80. Did the strike delay your intention to purchase?

81. [*If yes*] Did this affect your decision to participate in the strike?

VII. Economic concerns of renters and of those about to buy

82. Up to the time of the strike had you ever experienced any problems in meeting your rent?

Strikers only till Q.86

83. Did your loss of income during the strike mean that you could not pay your rent?

84. Did this in any way affect your participation in the strike?

85. Did you ask your landlord to postpone your rental payments whilst you were on strike?

86. [*If yes*] What was the response?

Purchaser owners

87. Up to the time of the strike had you experienced any problems in meeting your mortgage repayments?

Strikers only till Q.91

88. Did your loss of income during the strike mean that you could not meet your mortgage repayments?

89. Did this in any way affect your participation in the strike?

90. Did you ask your lending institution to postpone your mortgage repayments whilst you were on strike?

91. [*If yes*] What was the response?

Outright owners

92. Up to the time of the strike had you ever experienced problems in covering your housing costs?

Strikers only till Q.94

93. Did your loss of income during the strike affect your ability to cover your housing costs?

94. Did this in any way affect your participation in the strike?

All participants

95. Have you ever had to postpone or rethink any particular decisions due to the level of your housing costs?

96. Other people have suggested that the following sorts of decisions have been affected by their housing costs. How important were any of the following in your situation? a. Whether to get married or not; b. to live on your own; c. to buy a house; d. to furnish a house; e. to extend or improve a house; f. to have children; g. to buy a car; h. to go on holiday; i. to go on strike.

VIII. Tenure

All participants

97. Given complete freedom of choice what is your preferred housing option, owning or renting? Why?

    MADE IT / STATUS / COSTS / SAVINGS / FREEDOM / CONTROL / SECURITY?

98. Again with complete freedom of choice, which tenure would be the most likely in which you would establish a home, owning or renting? Why?

99. [*Home owners only*] Could you describe to me your feelings when you bought your first home?

100. Would you call where you now live home?

101. What does that word 'home' mean to you?

102. Do you feel sufficiently secure in your own home?

103. What does SECURITY / LACK OF SECURITY mean to you?

104. Is there anything particular about your own situation that contributes to those feelings of SECURITY / LACK OF SECURITY?

105. Do you feel you have sufficient control over what happens in and around your home?

106. What does that control mean to you?

107. Is there anything particular about your own situation that contributes to those feelings of CONTROL / LACK OF CONTROL?

108. Do you think ownership of a house as opposed to renting is an important part of those notions of 'home', 'security' and 'control'?

Home owners only

109. Do you think buying a house has been a good investment decision? In what way? TO MAKE MONEY / TO PROTECT SAVINGS / TO SAVE MONEY

110. Is the appearance (external and internal) of your house of importance to you?

111. Is the appearance of your garden of importance to you?

112. Is it important to you that your house should be seen to blend with the rest of the neighbourhood?

113. Why is this important to you? STATUS / HOUSE VALUE

Neighbourhood based concerns

114. How would you describe your attachment to this neighbourhood?

115. Why did you choose to move to this neighbourhood?
Due to choice of school?

116. How long have you lived in this neighbourhood?

117. How long do you intend living in this neighbourhood?

118. How would you describe your ability to influence events or developments in and around the neighbourhood? Why do you feel like that?

119. [*Home owners only*] Do you think that being a ratepayer affects how you view your neighbourhood?

120. [*Renters only*] Do you consider yourself a ratepayer of this neighbourhood? [*If yes, ask previous question*]

121. What for you would be the most important factors in creating your ideal neighbourhood?

122. What is it do you think that contributes to the standing or status of this neighbourhood?

123. Other people have suggested that they thought the following factors important. How important do you think they are? a. Appearance of other people's homes; b. appearance of other people's gardens; c. types of people; d. public amenities, parks; e. appearance and tidiness of streets.

124. If the Ministry of Housing announced plans to build some housing in your street how would you feel about the proposal?

125. How do you think this neighbourhood ranks in terms of its status, compared with Richmond, Hawthorn, Toorak?

126. What factors do you believe are the most important in shaping your views about their home?

127. And their neighbourhood?

128. How important do you think the following personal characteristics are in influencing your views about your home and neighbourhood? a. Sex; b. age; c. occupation; d. ethnicity; e. married or not; f. homeowner or not; g. having children.

129. [*Home owners only*] If the political party you don't normally vote for were to propose the re-introduction of income tax relief on mortgage interest repayments (i.e if the tax rate were say 30% you would only pay approximately two thirds of the interest you currently pay) would you be prepared to change your vote?

Appendix 2

NON-NUMERICAL UNSTRUCTURED DATA INDEXING SEARCHING AND THEORISING

The data from each of the case studies was analysed using a quali-tative data analysis package entitled NUDIST—Non-numerical Unstructured Data Indexing, Searching and Theorising. Having designed a series of 'index trees', based on formal logic, the data from the eighty-six interviews were indexed to be stored at a series of 'nodes', identifiable by a node number and name. For example, any statements by interviewees that related to home owning would be indexed under the 'home owning node' in the 'housing tenure index tree'. Having indexed all of the interview data, plus field notes, the data can then be manipulated very rapidly using a suite of analysis tools. One can thus get a print-out of, for example, all the comments by 'home owners' 'active' in the 'nurses strike' and 'under thirty years old' who related their 'strike activity' to the desire for a 'pay rise'. Each of the phrases in inverted commas would repre-sent nodes that would be 'intersected' so that one would have a print-out of quotes that only had each and every one of these indexed items in the quote. The manner in which these themes are related in the quote then forms the basis of the causal analysis.

Appendix 3

ABBREVIATIONS

This appendix lists abbreviations that describe the characteristics of interviewees in Chapters 5, 6, 7 and 8. Where a complete set of abbreviations is not stated for an individual, these data were not available.

about to buy = saving to purchase a house, at time of strike either renting or living in parental home

active = active in the observed social action

couple no children = two person household either married or in a de facto relationship who have no children

couple with children = two person household either married or in a de facto relationship who have at least one child

home duties = not in formal employment but responsible for household duties

in = did not go out on strike

in exempted area = worked in an 'essential' part of the hospital which was exempted by the Royal Australian Nurses Federation from the strike call

inactive = inactive in the observed social action

job representative = a Royal Australian Nurses Federation representative in the nursing work force

no tenure status = living at home with parents

non-ranf = not a member of the Royal Australian Nurses Federation

nw = Neighbourhood Watch case study

out = went out on strike

out long then in = out on strike for the major part of the strike but returned to work before the official union call to return to work

owner = home owner, either purchasing or owned outright

part time = part time nurse in the hospital

pensioner = main source of income is state benefits

pilot interview = this interview was conducted as a pilot interview but with the final format of the questionnaire

post-tertiary = completed a postgraduate qualification

powerline = powerline case study

purchaser owner over five years = a home owner who has been purchasing his/her home for more than five years

purchaser owner under five years = a home owner who has been purchasing his/her home for less than five years

ranf = member of the Royal Australian Nurses Federation

renter = private renter

renter (public) = renting from a Rental Co-operative or the Ministry of Housing

secondary = completed secondary education

single no children = single person household with no children

single no dependents = single person household with no dependents living at home

single with children = single person household with at least one child

strike = nurses strike case study

tertiary = completed tertiary degree

unemployed = not in formal employment

Occupational classifications follow those of the 1986 Census of Population and Housing, Australian Bureau of Statistics

occ 1 = occupational grade 1, managers and administrators

occ 2 = occupational grade 2, professionals

occ 3 = occupational grade 3, para-professionals

occ 4 = occupational grade 4, tradespersons

occ 5 = occupational grade 5, clerks

occ 6 = occupational grade 6, salespersons

occ 7 = occupational grade 7, plant and machine operators

20s, 30s, 40s, 50s = approximate age

1 income = a one income household

2 income = a two income household

1st = the first income earner or larger of the two household incomes

2nd = the second income earner or smaller of the two household incomes

$<10k = gross annual income less than $10,000

$10–15k = gross annual income between $10,000 and $15,000

$15–20k = gross annual income between $15,000 and $20,000

$20–25k = gross annual income between $20,000 and $25,000

$>25k = gross annual income more than $25,000

REFERENCES

Adams, J.S. (1984) The meaning of housing in America (Presidential Address) *Annals of the Association of American Geographers*, 74.4, 515–526.

Agnew, J. (1981) Home ownership and identity in capitalist societies. In *Housing and Identity*, J. S. Duncan (ed.) pp. 60–97. London: Croom Helm.

Australian Bureau of Statistics (ABS) (1987) *Crime and Crime Prevention Survey*, *Victoria*.

Badcock, B. (1989) Home ownership and the accumulation of real wealth. *Environment and Planning D: Society and Space*, 7.1, 69–92.

Badcock, B. (1992a) Adelaide's heart transplant, 1970–88: 1. Creation, transfer, and capture of 'value' within the built environment. *Environment and Planning A*, 24, 215–241.

Badcock, B. (1992b) Adelaide's heart transplant, 1970–88: 2. The 'transfer' of value within the housing market. *Environment and Planning A*, 24, 323– 339.

Badcock, B. and Browett, M. (1992c) Adelaide's heart transplant, 1970–88: 3. The deployment of capital in the renovation and redevelopment submarkets. *Environment and Planning A*, 24, 1167–1190.

Ball, M. (1983) *Housing Policy and Economic Power*. London: Methuen.

Ball, M. (1986) *Home Ownership: A Suitable Case for Reform*. London: Shelter.

Ball, M., Harloe, M. and Martens, M. (1988) *Housing and Social Change in Europe and the USA*. London: Routledge.

Barlow, J. and Duncan, S. (1988) The use and abuse of housing tenure. *Housing Studies*, 3.4, 219–231.

Bell, C. (1977) On Housing Classes. *Australian and New Zealand Journal of Sociology*, 13.1, 36–40.

Berry, M. (1977) Whose city? The forgotten tenant. *Australian and New Zealand Journal of Sociology*, 13.1, 53–59.

Berry, M. (1986) Housing provision and class relations under capitalism. *Housing Studies*, 1.2, 109–121.

261

Berry, M. (1988) To buy or rent? The demise of a duel tenure housing policy in Australia, 1945-1960. In *New Homes For Old*, R. Howe (ed.), Victoria: Ministry of Housing and Construction.

Bounds, M. (1989) *False expectations and derivative policies: analysing tenant participation*, Conference paper to The Australian Sociological Association, Melbourne, La Trobe University.

Bourdieu, P. (1984) *Distinction: A Social Critique of the Judgement of Taste*. London: Routledge Kegan Paul.

Bradbury, B., Rossiter C. and Vipond, J. (1987) Housing and Poverty in Australia. *Urban Studies*, 24, 95-102.

Bulmer, M. (1979) Concepts in the analysis of qualitative data. *Sociological Review*, 27.4, 651-677.

CAPIL (undated) *Capital Indexed Loans Study*. Victoria: Australian Institute of Family Studies and Ministry of Housing.

Castells, M. (1983) *The City and the Grassroots*. London: Edward Arnold.

Chapman, D. (1955) *The Home and Social Status*. London: Routledge Kegan Paul.

City of Collingwood (1989) *A Local Government Focus Special Feature*.

Clarke, S. and Ginsburg, N. (1975) The political economy of housing, *Political Economy and the Housing Question*. Workshop of the Conference of Socialist Economists.

Clyde Mitchell, J. (1983) Case and situation analysis. *Sociological Review*, 31, 187-211.

Commission of Inquiry into Poverty (1975) *Poverty in Australia, First Main Report* Canberra: AGPS.

Couper, M. and Brindley, T. (1975) Housing classes and housing values. *Sociological Review*, 23, 563-576.

Cox, K. R. (1982) Housing tenure and neighbourhood activism. *Urban Affairs Quarterly*, 18.1, 107-129.

Cox, K. R. (1989) The politics of turf and the question of class. In *The Power of Geography*, M. Dear and J. Wolch (eds), London: Unwin Hyman.

Cox, K. R. and McCarthy, J. J. (1980) Neighbourhood activism in the American city: behavioural relationships and evaluation. *Urban Geography*, 1.1, 22-38.

Cox, K. R. and McCarthy, J. J. (1982) Neighbourhood activism as a politics of turf: a critical analysis. In *Conflict, Politics and the Urban Scene*, K. R. Cox and J. J. McCarthy (eds), pp. 192-219. Harlow, Essex: Longman.

Davies, J. (1972) *The Evangelistic Bureaucrat*. London: Tavistock.

Davis, J. (1991) *Contested Ground: Collective Action in the Urban Neighbourhood*. Ithaca and London: Cornell University Press.

Davis, M. (1990) *City of Quartz: Excavating the Future in Los Angeles*. London: Verso.

De Leon, R. (1992) *Left Coast City: Progressive Politics in San Francisco, 1975-1991*. USA: University Press of Kansas.

Deverson, J. and Lindsay, K. (1975) *Voices from the Middle Class: a Study of Families in Two London Suburbs*. London: Hutchinson.

Dilthey, W. (1961) *Meaning in History*. London: George Allen and Unwin.

Duncan, J. S. (ed.) (1981) *Housing and Identity*. London: Croom Helm.

Duncan, S. (1990) Do house prices rise that much? A dissenting view. *Housing Studies*, 5.3, 195–208.

Dunleavy, P. (1979) The urban basis of political alignment: social class, domestic property ownership and state intervention in consumption processes. *British Journal of Political Science*, 9, 409–443.

Dunleavy, P. (1986) The growth of sectoral cleavages and the stabilisation of state expenditures. *Environment and Planning D: Society and Space*, 4, 129–144.

Dupuis, A. (1992) Financial gains from owner occupation: the New Zealand case 1970–88. *Housing Studies*, 7.1, 27–44.

Edel, M. (1982) Home ownership and working class unity. *International Journal of Urban and Regional Research*, 6, 205–222.

Edel, M., Sclar, E. D. and Luria, D. (1984) *Shaky Palaces: Home Ownership and Social Mobility in Boston's Suburbanisation*. New York: Columbia University Press.

Forrest, R. (1983) The meaning of home ownership. *Society and Space*, 15.1, 205–216.

Forrest, R. and Murie, A. (undated) *The affluent home owner: labour market position and the shaping of housing histories*. Mimeo.

Forrest, R., Murie A. and Williams, P. (1990) *Home Ownership: Differentiation and Fragmentation*. London: Unwin Hyman.

Gadamer, H. G. (1976) *Philosophical Hermeneutics*. New York: Universal.

Gardner, H. and McCoppin, B. (1986) Vocation, career or both? Politicisation of Australian nurses, Victoria 1984–86. *The Australian Journal of Advanced Nursing*, 4.1, 25–35.

Gerth, H. H. and Wright Mills, C. (1948) *From Max Weber: Essays in Sociology*. London: Routledge Kegan Paul.

Giddens, A. (1973) *The Class Structure of the Advanced Societies*. London: Hutchinson.

Giddens, A. (1982) *Profiles and Critiques in Social Theory*. London: Macmillan.

Giddens, A. (1984) *The Constitution of Society: Outline of the Theory of Structuration*. London: Polity Press.

Gray, F. (1982) Owner occupation and social relations. In *Owner Occupation in Britain*, S. Merrett with F. Gray, pp. 267–291. London: Routledge Kegan Paul.

Habermas, J. (1976) *Legitimation Crisis*. Tr. by T. McCarthy. London: Heinemann.

Haddon, R. (1970) A minority in a welfare state society. *New Atlantis*, 2, 80–133.

Halfpenny, P. (1979) The analysis of qualitative data. *Sociological Review*, 27.4, 799–825.

Halle, D. (1984) *America's Working Man: Work, Home and Politics among Blue-Collar Property Owners*. Chicago: University of Chicago Press.

Hamilton, S. W. (1976) Measuring changes in house prices. In *Recent perspectives in urban land economics: essays in honour of Richard U. Ratcliff and Paul E. Wendt*. M. A. Goldberg (ed.). Vancouver: Urban Land Economics Division, Faculty of Commerce and Business Administration, University of British Columbia.

Hamnett, C. (1988) Housing: the new rich. *New Society*, April 22, 10–11.

Harloe, M. (1984) Sector and class: a critical comment. *International Journal of Urban and Regional Research*, 8.2, 228–237.

Harloe, M. (1985) *Private Rented Housing in the United States and Europe*. Kent, England: Croom Helm.

Harvey, D. (1978) Labour, capital and class struggle around the built environment in advanced capitalist societies. In *Urbanisation and Conflict in Market Societies*, K. Cox (ed.), pp. 9–37. Chicago: Macroufa Press.

Harvey, D. (1989) From managerialism to entrepreneurialism: the transformation in urban governance in late capitalism. *Geografiska Annaler*, **71B(1)**, 3–17.

Harvey, D. (1989a) *The Condition of Postmodernity*. Oxford: Basil Blackwell.

Hayward, D. (1986) The Great Australian Dream reconsidered. *Housing Studies*, **1**, p. 213.

Holme, A. (1985) *Housing and Young Families in East London*. London: Routledge Kegan Paul.

Housing and Urban Land Development Association of Canada (HUDAC) (1978) *The filtering process in housing: a Vancouver case study, 1965–77*.

Ineichen, B. (1972) Home ownership and manual workers' lifestyles. *Sociological Review*, **20**, 391–412.

Jager, M. (1986) Class definition and the aesthetics of gentrification: Victoriana in Melbourne. In *Gentrification of the City*, N. Smith and P. Williams (eds), pp. 78–91. London: Allen and Unwin.

Jones, C. (1982) The demand for home ownership. In *The Future of Council Housing*, J. English (ed.). London: Croom Helm.

Jones, M. (1972) *Housing and Poverty in Australia*. Melbourne: Melbourne University Press.

Kant, I. (1978) *Anthropology from a Pragmatic Point of View*. Southern Illinois University Press.

Karn, V., Kemeny, J. and Williams, P. (1985) *Home Ownership in the Inner City*. Aldershot: Gower.

Kemeny, J. (1977) A political sociology of home ownership in Australia. *Australia and New Zealand Journal of Sociology*, **13.1**, 47–52.

Kemeny, J. (1980) Home ownership and privatisation. *International Journal of Urban and Regional Research*, **4.3**, 372–387.

Kemeny, J. (1981) *The Myth of Home Ownership*. London: Routledge Kegan Paul.

Kemeny, J. (1983) *The Great Australian Nightmare* Melbourne: Georgian House.

Kemeny, J. (1986) The ideology of home ownership. In *Urban Planning in Australia: critical readings*, J. B. McLoughlin and M. Huxley (eds). Melbourne: Longman Cheshire.

Kemeny, J. (1988) Defining housing reality: ideological hegemony and power in housing research. *Housing Studies*, **4.3**, 205–218.

Kendig, H. (1984) Housing careers, life cycle and residential mobility: implications for the housing market. *Urban Studies*, **21**, 271–283.

King, R. (1987) Monopoly rent, residential differentiation and the second global crisis of capitalism—the case of Melbourne, *Progress in Planning*, **28**, 195–298.

Kyle, F. (1987) Victorian Nurses Strike. *Scarlet Woman*, **23**, 3–6.

Lash, S. and Urry, J. (1987) *The End of Organised Capitalism*. Cambridge: Polity Press.

Lockwood, D. (1966) Sources of variation in working class images of society. *Sociological Review*, **14**, 249–267.

Low, N. and Moser, S. (1991) The causes and consequences of Melbourne's central city property boom. *Urban Policy and Research*, **9.1**, 5–27.

Lukes, S. (1974) *Power: A Radical View.* London: Macmillan.

Madge, J. and Brown, C. (1981) *First Homes: A Survey of the Housing Circumstances of Young Married Couples.* London: Policy Studies Institute.

Madigan, R. (1988) A new generation of home owners? Discussion Paper, Centre for Housing Research, University of Glasgow, Glasgow.

Manning, I. (1983) The distribution of wealth in Australia. *Current Affairs Bulletin*, **59**, p. 11

McAllister, I. (1984) Housing tenure and party choice in Australia, Britain and the United States. *British Journal of Political Science*, **14**, 509–522.

Munro, M. and McClennan, D. (1986) *Intra-urban changes in house prices: Glasgow 1972–83.* Mimeo.

Murie, A. (1991) Divisions of home ownership: housing tenure and social change. *Environment and Planning A*, **23.3**, 349–370.

New Spirit (1986) An official publication of the National Association of Town Watch, Inc. Spring.

Nicholson, J. and Weeks, P. (1984) A survey of the law governing private residential tenancies in Australia. In *Affordable and Available Housing: The Role of the Private Rental Sector.* C. Paris (ed.). Australian Institute of Urban Studies, Publication Number 117, Canberra.

O'Connor, J. (1973) *The Fiscal Crisis of the State.* New York: St Martins Press.

O'Malley, P. (1989) Redefining security: Neighbourhood Watch in context. *Arena*, **86**, 18–23.

Paris, C. (1984) Private rental housing in Australia. *Environment and Planning A*, **16**, 1079–1098.

Paris, C. and Williams, P. (1983) *Capitalism and Housing Provision.* Paper delivered to ANZAAS Congress, Perth, 19th May, URU, ANU, Canberra.

Parkin, F. (1972) *Class Inequality and Political Order.* London: Paladin.

Parsons, T. (1947) (ed.) *The Theory of Social and Economic Organisation.* New York: Free Press.

Patton, M. (1980) *Qualitative Evaluation Methods.* Beverly Hills: Sage.

Perin, C. (1977) *Everything in it's Place: Social Order and Land Use in America.* Princeton: Princeton University Press.

Powerline Review Panel (1989) *Final Report to the Victorian Government.* Melbourne: Government of Victoria.

Pratt, G. (1982) Class analysis and urban domestic property: a critical re-examination. *International Journal of Urban and Regional Research*, **6.4**, 481–501.

Pratt, G. (1986a) Against reductionism: the relations of consumption as a mode of social structuration. *International Journal of Urban and Regional Research*, **10.3**, 377–399.

Pratt, G. (1986b) Housing—consumption sectors and political response in urban Canada. *Society and Space*, **4**, 165–182.

Pratt, G. (1986c) Housing tenure and social cleavages in urban Canada. *Annals of the Association of American Geographers*, **76.3**, 366–380.

Pratt, G. (1986d) Why Canadian home owners are more conservative than tenants. *Urban Geography*, **7.3**, 187–209.

Pratt, G. (1987) Class, home and politics. *Canadian Review of Sociology and Anthropology*, **24.1**, 39–57.

Pratt, G. (1989) Incorporation theory and the reproduction of community fabric. In *The Power of Geography*, M. Dear and J. Wolch (eds). London: Unwin Hyman.

Preteceille, E. (1986) Collective consumption, urban segregation and social classes. *Society and Space*, 4, 145–154.

Rakoff, R. (1977) The meaning of the house. *Politics and Society*, 7, 85–104.

Rex, J. (1968) The sociology of a zone of transition. In *Readings in Urban Sociology*, R. Pahl (ed.). London: Pergamon

Rex, J. and Moore, R. (1967) *Race, Community and Conflict: A Study of Sparkbrook*. London: Oxford University Press.

Richards, L. (1985) *Little Boxes Made of Ideology? Women and Home ownership in the Suburban Estate*. Paper to the Women and Housing Conference, Adelaide University.

Richards, L. (1990) *Nobody's Home: Dreams and Realities in a New Suburb*. Melbourne: Oxford University Press.

Rickert, H. (1962) *Science and History: a critique of positivist epistemology*. Tr. by G. Reisman, (ed.) A. Goddard. Princeton, New Jersey: Van Nostrand

Rose, D. (1980) Toward a re-evaluation of the political significance of home ownership in Britain. *Housing, Construction and the State*, 71–76. London: Political Economy of Housing Workshop of the Conference of Socialist Economists.

Rosow, I. (1948) Home ownership motives. *American Sociological Review*, 13, 751–756.

Royal Trust Corporation of Canada (1983) *Royal Trust survey of Canadian house prices*.

Saunders, P. (1977) Housing tenure and class interests. *University of Sussex Urban and Regional Studies Working Paper* 6.

Saunders, P. (1978) Domestic property and social class. *International Journal of Urban and Regional Research*, 2, 233–251.

Saunders, P. (1979) *Urban Politics: A Sociological Interpretation*. London: Hutchinson.

Saunders, P. (1981) *Social Theory and the Urban Question*. 1st edition. London: Hutchinson.

Saunders, P. (1982) Beyond housing classes: the sociological significance of private property rights in means of consumption. *University of Sussex Urban and Regional Studies Working Paper* 33.

Saunders, P. (1984) Beyond housing classes: the sociological significance of private property rights in the means of consumption. *International Journal of Urban and Regional Research*, 8, 201–227.

Saunders, P. (1986) Comment on Dunleavy and Preteceille. *Environment and Planning D: Society and Space*, 4, 155–163.

Saunders, P. (1989) The meaning of 'home' in contemporary English culture. *Housing Studies*, 4.3, 177–192.

Saunders, P. (1990) *A Nation of Home Owners*. London: Unwin Hyman.

Saunders, P. and Williams, P. (1988) The constitution of the home. *Housing Studies*, 3, 81–93.

Savage, M. *et al.* (1987) 'Locality research': the Sussex programme on economic restructuring, social change and the locality. *Quarterly Journal of Social Affairs*, 3, 27–51.

Sayer, A. (1984) *Method in Social Science: A Realist Approach*. London: Hutchinson.

Seeley, J. *et al.* (1956) *Crestwood Heights*. Toronto: University of Toronto Press.

Soja, E. (1989) *Postmodern Geographies*. London: Verso.

Stretton, H. (1976) *Capitalism, Socialism and the Environment*. Cambridge: Cambridge University Press.

Stubbs, C. (1988) Property rights and relations: the purchase of council housing. *Housing Studies*, 2, 177–191.

Sullivan, O. (1989) Housing tenure as a consumption sector divide: a critical perspective. *International Journal of Urban and Regional Research*, 13.2, 183–200.

Thompson, E. P. (1978) *The Poverty of Theory and other essays*. London: Merlin Press.

Thorns, D. C. (1981) Owner occupation: its significance for wealth transfer and class formation. *Sociological Review*, 29.4, 705–728.

Thorns, D. C. (1989) The impact of home ownership and capital gains upon class and consumption sectors. *Environment and Planning D: Society and Space*, 7.3, 293–312.

Tonnies, F. (1955) *Community and Association*. London: Routledge Kegan Paul.

Turner, B. (1988) *Status*. Milton Keynes: Open University Press.

Victoria Police (1983) *Neighbourhood Watch Manual*.

Victoria Police (1986) *Neighbourhood Watch Crime Analysis*. Operations Department.

Victoria Police (1988) *Neighbourhood Watch Crime Analysis*. Operations Department.

Victoria Police (1989) *Neighbourhood Watch Crime Analysis*. Operations Department.

Victoria Police (1990) *Neighbourhood Watch Crime Analysis*. Operations Department.

Warde, A. (1990) Production, consumption and social change: reservations regarding Peter Saunders' sociology of consumption. *International Journal of Urban and Regional Research*, 14, 228–248.

Weber, M. (1947) *The Theory of Social and Economic Organisation*. T. Parsons (ed.), New York: Free Press.

Weber, M. (1948) (1974 reprint) *From Max Weber*. H. H. Gerth and C. Wright Mills (eds), London: Routledge Kegan Paul.

Weber, M. (1949) *The Methodology of the Social Sciences*. Glencoe: Free Press.

Weber, M. (1958) *The City*. Chicago: Free Press.

Weber, M. (1968) *Economy and Society*. New York: Bedminster Press.

Williams, N. (1989) Housing tenure, political attitudes and voting behaviour. *Area*, 21.2, 117–126.

Williams, P. (1984) The politics of property: home ownership in Australia, J. Halligan and C. Paris (eds). *Australian Urban Politics: critical perspectives*, pp. 167–192. Melbourne: Longman Cheshire.

Wilson, L. (1986) Neighbourhood Watch. *Legal Service Bulletin*, 11.2, 68–71.

Winter, I. (1993) Urban planning and the entrepreneurial state. *Urban Policy and Research*, **11.1**, 46–48.

Winter, I. and Brooke, T. (1993) Urban planning and the entrepreneurial state: the view from Victoria, Australia. *Environment and Planning C: Government and Policy*, **11**, 263–278.

Young, M. and Willmott, P. (1957) *Family and Kinship in East London*. Pelican edition (1962).

Znaniecki, F. (1934) *The Method of Sociology*. New York: Rinehart.

INDEX

For Product Safety Concerns and Information please contact our EU
representative GPSR@taylorandfrancis.com
Taylor & Francis Verlag GmbH, Kaufingerstraße 24, 80331 München, Germany

www.ingramcontent.com/pod-product-compliance
Lightning Source LLC
Chambersburg PA
CBHW070609270326
41926CB00013B/2475